Praise for *Building Integrations with MuleSoft*

In my 25+ years in technology, I've never seen integration explained so clearly. This practical guide transforms technical complexity into strategic business advantage—essential for modern enterprises.

—Justine Reilly, director, enterprise architecture, Salesforce, and former director of automation specialists, MuleSoft

Pooja and Diane offer an expertly crafted, practical blueprint drawn from their extensive MuleSoft training and real-world experience.

—Isabella Nararro, MuleSoft community manager, MuleSoft

With deep roots in the MuleSoft ecosystem, Pooja and Diane have created an invaluable guide for developers and architects alike. Drawing on years of hands-on experience, this book is packed with practical insights that will empower anyone building integrations with MuleSoft.

—Sabrina Marechal, MuleSoft community director, MuleSoft

Pooja and Diane exemplify what it means to be MuleSoft experts through their clear and detailed explanations guiding both beginners and advanced users to build integrations easily with MuleSoft.

—Sabrina (Hocket) Barnes, MuleSoft community advocacy and marketing manager, MuleSoft

This book is a masterful resource for developers and architects seeking to excel in enterprise integration. With its practical approach, this book transforms complex integration concepts into actionable insights, empowering readers to design scalable, reliable solutions. From prototyping APIs to mastering tools like Anypoint Studio and conquering DataWeave, the authors provide a comprehensive roadmap for tackling real-world challenges. Supported by detailed use cases, this guide dives deep into error handling, message orchestration, and deployment strategies, ensuring readers are equipped to handle the most demanding integration scenarios. Whether you're connecting legacy systems or deploying CI/CD pipelines, this book is your essential companion for leveraging MuleSoft's capabilities to unify data and streamline processes across the enterprise.

—*Jim Andrews, MuleSoft architect and author*

This book is a comprehensive, thoughtfully crafted guide for developers and architects who want to go beyond the basics and truly understand the power of MuleSoft. Pooja and Diane do an outstanding job of breaking down complex concepts—from API-led connectivity and integration patterns to the nuances of AsyncAPI, DataWeave and Unit Testing (MUnit)—without ever losing the reader in jargon. What sets this book apart is its balance of theory and practice: not only does it explain the why behind MuleSoft's design principles, it also provides real-world examples, best practices, and design insights that readers can immediately apply to their own projects. Whether you're just getting started or looking to deepen your expertise, this book is the perfect companion on your MuleSoft journey.

—*Simone Geib, director of product management, Salesforce*

An indispensable guide for anyone building modern enterprise integrations. This book brings API-led connectivity to life with clarity, precision, and practical examples—bridging foundational concepts with hands-on mastery in Anypoint Studio and Code Builder.

—*Ramsundernag Changalva,*
software engineering senior member technical staff, Salesforce

Pooja and Diane have done an amazing job creating a single resource containing all the essential information to enable you to create and deploy a MuleSoft API. If you are a MuleSoft developer, you need to get this book. Agentic AI needs integration to truly meet business goals. If your choice of an integration platform is MuleSoft, this book will teach you everything you need to know to develop MuleSoft APIs used by your agentic AI solution.

—*Brian Statkevicus, MuleSoft ambassador*
and MuleSoft practice director, Argano

Building Integrations with MuleSoft

Integrating Systems and Unifying Data in the Enterprise

Pooja Kamath and Diane Kesler

O'REILLY®

Building Integrations with MuleSoft

by Pooja Kamath and Diane Kesler

Published by O'Reilly Media, Inc., 1005 Gravenstein Highway North, Sebastopol, CA 95472.

O'Reilly books may be purchased for educational, business, or sales promotional use. Online editions are also available for most titles (*http://oreilly.com*). For more information, contact our corporate/institutional sales department: 800-998-9938 or *corporate@oreilly.com*.

Acquisitions Editor: Andy Kwan	**Indexer:** Ellen Troutman-Zaig
Development Editor: Corbin Collins	**Interior Designer:** David Futato
Production Editor: Elizabeth Faerm	**Cover Designer:** Susan Thompson
Copyeditor: nSight, Inc.	**Illustrator:** Kate Dullea
Proofreader: Miah Sandvik	

May 2025:   First Edition

Revision History for the First Edition
2025-05-09:   First Release

See *http://oreilly.com/catalog/errata.csp?isbn=9781098158293* for release details.

978-1-098-15829-3

[LSI]

Table of Contents

Preface

In today's ever-changing digital landscape, disruption is widespread, and creating a composable enterprise enables organizations to adapt to changing landscapes. This is made possible by creating reusable assets to foster agility and adaptability. Enterprises like this help democratize automation and drive innovation. Just like integration connects applications and data to generate insights and improve observation of business impact, automation relies on this integration to create a network of capabilities. The ability to scale rapidly and develop truly connected experiences is important for organizations to remain competitive. As businesses strive to automate their systems quickly and seek to create assets that can be combined to deliver a distinctive customer experience, companies are exploring technologies that complement rapid innovation.

Welcome to the world of integration! MuleSoft is a robust integration platform consisting of products like CloudHub, Mule as an ESB, Anypoint Studio, Enterprise Management Console, DataWeave, and Anypoint Enterprise Security. Together, these products provide organizations with essential connectivity solutions, streamlined development, comprehensive management, and enhanced security for seamless integration and interoperability across their enterprise. MuleSoft stands as the ultimate solution for seamlessly integrating applications and unifying data. Powered by the Mule runtime engine, MuleSoft ensures exceptional performance, outperforming other comparable approaches by up to five times. Additionally, with the aid of Anypoint templates, MuleSoft empowers organizations with unmatched productivity and accelerated time to market, enabling these organizations to stay ahead in today's fast-paced business landscape.

MuleSoft helps organizations create an API portal for their software ecosystem, personalize new digital experiences using templates that can be viewed via Anypoint Exchange, and provide interactive documentation for developers so they can solicit feedback from users while building assets. It also has a vibrant community where the users can engage with other developers and architects to post questions and access publicly shared knowledge.

The world of integration is evolving faster than ever. We stand at the intersection of API-led connectivity, hyperautomation, and AI-driven innovation, transforming how businesses connect, scale, and automate. What once required months of custom development can now be achieved in days with the right tools, frameworks, and strategies. This book is designed to guide you through the entire process of designing, building, and deploying effective MuleSoft application programming interfaces (APIs). As you progress, you will learn practices and principles to create connected experiences for your enterprise. You will also gain skills in a wide range of MuleSoft developer tools, including tools for design, documentation, development, testing, and deployment. By the time you work through this book, you should have enough experience to develop an API from concept to launch. This book is more than a guide—it's a blueprint for the future of integration, automation, and intelligent systems. Welcome to the journey. Let's build the future together.

Who Should Use This Book?

This book is for developers and architects looking to get up to speed on developing integrations using MuleSoft. Most of the content used here is from the training material we have created and used over the years. This book also contains our learnings from past project experiences.

This book can also serve as a comprehensive reference guide for fundamental topics such as API design methods, the API build process, testing, and other stages of API development using MuleSoft. This is why it is a valuable resource for senior software architects and API product managers who aim to provide consistent guidance to their teams.

What's Covered and What's Not

The goal of this book is to give you a linear coverage of what is required to get up and running and launch an API to production. We understand that software development is an iterative process, and in the real world you will have to bounce back and forth between processes for the successful delivery of applications. MuleSoft is a very big topic with a lot of products; we won't be able to cover it all. With the help of a use case, we will learn how to create an API, develop, test, and deploy it. We won't be covering topics related to the broader topic of API management. Things like API Gateways, portals, monitoring, and overall governance are out of scope for us in this book.

Conventions Used in This Book

The following typographical conventions are used in this book:

Italic
> Indicates new terms, URLs, email addresses, filenames, and file extensions.

`Constant width`
> Used for program listings, as well as within paragraphs to refer to program elements such as variable or function names, databases, data types, environment variables, statements, and keywords.

`Constant width bold`
> Shows commands or other text that should be typed literally by the user.

`Constant width italic`
> Shows text that should be replaced with user-supplied values or by values determined by context.

> This element signifies a tip or suggestion.

> This element signifies a general note.

> This element indicates a warning or caution.

Using Code Examples

Supplemental material (code examples, exercises, etc.) is available for download at *https://github.com/poojapkamath/Building-Integrations-with-MuleSoft*.

If you have a technical question or a problem using the code examples, please send email to *support@oreilly.com*.

This book is here to help you get your job done. In general, if example code is offered with this book, you may use it in your programs and documentation. You do not need to contact us for permission unless you're reproducing a significant portion of the code. For example, writing a program that uses several chunks of code from this book does not require permission. Selling or distributing examples from O'Reilly books does require permission. Answering a question by citing this book and quoting example code does not require permission. Incorporating a significant amount of example code from this book into your product's documentation does require permission.

We appreciate, but generally do not require, attribution. An attribution usually includes the title, author, publisher, and ISBN. For example: "*Building Integrations with MuleSoft* by Pooja Kamath and Diane Kesler (O'Reilly). Copyright 2025 Pooja Kamath and Diane Kesler, 978-1-098-15829-3."

If you feel your use of code examples falls outside fair use or the permission given above, feel free to contact us at *permissions@oreilly.com*.

O'Reilly Online Learning

For more than 40 years, *O'Reilly Media* has provided technology and business training, knowledge, and insight to help companies succeed.

Our unique network of experts and innovators share their knowledge and expertise through books, articles, and our online learning platform. O'Reilly's online learning platform gives you on-demand access to live training courses, in-depth learning paths, interactive coding environments, and a vast collection of text and video from O'Reilly and 200+ other publishers. For more information, visit *https://oreilly.com*.

How to Contact Us

Please address comments and questions concerning this book to the publisher:

O'Reilly Media, Inc.
1005 Gravenstein Highway North
Sebastopol, CA 95472
800-889-8969 (in the United States or Canada)
707-827-7019 (international or local)
707-829-0104 (fax)
support@oreilly.com
https://oreilly.com/about/contact.html

We have a web page for this book, where we list errata, examples, and any additional information. You can access this page at *https://oreil.ly/bldg-integ-mulesoft*.

For news and information about our books and courses, visit *https://oreilly.com*.

Find us on LinkedIn: *https://linkedin.com/company/oreilly-media*.

Watch us on YouTube: *https://youtube.com/oreillymedia*.

Acknowledgments

We are grateful to all those who helped us while we were writing this book: the staff at O'Reilly, especially Corbin Collins and Elizabeth Faerm, whose efforts kept us on track. We are grateful to Simone Geib, who provided deep technical expertise and patient guidance on the content for this book. We thank our reviewers Ramsundernag Changalva, Shivani Marrero, Tahn Amuchastegui, Audrey Honeycutt, and Ethan Port for their expert reviews of our treatment of the subject matter.

CHAPTER 1

The World of Integrations

Welcome to the world of integrations, where the magic of connecting systems, data, and people transforms what we can accomplish. We are getting more connected and faster than ever, and integration is no longer just nice to have—it's essential. This book is your guide to understanding what makes integration tick and how MuleSoft can help you build solutions to tackle real-world challenges. Whether you're diving in for the first time or you're already deep in the integration game, we're excited to be on this journey with you.

MuleSoft is indeed like that trusty, hardworking mule, doing the heavy lifting so you don't have to (and with way fewer hay bales involved). It's not just a platform; it's a game changer that helps bring innovation, speed, and flexibility into your integrations. With AI-driven tools like Intelligent Document Processing and AI-assisted flow building, MuleSoft is keeping us all on the cutting edge by making automating data capture and building adaptable workflows easier than ever. By blending API-led connectivity with these new AI-powered tools, MuleSoft empowers you to create integrations that move at the speed of today's digital pace and do it with style.

Integration is a journey, one that will totally transform how you approach building and scaling. Each chapter in this book invites you to learn, experiment, and build something impactful. MuleSoft's possibilities are vast, and with these new AI capabilities, there's never been a better time to hitch up that digital mule and get to work. Let's make your integration vision a reality.

Imagine each integration as part of a bigger puzzle. Build reusable APIs for each layer: experience, process, and system. It's like playing with Legos: once the pieces exist, you mix, match, and boom—everything just clicks! Who doesn't love building something that actually works without extra duct tape?

Super Routes Logistics

In this book, we'll be helping a fictional logistics company, Super Routes Logistics (SRL), integrate their proprietary cost-analysis software with MuleSoft to offer real-time quotes and delivery times to customers. They want to include variables such as traffic conditions, package load, and even driver availability in the analytics model. Their goal is to optimize operations and reduce costs. Now, these guys aren't your run-of-the-mill delivery service. No, they're in the regional freight and delivery game, and they've got big plans. They want to flip the logistics world on its head using some really smart tech, but they want to do this while helping small- to medium-sized businesses. SRL knows that these smaller companies often get the short end of the stick or can't afford the big logistics players, which is SRL's differentiator. They offer shipping solutions that are easy on the wallet, super efficient, and totally transparent. This way, businesses can focus on what they do best—running their businesses—while SRL handles all the shipping headaches.

Milestones

Founded in 2010, SRL has rapidly ascended as a leader in the logistics and supply chain industry. Below are some milestones the company is proud of:

2011
    Launched operations in North America

2012
    Introduced customer portal

2013
    Purchased Salesforce license for customer management

2019
    Introduced proprietary cost-analysis software

2020
    Achieved a 97% customer satisfaction rate

2023
    Purchased MuleSoft licenses and intends to use the product to implement its real-time analytics shipping solution

Transformation Goals

Here are the goals of the company:

Real-time analytics
Use real-time data analytics to optimize routes and delivery schedules, taking into account impactful variables such as traffic, weather, and package load.

Dynamic pricing
Improve cost-analysis software to offer competitive, real-time pricing options to customers, ensuring transparency and fairness.

Scalability
Build a modular technology infrastructure that will allow them to easily scale their operations to meet the demands of their growing customer base and geographic reach.

Business Challenges

SRL is facing common challenges seen in businesses undergoing modernization. Here's what they need to address:

Lack of real-time data
Building applications that can receive and process real-time data.

Complex variables
Multiple factors like package load, traffic, and driver availability must be considered in real time to optimize operations.

Inefficient quoting system
Using real-time data and complex variables to calculate correct quotes. Currently, this is not possible because the cost analysis software does not have access to real-time data.

Current state
The current state of the systems is as shown in Figure 1-1.

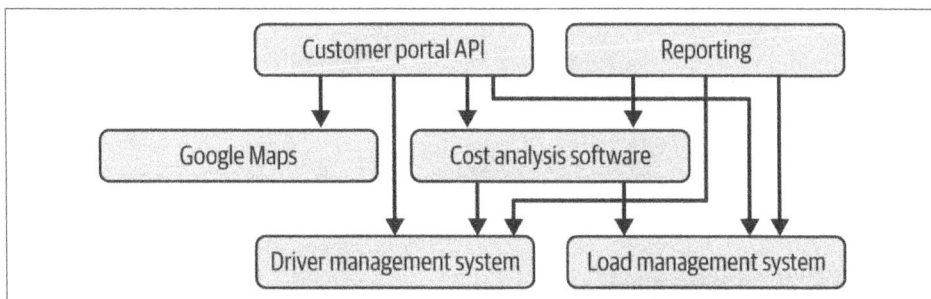

Figure 1-1. SRL current state

Creating a diagram manually is painful and time-consuming. So, we used Mermaid (*https://mermaid.js.org*) to render the API-led connectivity diagram. It's basic—feel free to customize it to your liking using CSS styling.

Below is the Mermaid source code we used to render Figure 1-1:

```
----
graph TD

    A[Customer Portal API]

    B[Google Maps]
    C[Driver Management System]
    D[Load Management System]
    E[ Cost-Analysis Software]
    F[Reporting]

  A --> B
  A --> C
  A --> D
  A --> E
  E--> D
  E --> C

  F --> C
  F --> D
  F --> E
----
```

From Spaghetti Links to Smart APIs: The Evolution of Integration

Our journey into the world of integration begins with the simplest of needs: sharing data between two systems. At first glance, that sounds easy enough. But as any integration architect knows, getting systems to talk involves more than just connecting the dots. Data formats, input and output structures, security, and the unique quirks of each system all come into play. Over time, as technology evolved and businesses grew, integration methods adapted, progressing through different architectural styles designed to meet the challenges of their day.

First, we'll explore point-to-point (P2P) integrations, a straightforward yet messy solution that connects systems in pairs. It gets the job done but quickly becomes a tangled web as more systems join the network. And yes, we've written some of that spaghetti code ourselves. Next comes the enterprise service bus (ESB), a step up that centralizes integrations and cuts down on the chaos but still has limitations.

Finally, we arrive at API-led connectivity, the modern approach that offers flexibility, scalability, and order in an otherwise chaotic digital world.

Let's dive into the evolution of integration, looking at the good, the bad, and the lessons we've learned along the way.

Point-to-Point Integration

Point-to-point (P2P) integrations are all about getting two systems to exchange data through custom code that's tailor-made for each pair. The developer picks a programming language that fits the project, writes some code, and ta-da—the systems are talking. The main perk here is that it's fast and straightforward, perfect for small projects or isolated connections that don't need a complex setup.

But as more systems are added, P2P's quirks start showing. Maintenance becomes a hassle, especially if the original developer is nowhere to be found and the code is in some dusty legacy language. Each new system needs its own custom connection, and soon you're looking at a tangled network of links, a mess we lovingly call *spaghetti integration*. Look at Figure 1-2; each line represents a direct integration between two systems, creating a web of dependencies that's hard to manage as connections multiply.

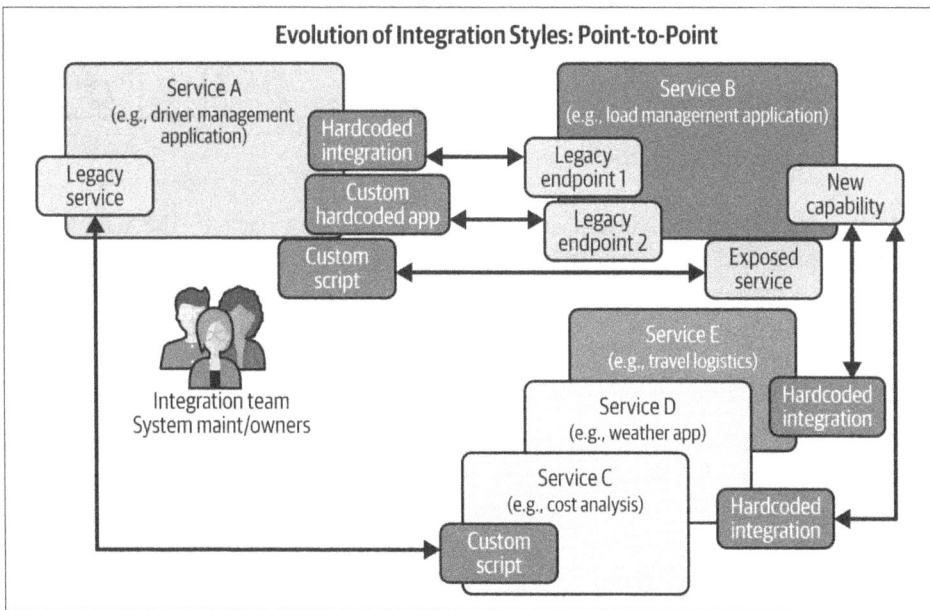

Figure 1-2. Point-to-point integration

And here's the real kicker: if one system connected to several others needs replacing, every affected connection has to be reworked. As shown in Figure 1-3, P2P integrations quickly spiral into a complex mess, lacking governance, scalability, and a streamlined way to handle growth. Although this approach might have once worked as a quick fix, today's fast-paced digital world demands something more organized, flexible, and scalable than this tangled solution.

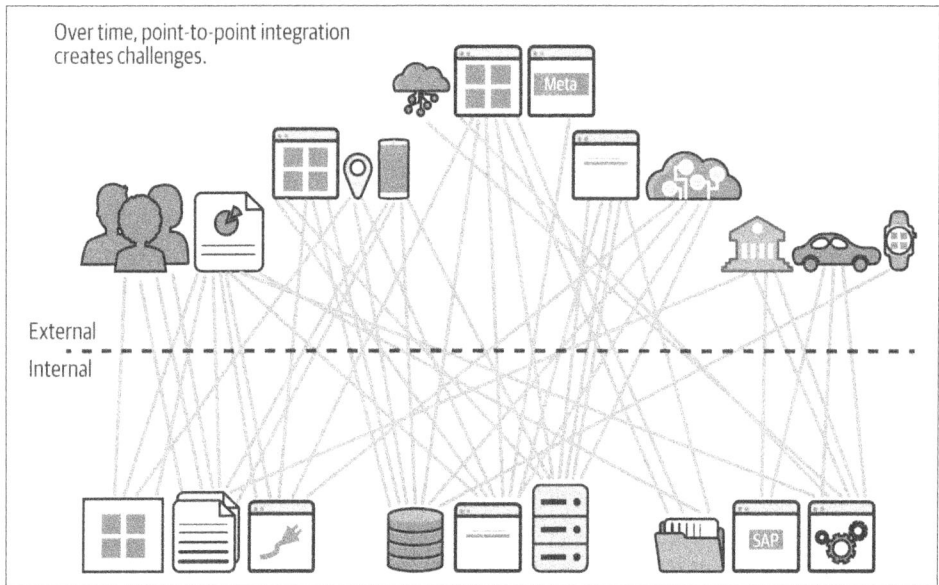

Figure 1-3. Spaghetti integration

P2P integrations got us started, and they were lifesavers back in the day. But as businesses grew and needed more connections, what started as a simple setup quickly turned into a massive headache. Every new system meant adding more custom code, more connections, and a lot more maintenance. It became clear that P2P just wasn't cut out for the big leagues. We needed a better way to keep everything running smoothly without all the hassle.

Enter the enterprise service bus (ESB), the hero of our next section. The ESB brought order to the chaos by acting as a central hub for system communication, taking us from individual connections to a streamlined, organized approach. We'll dive into how the ESB transformed integration, making it easier to scale and manage integration, and keep sanity intact.

Enterprise Service Bus

Think of the *enterprise service bus* (ESB) as the traffic controller of integrations—all those connections that used to be scattered across different systems now run on a single platform. In this setup, everything's centralized, making it a whole lot easier to keep track of what's going on. MuleSoft's runtime environment is perfect for ESB, especially with the Anypoint Platform's control plane, which lets you manage and monitor everything from one place, as shown in Figure 1-4. ESB promotes sharing assets, makes system changes a breeze, and gives you centralized control over governance, security, monitoring, and more.

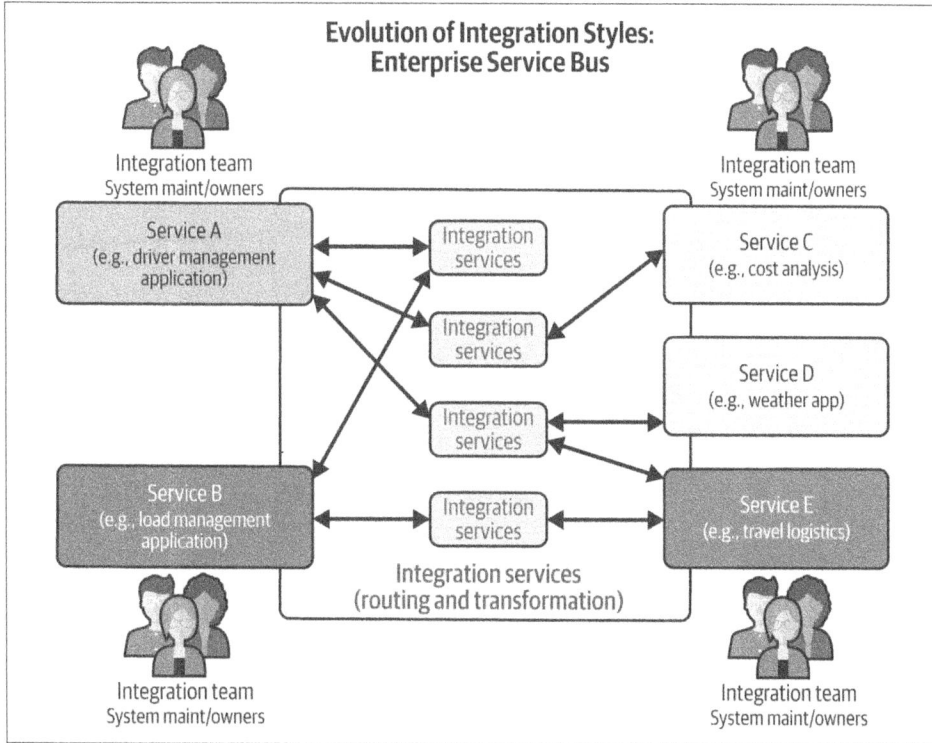

Figure 1-4. ESB integration

Of course, there are a few trade-offs. The biggest risk with an ESB setup is if the platform goes down, it's like hitting the brakes on every integration running through it. Everything is centralized, so one point of failure can freeze the whole network, bringing all those connected systems to a screeching halt. Sure, there are high availability and failover strategies to help prevent this, but they come with extra cost and complexity and need to be factored in.

Then there's the challenge of scalability. While the ESB brings much-needed organization to the P2P mess, as more systems get connected and demands grow, the ESB can start to feel the pressure. Scaling up to keep up with this load isn't as simple as flipping a switch; it takes serious infrastructure and resources. And when the ESB gets overloaded with too many transactions, bottlenecks happen that can slow everything down and impact performance.

But let's talk about the pros. There's a reason the ESB was such a game-changer: with all integrations flowing through a single hub, governance, security, and monitoring have become way easier. You get centralized control, which means you can enforce policies, manage security protocols, and have visibility across every connection—super handy for compliance and troubleshooting. Plus, the ESB promotes reusability. Instead of building the same services over and over, you can share assets across integrations, saving time and cutting down on duplicate work.

Other big wins: quick changes and updates. If you need to update a central service or tweak a policy, you only have to do it once on the ESB, and it's rolled out across all connected systems. No more modifying each integration individually; just one update, and boom, it's everywhere.

Although the ESB brings some serious perks like organization, reusability, and centralized control, it does come with its own set of challenges: potential bottlenecks, higher costs, and some scaling hurdles. It was a major upgrade from P2P, but, as we'll see, the evolution didn't stop there. API-led connectivity is the next big leap in integration strategy, designed to handle these challenges and take things up a notch.

API-Led Connectivity

Now we arrive at the third and most game-changing integration style: API-led connectivity. Here's the big idea: forget the spaghetti mess and single-platform bottlenecks. This approach is about building purpose-driven, reusable APIs that make integration a breeze. At its core, an *application programming interface* (API) is like an agreement between systems, defining exactly how they will work together. With clear rules for inputs, outputs, and data types, each connection is efficient, consistent, and ready to play well with others, as you will see in Chapter 2. And while there are a few different flavors of APIs, RESTful APIs have taken the spotlight. They're reliable, and easy to implement, and their structured methods keep development smooth and reusable, promoting self-service and rapid adoption.

MuleSoft takes API-led connectivity to another level by introducing a separation of concerns that makes integration downright organized. Instead of packing everything into one massive integration layer, as P2P did, MuleSoft breaks functionality into three distinct API layers: Experience APIs (EAPIs), Process APIs (PAPIs), and System APIs (SAPIs). Each layer is like its own team with a specific role:

EAPIs
Connect with end users and devices such as mobile apps or web servers

PAPIs
Handle data transformations and business logic in the background

SAPIs
Provide access to core systems such as databases or legacy platforms

This setup not only keeps things clean, but it also makes scaling and managing integrations much easier.

Here's the thing: switching to API-led connectivity requires a mindset shift, and it can feel like a leap for teams used to P2P or ESB. Some folks find the new structure a bit of a challenge and are tempted to go back to the old ways. But that's where MuleSoft's Center for Enablement (C4E) shines. The C4E is like your integration dream team, providing guidance, support, and best practices to help you maximize API-led connectivity. It's the secret that helps teams avoid technical debt, boost reusability, and build a setup that's ready for whatever comes next.

Each time you need an API, the first move is to see if there's already one available to reuse. If there is, grab it and go. If not, build a new one from scratch with an eye on reusability, knowing it'll likely be a valuable asset down the line. Every project produces API building blocks that can be used in future projects, speeding up delivery and creating a flexible, scalable network over time. By adopting API-led connectivity, you're not just creating isolated integrations—you're building a whole ecosystem of RESTful APIs that are designed to grow with you, adapt to new needs, and make digital transformation as smooth as it gets. Figure 1-5 shows an example of API-led connectivity architecture style.

By following API-led connectivity, you're not just hooking up systems—you're stepping into the role of a true change agent. This isn't just about wiring things together; it's about building a smart, adaptable network that can flex and grow with your organization. MuleSoft's API-led approach puts you on the cutting edge, armed with tools to scale, pivot, and lead the charge in digital transformation. And guess what? This is the exact style you'll learn to master in this book.

But here's where it gets even better: as you implement APIs with this approach, you're not just creating isolated integrations; you're building something bigger—a true application network. This network enables seamless connections across your entire organization, allowing data and services to flow where they're needed when they're needed. "Application Network" on page 10 dives into what an application network means and why it's the backbone of modern, agile organizations.

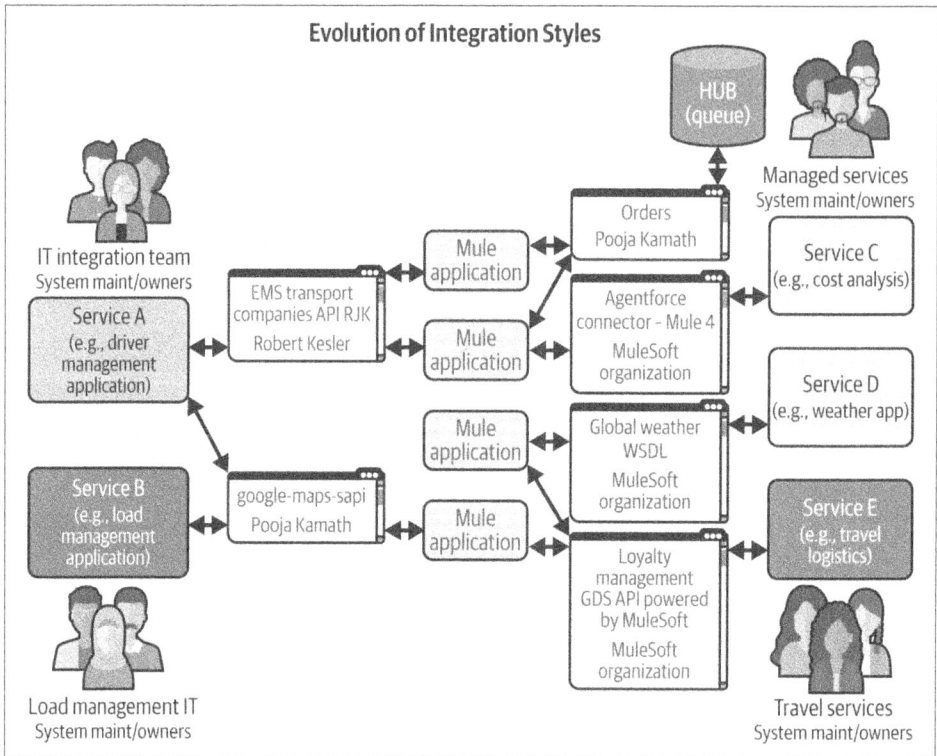

Evolution of Integration Styles

HUB (queue)

Managed services
System maint/owners

IT integration team
System maint/owners

Service A
(e.g., driver management application)

EMS transport companies API RJK
Robert Kesler

Mule application

Orders
Pooja Kamath

Service C
(e.g., cost analysis)

Mule application

Agentforce connector - Mule 4
MuleSoft organization

Service D
(e.g., weather app)

Mule application

Global weather WSDL
MuleSoft organization

Service B
(e.g., load management application)

google-maps-sapi
Pooja Kamath

Mule application

Service E
(e.g., travel logistics)

Loyalty management
GDS API powered by MuleSoft
MuleSoft organization

Load management IT
System maint/owners

Travel services
System maint/owners

Figure 1-5. API-led connectivity

Application Network

An *application network* is like a connected ecosystem where all your apps, systems, and even AI components talk effortlessly through a network of APIs. Instead of dealing with one-off connections or a centralized bottleneck, you're building a flexible, plug-and-play system where each API serves a specific purpose—whether it's fetching data from a legacy system, handling business logic, processing documents with AI, or powering a mobile app. The beauty of an application network is that as new apps, AI services, or intelligent processing tools come on board, they slot right in without disturbing the existing flow. No more backtracking or reworking old connections—everything just fits.

And this modular setup isn't just about saving time; it's about creating a network that grows and adapts. Need to add an AI-driven feature like Intelligent Document Processing? Easy. This network can handle complex data extraction, automation, and processing workflows that scale with you. An application network gives you that smooth, connected flow, transforming what used to be a tangled mess into a streamlined, adaptable powerhouse. It's the backbone of a truly agile organization, empowering you to stay flexible, move fast, and innovate like never before (see Figure 1-6).

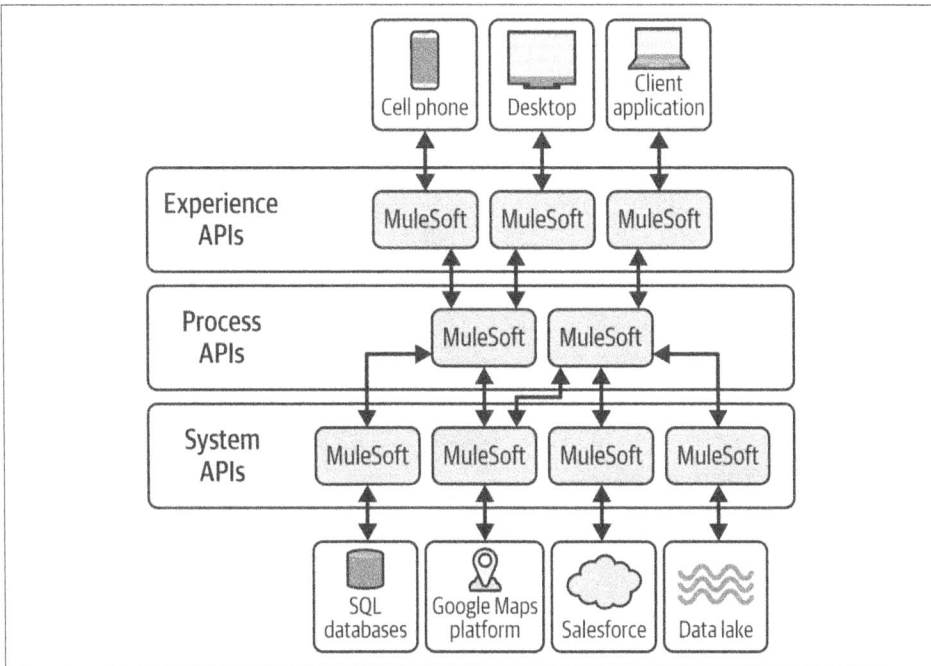

Figure 1-6. Application network

To build this kind of agility, it's not just about having APIs—it's about designing them the right way. The structure of your application network depends heavily on the connectivity pattern you choose. That's where API-led design comes in. Before identifying which APIs make up your use case, we need to understand how different API layers support our goals.

It is essential to understand that these patterns are not "one size fits all" and can vary depending on your goals. Sometimes, engineers and architects create three-layer API-led connectivity patterns even when it is unnecessary. If your end goal is to create an application network for your organization, it is crucial to use the appropriate API-led connectivity pattern. This pattern could have one, two, or three layers or be a combination of event-driven and layered architecture. What matters is that it achieves the following:

- Each asset has a clear purpose.
- The assets can be combined with other capabilities to extend functionality.

- The assets are easy to find and manage.
- The assets describe the elements and actions that make up the core functions and operations of your business.

Our objective for SRL is to create a real-time quote generation solution using the aforementioned guidance. To integrate SRL's proprietary cost-analysis software with MuleSoft, it's important to include variables like traffic conditions, package load, and driver availability in the analytics model to optimize operations and reduce costs. So, at a minimum we need to build the following applications:

Google Maps API
   This API will be integrated with Google Maps to receive current traffic conditions and estimated times of arrival.

Driver management API
   This API will integrate with SRL's in-house workforce management system. For our sample project we can mock the data in a local database.

Load management API
   This API will integrate with SRL's in-house driver management system. Like for the driver management API, the data will be mocked in a local database.

Cost analysis API
   This is an existing API that SRL uses to process quotes. This API will be enhanced to use information from the traffic system, workforce management system, and package load system to improve quotes and package delivery systems.

Real-time quote generation API
   This API will process quotes for packages using traffic, load, and driver information.

Route optimization API
   This API will process package arrival, delay, vehicle routing information, and other systems.

Now, let's categorize these into experience, process, and system APIs:

Experience layer
   This is the presentation layer; the customer portal API and driver portal API will be in the experience layer. Per our use case these APIs already exist, and customers use them to access quotes and delivery information.

Process layer

This layer consists of APIs that are internal to the business and will gather and process data from different systems. APIs in this layer do not have to worry about system integration or client integration. They are isolated from direct outside exposure. This must be considered when planning for the security and governance of these APIs. The quote generation API and route optimization API will be our process APIs.

System layer

This layer consists of APIs that can access the system of records and resurface data. In our case, these are the Google Maps API, driver management API, load management API, and truck API.

Applying API-led connectivity architecture style, we see the SRL APIs identified, as in Figure 1-7.

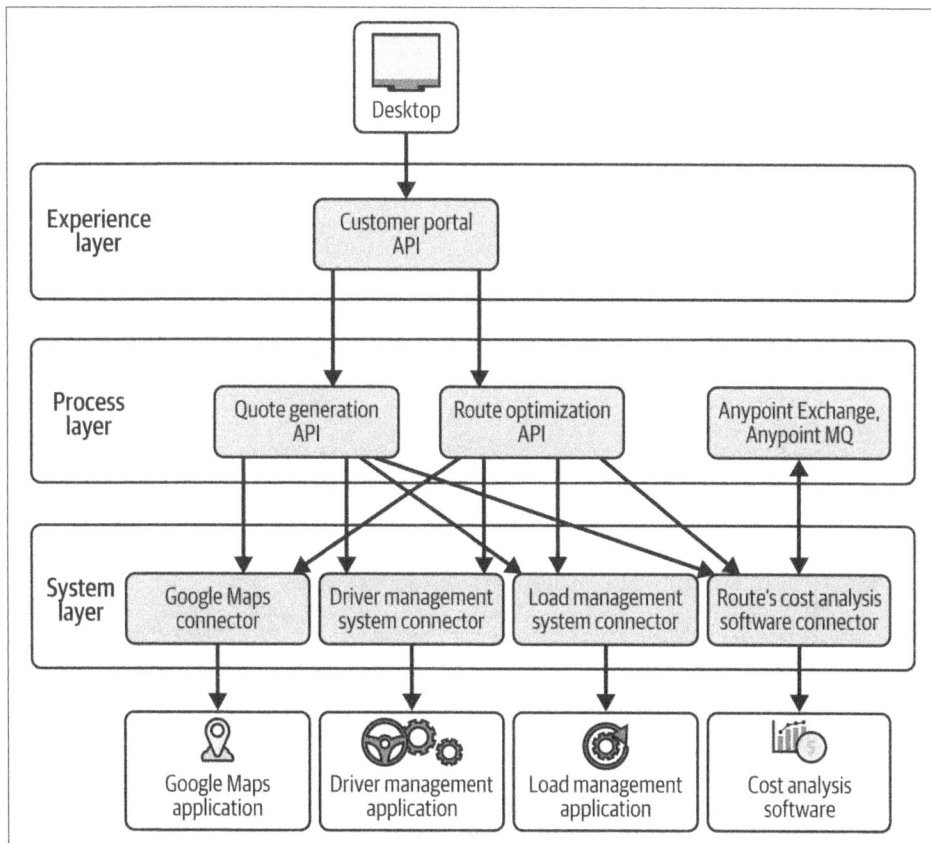

Figure 1-7. API-led connectivity

Here is the code we used to render Figure 1-7 in Mermaid:

```
graph TD
  subgraph ExperienceLayer[Experience Layer]
    A[Customer Portal API]
  end
  subgraph ProcessLayer[Process Layer]
    B[Quote Generation API]
    C[Route Optimization API]
   subgraph
    D[[Anypoint Exchange, Anypoint MQ]]
   end
  end
  subgraph System Layer[System Layer]
    F[Google Maps Connector]
    G[Driver Management System Connector]
    H[Load Management System Connector]
    We[Route's Cost-Analysis Software Connector]

  end
  A --> B
  A --> C
  B --> F
  B --> G
  B --> H
  B --> WE
  C --> F
  C --> G
  C --> H
  C --> WE
  F--> J[Google Maps Application]
  G--> K[Driver Management Application]
  H --> L[Load Management Application]
  WE --> M[Cost Analysis Software]
  D <--> WE
```

> There is an API-led connectivity template that MuleSoft shares with its customers, and you can customize that to create API-led connectivity pattern diagrams for your use cases.

Beyond the three layers, we often see event-driven architecture integration connecting with this design at various points. For SRL, we are utilizing MuleSoft's Anypoint MQ to broadcast quote data across the organization. This will make the quote data accessible to other users and analytics platforms.

Discovery

The discovery process is all about gathering the information needed to design a solid MuleSoft solution. Even if you're handed what seems like comprehensive project documentation, it's still crucial to perform your own discovery. Start by asking questions—lots of them—and documenting everything you learn. This information becomes the foundation for creating sequence diagrams, context diagrams, and detailed API stories that guide the development process.

Broadly, the real-time quote generation solution will behave as follows:

1. Customer initiates a request for a shipping quote via the Customer Portal.
2. Customer portal forwards the quote request to the MuleSoft integration layer.
3. MuleSoft integration layer sends parallel asynchronous requests to:
    a. Google Maps API for real-time traffic data.
    b. Driver management system for driver availability.
    c. Load management system for package load status.
4. Google Maps API responds with real-time traffic data.
5. Driver management system responds with driver availability data.
6. Load management system responds with current package load status.
7. MuleSoft integration layer:
    a. Transforms and aggregates the data using DataWeave.
    b. Sends the aggregated data to OptimoRoute's cost-analysis software.
8. MuleSoft integration layer:
    a. Receives the calculated quote from the cost-analysis software.
    b. Puts the quote into Anypoint Message Queue (MQ) for future analytics and auditing.
9. Cost-analysis software processes the data and calculates the real-time quote.
10. Customer portal receives the real-time quote from the MuleSoft integration layer.
11. Customer sees the real-time shipping quote displayed on the portal.

SRL has a customer portal that is tightly coupled with the cost-analysis software. The goal is to uncouple it and build a MuleSoft integration layer between the customer portal and the application systems that SRL uses. Some examples of good questions to ask during discovery include:

- What is the volume of quote requests that come through daily?
- How can you unlock data from the cost-analysis software?

- Are there any security controls that would impact integration with load management APIs or driver management APIs?
- Does the enterprise have an error-handling strategy?
- Should there be an alert if quote generation fails?
- Is there a need for a retry mechanism?

The example we gave you is just a starting point. For a full picture, you must both dig deep into the documentation and have some face-to-face chats with the customer. After we have a good grasp on things, we loop back with everyone we've been talking to during this discovery phase. This is usually when any missing pieces or manual steps we should have caught before are found. For example, after sharing the documentation with the logistics manager, we might be told, "When a quote is generated and a driver lined up, the front-desk associate, Krysta, must get an email copy. That way, she can give the driver a ring and set a reminder."

After the discovery is complete, it's time to create a sequence diagram.

Writing Sequence Diagrams

Sequence diagrams are interaction diagrams that keep the project on track and the implementation team in the loop. We like to start with a big-picture sequence diagram for the whole solution. Then, we get into the nitty-gritty and create diagrams for each piece. As time-consuming as this is, we assure you, it's worth the effort. You'd be surprised how many mini-cycles can pop up within each major step, and you don't want to overlook those.

Well-crafted sequence diagrams can be the difference between a successful MuleSoft project and one that falls short. They not only provide clarity during development but also help onboard new developers quickly by visualizing how systems interact. Sequence diagrams follow the unified modeling language (UML) standard.

The key components are:

- Lifelines represent the major players in the solution, such as systems or components. They appear as vertical dashed lines.
- Activation bars show when an object or system is performing an action and are drawn as vertical rectangles on the lifelines.
- Messages represent the communication between activation bars and are illustrated with arrows.
- Control behaviors include loops, conditions, and other flow control mechanisms that represent the system's complex logic.

Sequence diagrams are read from top to bottom. Lifelines are horizontal, and the arrows or lines going up and down are the interactions or method calls. Figure 1-8 shows an example sequence diagram for our use case.

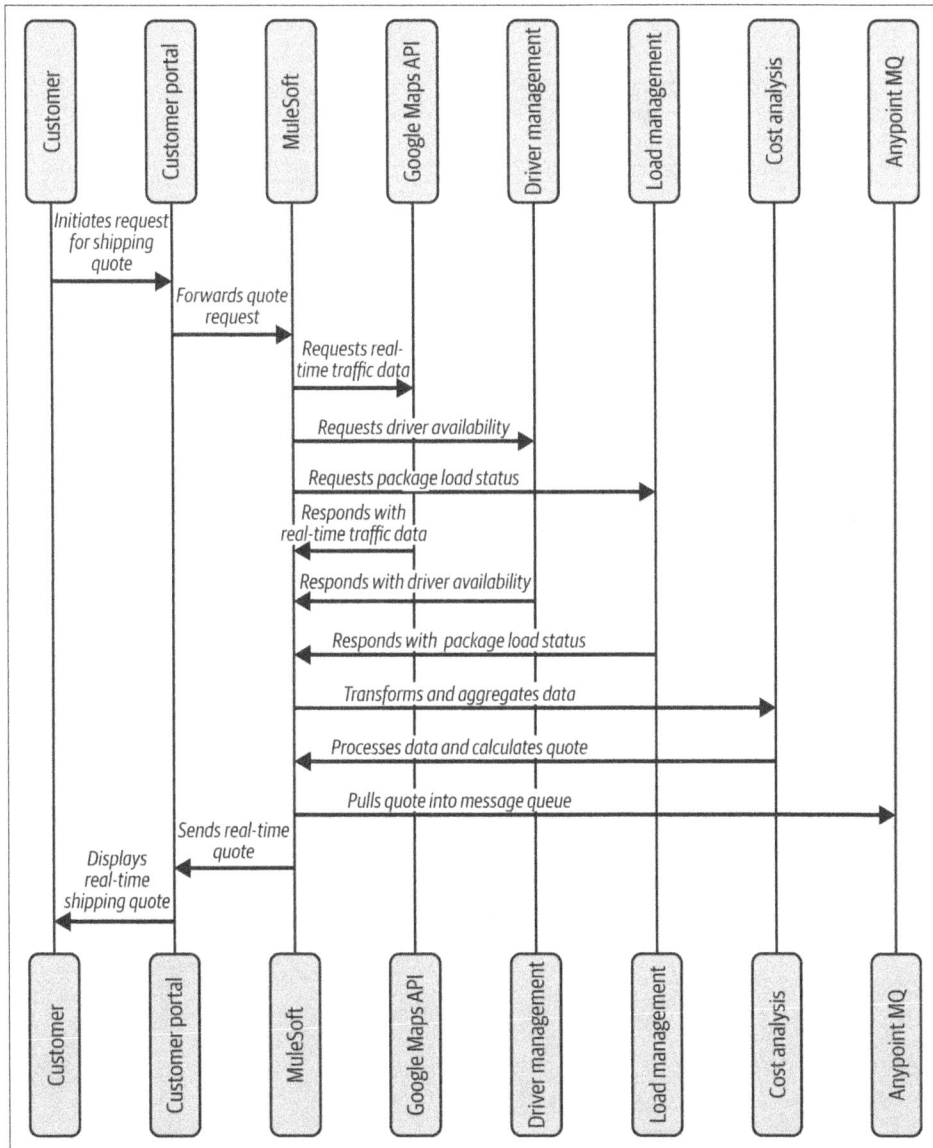

Figure 1-8. SRL sequence diagram

Here is the Mermaid code for Figure 1-8:

```
sequence diagram
  participant Customer
  participant CustomerPortal
  participant MuleSoft
  participant GoogleMapsAPI
  participant DriverManagement
  participant LoadManagement
  participant CostAnalysis
  participant AnypointMQ

  Customer->>CustomerPortal: Initiates request for shipping quote
  CustomerPortal->>MuleSoft: Forwards quote request
  MuleSoft->>GoogleMapsAPI: Requests real-time traffic data
  MuleSoft->>DriverManagement: Requests driver availability
  MuleSoft->>LoadManagement: Requests package load status
  GoogleMapsAPI->>MuleSoft: Responds with real-time traffic data
  DriverManagement->>MuleSoft: Responds with driver availability
  LoadManagement->>MuleSoft: Responds with package load status
  MuleSoft->>CostAnalysis: Transforms & aggregates data
  CostAnalysis->>MuleSoft: Processes data & calculates quote
  MuleSoft->>AnypointMQ: Puts quote into Message Queue
  MuleSoft->>CustomerPortal: Sends real-time quote
  CustomerPortal->>Customer: Displays real-time shipping quote
```

Writing API Context Diagrams

API context diagrams are a special type of context diagram focusing on the API and its interaction with external elements. After you've defined processes with sequence diagrams, an API context diagram serves as a reality check. It can also help you spot gaps and inconsistencies within a project. We like to write API context diagrams for all APIs we are developing. This serves as documentation later for the API itself. Like the sequence diagrams, API context diagrams help to onboard developers quicker and reduce resource drain by catching inconsistencies earlier in the project cycle. Figure 1-9 shows an API context diagram for the Driver Management API.

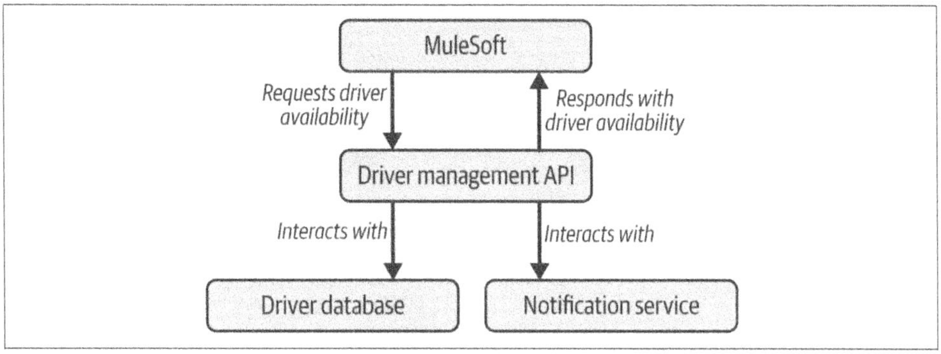

Figure 1-9. Driver Management API context diagram

Here is the Mermaid code we used to render Figure 1-9:

```
graph TD
  MuleSoft -->|Requests Driver Availability|
  DriverManagementAPI[Driver Management API]
  DriverManagementAPI -->|Responds with Driver
  Availability|
  MuleSoft DriverManagementAPI -->|Interacts with|
  DriverDatabase[Driver Database]
  DriverManagementAPI -->|Interacts with|
  NotificationService[Notification Service]
```

Both sequence diagrams and API context diagrams serve as documentation for the API stories that will be discussed next.

Writing Stories

API stories are essential for Agile project development.

To write API stories, follow the template provided by Mike Amundsen in *Design and Build Great Web APIs* (Pragmatic Bookshelf). In our case for the Driver Management API, the story would look something like Figure 1-10.

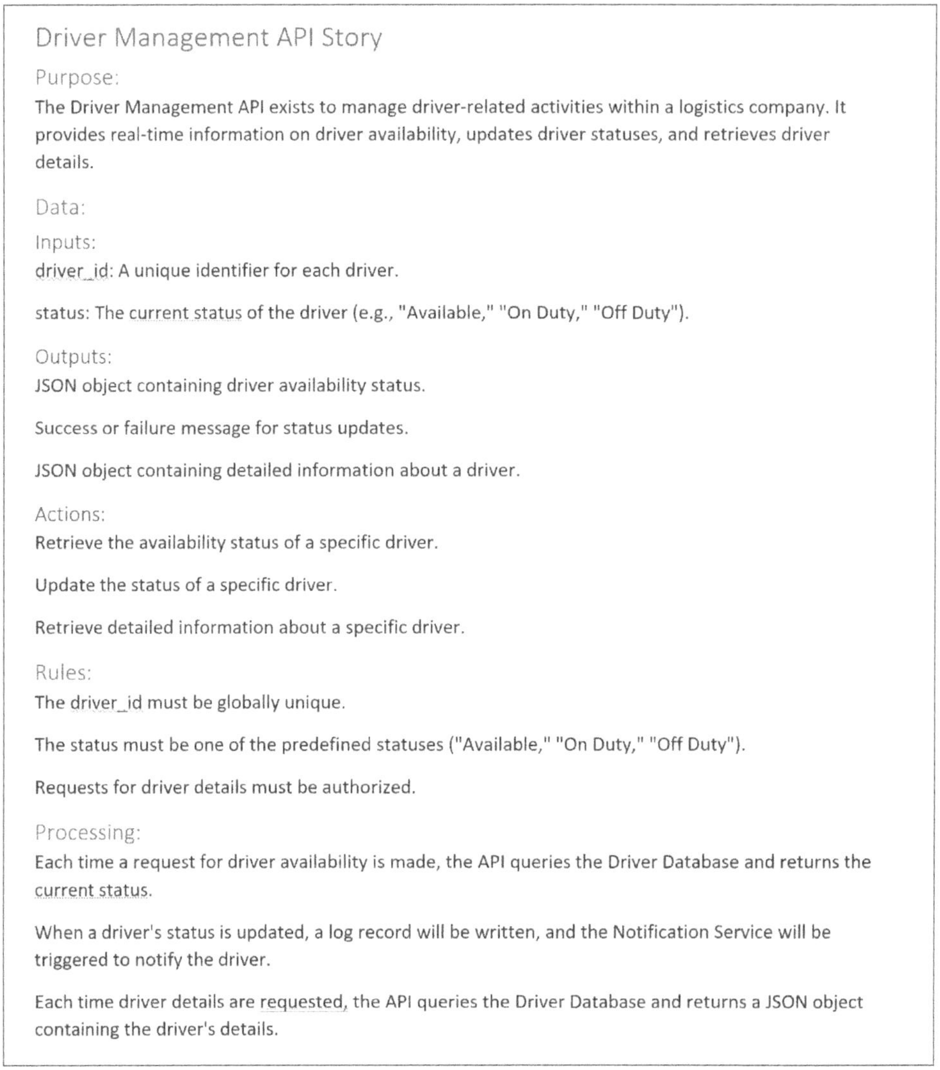

Driver Management API Story

Purpose:

The Driver Management API exists to manage driver-related activities within a logistics company. It provides real-time information on driver availability, updates driver statuses, and retrieves driver details.

Data:

Inputs:

driver_id: A unique identifier for each driver.

status: The current status of the driver (e.g., "Available," "On Duty," "Off Duty").

Outputs:

JSON object containing driver availability status.

Success or failure message for status updates.

JSON object containing detailed information about a driver.

Actions:

Retrieve the availability status of a specific driver.

Update the status of a specific driver.

Retrieve detailed information about a specific driver.

Rules:

The driver_id must be globally unique.

The status must be one of the predefined statuses ("Available," "On Duty," "Off Duty").

Requests for driver details must be authorized.

Processing:

Each time a request for driver availability is made, the API queries the Driver Database and returns the current status.

When a driver's status is updated, a log record will be written, and the Notification Service will be triggered to notify the driver.

Each time driver details are requested, the API queries the Driver Database and returns a JSON object containing the driver's details.

Figure 1-10. API story for Driver Management API

Now that we have a complete set of project documents, let's add them to a folder called *project documents*.

Integration Essentials: The Tools You Need to Succeed

In this section, we're gearing up with the essentials you'll use throughout the book. We'll dive into the core tools of the MuleSoft ecosystem: Anypoint Platform, Anypoint Studio, and the all-new Anypoint Code Builder (ACB). You'll also pick up the basics for managing code and performing unit testing, all while keeping our sample use case for SRL front and center. The goal is to give you a solid foundation in these tools so you can build MuleSoft applications that aren't just functional—they're production-ready and built to perform. Let's get started and put together the toolkit that'll take your integration game to the next level.

MuleSoft's Anypoint Platform

MuleSoft's Anypoint Platform is a comprehensive, full lifecycle API management tool that supports every stage of your API journey, from design to deployment. To get started, simply log in (*https://oreil.ly/x2s6h*). If you don't have an account, you can sign up for a free 30-day trial. For the rest of this book, we'll assume you're logged into the Anypoint Platform and ready to go.

Before we get into the platform's capabilities, let's take a moment to review some fundamentals of cloud architecture within the Anypoint context. MuleSoft's Anypoint Platform is built on two powerhouse components: the control plane and the runtime plane. Each one brings something essential to the table, working together to keep your integrations running smoothly and ready to scale.

Control plane

The *control plane* is the brains of the operation. It's where you design, manage, and monitor your APIs and integrations. Accessible through the Anypoint Platform's web interface, this is your go-to for everything from API creation and version control to policy enforcement and access management. With tools like Anypoint API Manager and Anypoint Exchange, the control plane gives you complete visibility and, yes, *control* over your application network. It's also packed with security, governance, and monitoring features, making it easy to enforce standards, track performance, and manage access—all in one place. Think of the control plane as your command center, giving you centralized control to manage the full lifecycle of your integrations.

Runtime plane

The *runtime plane* is where Mule servers operate, enabling the real-time execution of your integrations and APIs. Designed for flexibility, the runtime plane supports various deployment models.

In CloudHub, each application runs within its own isolated container, with a dedicated Mule runtime instance per application—commonly referred to as a "one application, one runtime" model. In contrast, on-premises servers and preferred cloud providers follow a "many applications, one runtime" approach, where a single Mule runtime can host and manage multiple applications. This versatility allows organizations to adopt hybrid setups that align with their infrastructure preferences and scalability requirements.

Together, the control plane and runtime plane are the dynamic duo of Anypoint, each handling its own essential part to keep your integrations on point. The control plane manages and governs, while the runtime plane takes care of execution. Understanding how these planes work together is key to building an efficient, scalable application network that's ready to tackle whatever your business throws at it.

Anypoint Platform APIs

There is a special group of APIs that serve as the driving force behind the MuleSoft Anypoint Platform, providing essential capabilities that keep your integrations running smoothly. These powerful APIs enable you to manage, monitor, and automate your integration processes with ease, supporting automation, CI/CD pipelines, and much more (see Figure 1-11).

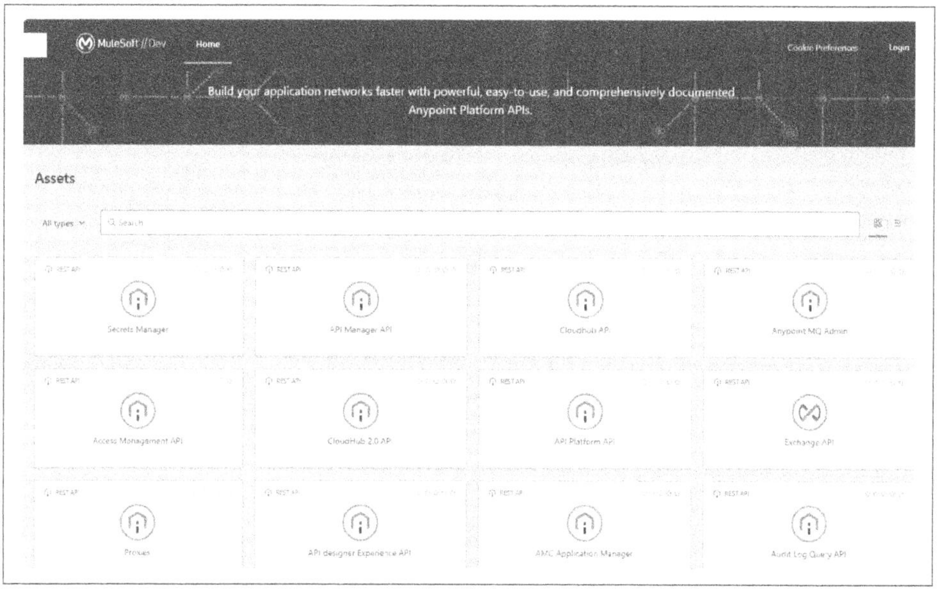

Figure 1-11. Anypoint Platform APIs

With these APIs, you can effortlessly create, update, and oversee your integrations, handling everything from policy settings to performance metrics—all while keeping everything organized and efficient. Plus, you can manage user access and permissions, ensuring that the right people have the keys (IDs and secrets) to your kingdom.

These APIs also give you access to vital analytics and monitoring tools that provide insights into usage patterns and error rates, helping you maintain the health of your integrations. And with the ability to automate your deployment processes and streamline CI/CD pipelines, launching your applications becomes faster and more efficient.

Finally, connecting with other systems and tools is a breeze, allowing you to expand your integration capabilities without any hassle. With Anypoint Platform APIs, you unlock a world of possibilities that transform your integration strategy and set you up for success.

Getting Started with the Anypoint Platform

Now that you understand the importance of Anypoint Platform APIs, let's look at how to effectively use the Anypoint Platform itself. This powerful tool is your gateway to designing, managing, and deploying your integrations. The following sections explore its key features, including Anypoint Studio for development, Anypoint Exchange for asset sharing, and a part on how to leverage the platform's capabilities to build a robust application network.

Simply put, the Anypoint Platform offers tools to design, build, and manage APIs and integrations. The Anypoint Platform landing page in Figure 1-12 shows the different components available for use.

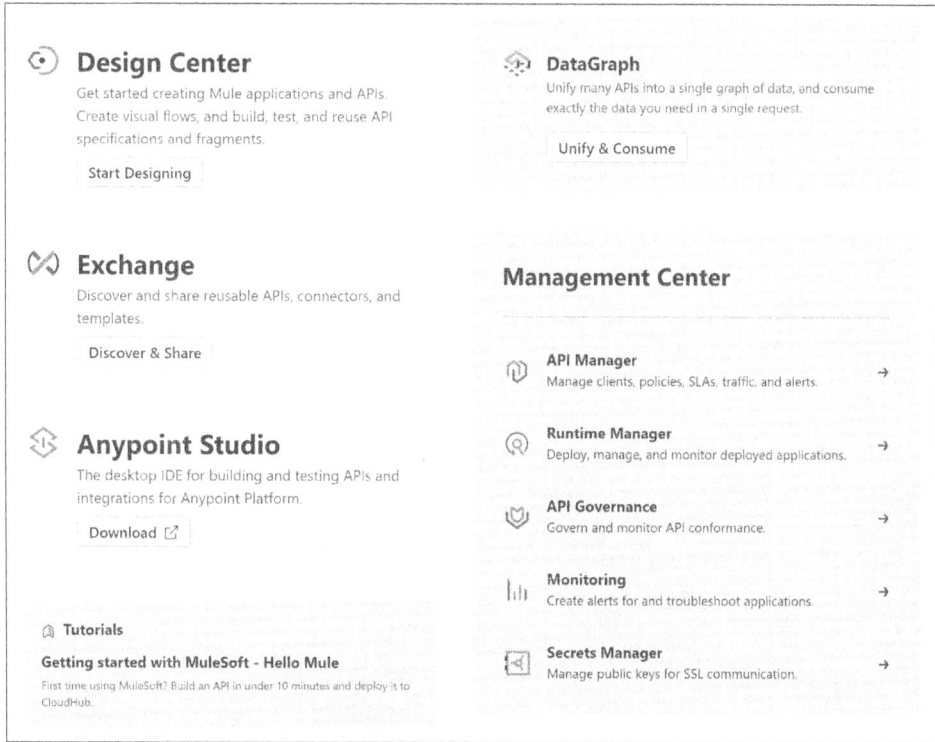

Design Center
Get started creating Mule applications and APIs. Create visual flows, and build, test, and reuse API specifications and fragments.

Start Designing

Exchange
Discover and share reusable APIs, connectors, and templates.

Discover & Share

Anypoint Studio
The desktop IDE for building and testing APIs and integrations for Anypoint Platform.

Download

Tutorials

Getting started with MuleSoft - Hello Mule
First time using MuleSoft? Build an API in under 10 minutes and deploy it to CloudHub.

DataGraph
Unify many APIs into a single graph of data, and consume exactly the data you need in a single request.

Unify & Consume

Management Center

API Manager
Manage clients, policies, SLAs, traffic, and alerts.

Runtime Manager
Deploy, manage, and monitor deployed applications.

API Governance
Govern and monitor API conformance.

Monitoring
Create alerts for and troubleshoot applications.

Secrets Manager
Manage public keys for SSL communication.

Figure 1-12. Anypoint Platform landing page

Let's explore some of these capabilities needed to develop a real-time analytics solution for our fictitious SRL company:

Design Center

The Anypoint Design Center is a powerful and intuitive web-based tool that allows you to design, build, and document your APIs in a collaborative environment.

API Designer

API Designer is a powerful web-based tool that developers use to design and define APIs with clarity and precision. It enables you to create detailed API specifications using RESTful API Modeling Language (RAML) or Open API Specification (OAS), making it easy to outline how different applications will communicate. Think of it as your digital sketchpad for mapping out seamless data flow and interactions.

We'll be using API Designer extensively as we work through our sample use case, covering each step in detail to ensure a clear and effective API design. Whether you prefer the text editor for direct coding or the visual editor for a more hands-on approach, API Designer provides both options, giving you flexibility as you build powerful, production-ready APIs.

Anypoint Exchange

Anypoint Exchange is a centralized repository and marketplace that takes collaborative API development and integration work to the next level. It's packed with a variety of prebuilt API specifications, connectors, templates, and more, all designed to jump-start your projects and streamline development, saving you valuable time and effort. We'll be diving into Anypoint Exchange in detail soon, exploring how it supports efficient, reusable, and scalable integration solutions.

API Manager

API Manager is the go-to tool for managing APIs, giving you control over the entire lifecycle. We'll be using it to not only oversee but also govern and secure the APIs we're developing for our hypothetical logistics enterprise. With API Manager, you'll have everything you need to ensure that your APIs are compliant, protected, and performing at their best.

Runtime Manager

Runtime Manager is the command center for deploying, managing, and monitoring your Mule applications and APIs. Whether on prem, in CloudHub, or in a hybrid setup, it provides complete visibility and control, ensuring your integrations run smoothly and securely.

Monitoring

Anypoint Monitoring provides real-time visibility into the performance and health of your Mule applications and APIs. With powerful analytics, alerts, and dashboards, it helps you proactively manage and troubleshoot issues, ensuring optimal performance across your integration landscape.

Anypoint Code Builder

ACB is MuleSoft's new integrated development environment (IDE) and uses visual code for the design and development of APIs. ACB is a cloud-based IDE for building, testing, and deploying APIs and integrations, enhanced with AI Flow Builder. This feature uses AI to suggest flow designs, automate repetitive tasks, and streamline the development process. With smart code suggestions, debugging tools, and seamless integration within the Anypoint Platform, it empowers you to create, refine, and manage APIs with speed.

> If you cannot access or view the features mentioned here, it indicates that you don't have the necessary permission. If so, contact your Anypoint Platform administrator for assistance. However, if you've signed up for a trial account, you should have access to all the tools and services offered by Anypoint Platform.

Next we'll look at Anypoint Exchange and Anypoint Studio. To begin with, we'll just review these tools to get a better understanding of how they work. Think of it as speed dating for technology. We'll get to know the features and functions but without making any commitments for now, starting with Anypoint Exchange.

Anypoint Exchange

Anypoint Exchange is a carefully organized library of reusable resources. We already discussed the concept of an application network and emphasized how it should enable users to autonomously find and repurpose various assets. Anypoint Exchange precisely serves this function. And because of this, Anypoint Exchange integrates closely with other tools within the MuleSoft ecosystem. This is the first place you should look before you begin the development of applications. The essence of an application network is to capitalize on work that's already been done, rather than redundantly creating new P2P integrations. Learning how to leverage Anypoint Exchange efficiently will help you discover integration assets such as connectors, templates, and examples that are already available, so you can focus your efforts on innovation.

Anypoint Exchange is a searchable catalog where you can perform keyword searches and filter, sort, and save search results. When you perform a search in Anypoint Exchange, it scours a variety of elements to find what you're looking for. These elements include the asset's name, its description, the contact's name, and the email associated with it, as well as any tags or categories. Additionally, the search also combs through the content present on the asset's portal pages. If you're dealing with OAS and RAML API specifications, rest assured it also looks into the properties defined there.

> Anypoint Platform uses metadata and descriptive information to help you discover appropriate assets for your project, accelerating development cycles.

Anypoint Studio

Anypoint Studio is MuleSoft's go-to workspace for developers, built on the reliable Eclipse platform and loaded with tools to make Mule application development smooth and efficient. A good IDE needs to support real-time, local testing, and Anypoint Studio does just that. It integrates seamlessly with Anypoint Exchange, so you can kick off projects with ready-to-use templates and examples right at your fingertips. You can also import resources directly from your Anypoint Platform account, making it easy to bring everything you need into one place. Plus, Anypoint Studio has built-in unit testing, debugging tools, and native capabilities for deploying applications to CloudHub—everything you need to streamline your development workflow.

> Anypoint Studio 7.x is compatible exclusively with Mule 4.x projects. This is due to differences in project structure, export formats, and underlying scripting languages, making it incompatible with Mule 3.x runtimes or older versions. So, unless you are working on Mule 3.x migrations, you should be using Mule 4.x only.

With Anypoint Studio successfully installed and ready to use, let's explore what happens when you open it for the first time. As shown in Figure 1-13, three different capabilities are available:

Workspace Name
> Anypoint Studio is just like Eclipse in that you can switch workspaces. We advise you to use a dedicated workspace for a project to minimize confusion.

Package Explorer

This is where you will see the project and all its structural elements. Right now, it is blank because we have not done anything. If you click the "Create a Mule Project" link, you will see it populated with the elements of the project.

Mule Palette

Mule Palette is where all your MuleSoft components and connectors will show up. We will be using this a lot, so it's a good idea to take some time to get familiar with it.

There are other parts to Anypoint Studio, as you can see in the landing page shown in Figure 1-13, and when we do hands-on exercises, we will explore them in detail.

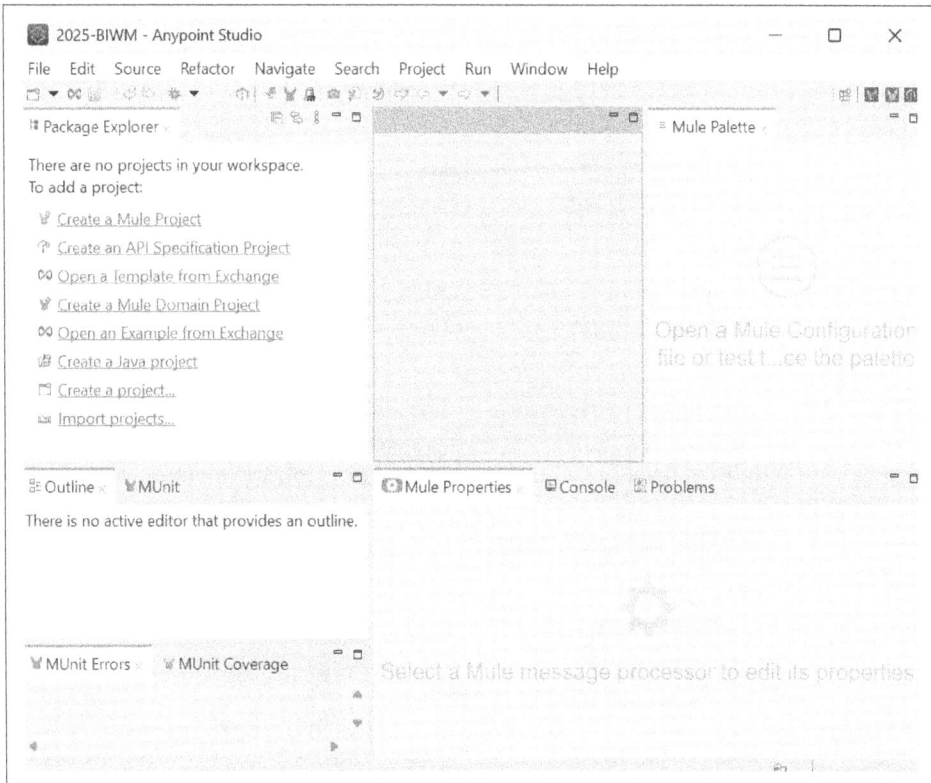

Figure 1-13. Anypoint Studio landing page

Anypoint Code Builder

ACB is a new IDE for developers, as shown in Figure 1-14. Using this IDE, you can create and launch APIs, integrations, and automation seamlessly within a unified environment. This advanced tool offers developers a suite of capabilities:

API design across specifications
Create APIs with versatility, accommodating various specifications and requirements.

Built-in mocking service for API testing
Validate and test the functionality of APIs seamlessly with the aid of the integrated mocking service.

Automated API logic implementation
Streamline the development process by automatically implementing API logic based on existing specifications.

Building integrations across applications, systems, and data
Construct integrations effortlessly, connecting diverse applications, systems, and data sources seamlessly.

ACB is built on Visual Studio Code (VS Code), whereas Anypoint Studio runs on Eclipse—two popular development environments that add familiarity and flexibility to the MuleSoft ecosystem.

VS Code is a lightweight, cross-platform editor known for its speed and versatility. It supports multiple languages and offers features like IntelliSense for smart code completion, a built-in terminal, and robust Git integration, making it ideal for cloud-based development. ACB leverages these strengths, enabling API design and development directly in the cloud, with a minimal learning curve for teams familiar with VS Code.

Eclipse is a powerful, extensible IDE widely used for Java and enterprise applications. As a desktop-based environment, it provides deep support for debugging, testing, and performance monitoring. Anypoint Studio's foundation on Eclipse brings these capabilities to MuleSoft, offering efficient Mule application development with tools for testing, deployment, and resource management.

By building on VS Code (as shown in Figure 1-14) for cloud development and Eclipse for robust desktop work, these tools streamline both API design and integration projects, creating a seamless experience for developers.

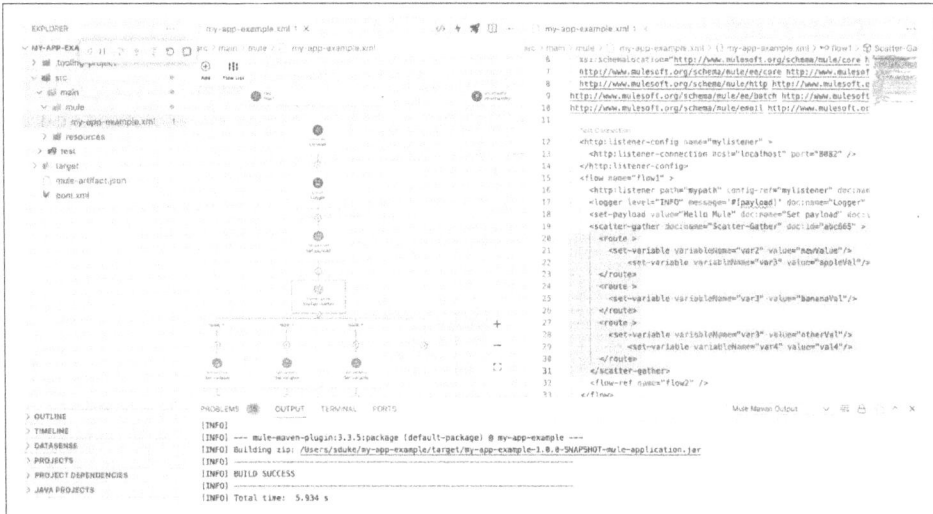

Figure 1-14. An ACB graphical canvas

Maven

Maven is a powerful build automation and project management tool designed for Java-based applications, including MuleSoft projects. It simplifies dependency management, project structuring, and build execution. Anypoint Studio and Maven work together seamlessly to make your development process more efficient. With Maven integrated directly into Anypoint Studio, managing dependencies becomes effortless and ensures that your builds are consistent.

If you require more control over your Maven settings, you can use your custom Maven within Anypoint Studio. This is particularly useful if you need to integrate your Mule app with other Maven-based systems such as your CI/CD pipelines.

POM and Its Elements

When you use Maven in your projects, you might come across a file named *pom.xml*. This is not just a configuration file; it is a blueprint Maven uses for building, packaging, and deploying your project. Maven's Project Object Model (POM) lists all the dependencies and respective versions required for your project. This helps Maven handle the downloads of your application's plug-ins and dependencies efficiently. POM is especially useful when integrating with third-party libraries or modules in your application. Additionally, the POM file defines build lifecycles for projects. This is used to validate projects, compile code, run MUnit tests before deployments, and inject plug-ins into projects. MUnit is MuleSoft's unit testing framework, designed to ensure reliability and stability by allowing developers to create and automate tests for their Mule applications. It enables mocking dependencies, validating payloads, and checking error handling, ensuring that integrations work as expected before deployment. The POM file includes all the necessary details, such as name, version, and description, which you require when pushing artifacts to a code repository. It also allows you to set environment-specific variables, making switching between development, testing, and production environments easy.

The POM file includes several core elements that provide essential metadata and configuration options for a Maven project. Here are the core POM elements:

<modelVersion>

Usually *x.x.x*, where *x* represents a number between 0 and 9; this specifies the POM model version.

<groupId> *and* <artifactId>

These are your project's unique identifiers; artifactId is your project's name, and groupId is usually your organization's domain name flipped.

<version>

Your project's version, plain and simple.

<dependencies>

Lists the libraries you'll need, for example, MUnit, Anypoint MQ, and so on.

<plugins>

The plug-ins you'll need for tasks like compiling, packaging, and testing.

<properties>

These are reusable variables within the POM.

Here is an example POM file with core elements visible:

```
<project>
  <modelVersion>4.0.0</modelVersion>
  <groupId>com.superRouteLogistics</groupId>
  <artifactId>sys-weather-api</artifactId>
  <version>1.0</version>

  <dependencies>
    <!-- Your dependencies go here -->
  </dependencies>

  <build>
    <plugins>
      <!-- Your plugins go here -->
    </plugins>
  </build>
</project>
```

Repositories

The Maven repositories are your go-to spots for all project artifacts—libraries, plugins, you name it. You've got three main types:

Local repository
> This is where Maven stores all the stuff it downloads for the first time. It's usually in the *.m2/repository* in your home directory.

Central repository
> Hosted by the Maven community, this is your one-stop shop for commonly used libraries.

Remote repositories
> These are custom repos, often maintained by organizations for their specific needs.

Maven checks *pom.xml* for your project's dependencies and looks for those dependencies in your local repo first. If it's not local, Maven fetches it from a remote repo and stores the dependency locally for future use. Finally, Maven uses these dependencies to build your project.

Maven's Lifecycle

Maven follows a build lifecycle with phases such as validate, compile, test, and install. There are three built-in lifecycles.

Default

Handles project deployment. The main phases in this lifecycle include:

Validate
> Checks if you've got all you need for the build.

Compile
> Compiles the source code. Syntax errors, beware!

Test
> Runs unit tests. If one fails, the build fails.

Package
> Packs the compiled code into a runnable format.

Verify
> Checks if the package is set up correctly.

Install
> Makes the package available locally.

Deploy
> Sends the package to a remote repo for sharing.

Clean

Cleans up your project by removing build-time files. The primary phase in this lifecycle is the clean phase. When you run `mvn clean`, it triggers the clean phase of the clean lifecycle, which typically deletes the project's target directory. The main phases in this lifecycle include the following:

Pre-clean
> Executes processes needed before the actual project cleaning.

Clean
> Removes all files generated by the previous build.

Post-clean
> Executes processes needed to finalize the project cleaning.

Site

Generates your project's documentation. The main phase in this lifecycle is the site phase. When you run `mvn site`, it triggers the site phase of the site lifecycle, which generates project documentation, including any reports defined in the POM. The main phases in this lifecycle are as follows:

Pre-site
> Executes processes needed before the actual project site generation.

Site
> Generates project documentation and reports as defined in the POM.

Post-site
> Executes processes needed to finalize the site generation.

Site-deploy
> Deploys the generated site documentation to a specified web server.

To sum it up: every lifecycle is equipped with distinct phases designed for its unique role. To kick off these phases, you invoke them. For example, if you run `mvn install`, Maven goes through every phase leading up to and including installation.

Summary

We've journeyed through the foundations of integration, looking at where we started and how we got here. As our world gets more connected, integration has transformed from a "nice-to-have" to an essential driver of digital success. Whether you're new to this field or already deep in the integration game, this chapter lays the groundwork for creating powerful, scalable solutions using MuleSoft.

Back in the early days, integrations were often a tangled mess of point-to-point connections—a necessary but chaotic setup. Over time, we moved to centralized solutions like the enterprise service bus, which added structure but didn't fully solve the need for flexibility. Now, with API-led connectivity and advanced tools like MuleSoft, we're poised to meet the demands of a fast-paced digital world with a streamlined, reusable, and scalable approach.

But MuleSoft isn't just keeping up—it's setting us up for the future. Think of it as the powerhouse "mule" doing all the heavy lifting (minus the hay). With AI-driven features like Intelligent Document Processing and AI-powered flow building, MuleSoft leads the way, making integrations faster, smarter, and more adaptable. It's not just a platform; it's a game-changer for building systems that are ready to evolve with the times.

So, are you ready to roll up your sleeves and get hands-on? The journey ahead is full of opportunities to learn, build, and innovate. With MuleSoft's robust toolkit, you'll be empowered to create integrations that not only meet today's demands but are future-ready. Chapter 2 continues the journey of shaping the future of connectivity—one API, one connection, and one solution at a time.

Prototyping APIs

We want the integrations in this book to be created as part of an application network so other users in the enterprise can find, use, and share the applications. We also want the user story to be captured into an interactive API specification, which will ensure that the API is built for business requirements and is not just an afterthought to service the backend. This approach to asset creation will encourage reuse and drive integration success.

In recent years, *spec-driven development* has emerged as a significant trend in contemporary business systems. We've observed a correlation between spec-driven development and continued success in creating robust, scalable, and successful application networks. Previously, API development was *implementation driven*, with developers quickly prototyping endpoints without initially considering an API specification. But as the code evolved, it caused a lot of problems due to outdated documentation and specifications. Keeping up with all the layers of software development became increasingly difficult. IT began to grow rapidly, and as a result, the product teams struggled to keep up with the disruptions, leading to a significant backlog.

Spec-driven development allows developers to design specifications. It is a process that enables developers to design a specification first, write code according to the design, and then maintain the specification. MuleSoft, with its tools like Anypoint Platform and Anypoint Exchange, takes this process to the next level. It allows developers to design the specification and use the mocking service to test the API. This helps to improve the API specification and get business buy-in even as part of continuous API development. Anypoint Platform also makes it easier to manage and maintain APIs and apply security measures. With MuleSoft Anypoint Studio or ACB, developers can use the approved specification to autocreate HTTP routing code, which accelerates the application development process.

This chapter introduces API design using MuleSoft at a basic practitioner level. It shows you how to use the Anypoint Platform and, in particular, how to use API Designer and Anypoint Exchange to create and publish API specifications. It also demonstrates different languages for writing API specifications, such as RAML and OpenAPI Specification (OAS; formerly Swagger), to write API specifications. We will also compare the differences between RAML and OAS.

> There are many API design tools available in the market, with the most popular being OAS, Postman, APIdog, Paw, Apigee, Spotlight, and Apiary, among many others. Remember that the choice of tool depends on your specific needs, team preferences, and the complexity of your API project. We highly recommend you use API Designer, available on MuleSoft's Anypoint Platform, because it helps with seamless integration and code building.

This is an important chapter, but it's not a comprehensive guide to Representational State Transfer (REST) APIs. Instead, it gives you sufficient exposure to be able to work through the solutions contained in the rest of this book and develop robust MuleSoft APIs. For more in-depth information, there are many good books on the topic, such as *REST in Practice* by Jim Webber et al. (O'Reilly).

API Fundamentals

Before we jump in and start designing the APIs, let's first look at API fundamentals. API stands for *application programming interface*. APIs are integration points, basically sets of rules and protocols that allow different software applications to communicate with each other. Let's say you are at a restaurant and want to order shawarma. You don't need to know how the kitchen operates or who the chef is. All you need is to ask for the menu and then tell the server what you want. In this case, you're the client, the server is the API, the menu is the resource serviced, and·the kitchen is the backend system. They handle your requests and deliver responses while taking care of all the complex processes behind the scenes.

An API consists of *endpoints*, specific URLs that represent resources or functionalities provided by the API, and *methods* that define the actions you can take on these endpoints, such as GET data or POST requests. When you make a request, you can include parameters to provide context or criteria for the desired operation. The response you get back will include the outcome along with any requested data or metadata. Authentication and authorization mechanisms ensure that your access to resources is secure, while documentation explains the API's endpoints, methods, authentication methods, and usage examples.

API Types

There are three main types of APIs:

Open APIs
> These are freely accessible to the public with minimal restrictions, allowing developers to leverage their functionalities without constraints. A prime example is the Google Maps API, which allows developers to integrate mapping and location-based services into their applications.

Partner APIs
> Partner APIs require specific access rights and are often exposed through dedicated API developer portals. These APIs, like those offered by social media platforms such as Facebook or X, enable developers to access restricted data or features by obtaining partnership agreements.

Internal APIs
> Also known as *private APIs*, these remain hidden from external users and function solely within internal systems to facilitate communication between different components or services. Examples include APIs used by large enterprises like Amazon or Netflix, which streamline internal operations and enhance efficiency without external exposure.

The set of rules, conventions, and standards that govern how different software applications communicate and interact with each other over a network are together called a *protocol*. API protocols are important because they help in consistent communication. They guide how requests should be formatted and structured, what methods or operations are supported, and how errors are handled.

There are several API protocols that developers use, such as REST, Simple Object Access Protocol (SOAP), WebSocket, GraphQL, and Google Remote Procedure Call (gRPC). Each protocol has its unique characteristics, benefits, and ideal use cases, allowing developers to create software for various needs and requirements. However, SOAP and REST are the two main web service protocols. Complying with the established protocols' rules and guidelines helps developers ensure that their applications can communicate with other applications on the network.

SOAP Web Services

SOAP web services use Extensible Markup Language (XML) to exchange information over the internet. When you send a message using SOAP, it's like putting it in a special envelope. This envelope has different sections, like the address (where the message is going), any extra notes (like a header), and the main message itself (the body). These sections help keep everything organized and make sure the message gets to where it needs to go.

Now, the cool thing about SOAP is that it works with standard internet protocols like HTTP or SMTP, which means it can be used with all sorts of different systems and technologies, making it platform- and operating-service-independent. Plus, it's secure because it can encrypt messages, make sure they're from the right person (authentication), and keep them safe from tampering (message integrity). You can secure SOAP messages without using policy sets for configuration by using the Web Services Security APIs (WSS API). To configure the client for request encryption on the generator side, use the WSSEncryption API to encrypt the SOAP message. The WSSEncryption API specifies which request SOAP message parts to encrypt when configuring the client.

SOAP also lets you send complex data and organize it neatly, which is handy for big companies with lots of different systems that need to talk to each other. So, whether you're building a big enterprise system or just want your apps to play nice together, SOAP is there to make sure everything runs smoothly.

Let's say we want to retrieve geolocation information for Sherlock Holmes's address because we have to deliver a package to Mr. Holmes. We'd make a SOAP request like in Example 2-1.

Example 2-1. SOAP call to GET address

```
<soapenv:Envelope
xmlns:soapenv="http://schemas.xmlsoap.org/soap/envelope/"
xmlns:web="http://www.example.com/webservices">
    <soapenv:Header/>
    <soapenv:Body>
        <web:GetGeolocation>
            <web:Address>221B Baker Street</web:Address>
        </web:GetGeolocation>
    </soapenv:Body>
</soapenv:Envelope>
```

REST Web Services

REST is an architectural style, where the client and server exchange representations of resources. When you use RESTful web services, you interact with resources (like data or functionalities) using standard actions, such as GET (to fetch data), POST (to create new data), PUT or PATCH (to update existing data), and DELETE (to remove data). One important thing about REST is that it keeps things simple by not remembering the client state from previous requests (meaning it is *stateless*). This makes it faster and more efficient. Also, clients can cache previous responses, so they don't have to ask for the same information over and over again.

In REST, everything is a resource. *Resources* can be objects, data, or services. REST also relies on URLs to identify resources, just like addresses tell you where a place is. For example, to get geocode for an address, call *https://maps.com/geocode*.

Accessing or modifying resources is done through a specific set of operations, and RESTful web services respond with an HTTP status code that indicates the outcome of the operation (success, failure, or update). This section is a brief explanation of how it works.

GET

Imagine you're using a mapping app and you want to find the location of a specific restaurant, say Torchy's Tacos. You open the app and type "Torchy's Tacos" in the search bar. The app then retrieves the current location of Torchy's Tacos and displays it on the map. In this scenario, your search request to the mapping app is like a GET request, and the app's response, showing the location of Torchy's Tacos, is like the server's response, providing you with the current state of the resource (the restaurant's location) in a representation (the map).

In Example 2-2, the HTTP method GET is used to indicate that the request is for retrieving data from the server. The URL path */locations/torchys_tacos* specifies the resource that needs to be retrieved, which in this case is the location information for Torchy's Tacos.

Example 2-2. GET request to get the location for Torchy's Tacos

```
GET /locations/torchys_tacos
```

When the server receives this request, it responds with the details of Torchy's Tacos, as shown in Example 2-3, typically in JSON format.

Example 2-3. Success response for the GET request

```
HTTP/1.1 200 OK
Content-Type: application/json
{
  "name": "Torchy's Tacos",
  "address": "123 Main Street",
  "category": "Restaurant",
  "latitude": 40.7306,
  "longitude": -73.9352
}
```

In Example 2-3, 200 OK indicates that the request was successful, and the server is returning the requested data. Content-Type: application/json specifies that the response body is in JSON format. The body contains the details of Torchy's Tacos, including its name, address, category, latitude, and longitude.

POST

Now let's say you discover a new café that's not on the map yet, and you want to add it. You open the app, go to the Add Location section, and fill out a form with all the details about the café—its name, address, opening hours, and so on. You then submit the form, and the app adds the café to its database and displays it on the map. A POST body is shown in Example 2-4. In this scenario, filling out the form and submitting it to the mapping app is like sending a POST request to the server, asking it to create a new resource (the café) based on the information provided.

Example 2-4. POST request to add a location

```
POST /locations

{
  "name": "Oreilly Cafe",
  "address": "331 Coffee Street",
  "category": "Café",
  "latitude": 40.7128,
  "longitude": -74.0060
}
```

When you send a POST request to create a new location, the server responds with a confirmation message or the newly created resource. Example 2-5 shows an HTTP response for the POST call.

Example 2-5. POST response

```
HTTP/1.1 201 Created
Content-Type: application/json
{
  "message": "Location created successfully",
  "location_id": "123"
}
```

DELETE

Continuing with the mapping app analogy, let's say you find an old location on the map that's no longer there, like a closed-down bakery called Creative Catering Shop. You tap on the location and select Delete. The app then removes the bakery from its database and updates the map accordingly, removing the location from view. This act of deleting the outdated location from the map is like sending a DELETE request, as shown in Example 2-6 to the server, asking it to delete the resource (the bakery's location) from its records.

Example 2-6. DELETE request to delete the bakery's location

```
DELETE /locations/creative_catering_shop
```

PUT

Imagine you come across a location on the map with the wrong name listed—instead of "Torchy's Tacos," it says, "Joe's Pizzeria." You tap on the location, select Edit, and correct the name to "Torchy's Tacos." The app then updates its database with the corrected information and displays the updated name on the map. This process of providing corrected information and updating the map is like sending a PUT request to the server. A PUT body is shown in Example 2-7, asking it to replace the entire resource (the location's information) with the new information provided. Example 2-7 is an example of the JSON payload you might send.

Example 2-7. PUT body to correct a resource

```
PUT /locations/123

{
  "name": "Torchy's Tacos",
  "address": "331 Taco Street",
  "category": "Restaurant",
  "latitude": 40.7306,
  "longitude": -73.9352
}
```

When the server receives this request, it updates the existing resource (location) for Torchy's Tacos with the new address and gives the response shown in Example 2-8.

Example 2-8. PUT response

```
HTTP/1.1 200 OK
Content-Type: application/json

{
  "message": "Location replaced successfully"
}
```

PATCH

Finally, let's say you discover a small error in the address of a location—instead of "123 Main Street," it should be "123 Main Avenue." You tap on the location, select Edit, and correct the address. The app then updates its database with the corrected address without changing anything else. This act of making a small correction to the existing information is like sending a PATCH request to the server, asking it to make a partial update to the resource (the location's address).

When you send a PATCH request to update part of a location's information, the server responds with a confirmation message or the updated resource. Example 2-9 shows the HTTP response for a PATCH call.

Example 2-9. PATCH response

```
HTTP/1.1 200 OK
Content-Type: application/json

{
  "message": "Location updated successfully",
  "updated_fields": ["address"]
}
```

A good API should return status codes that align with the HTTP specifications. Table 2-1 has a list of common HTTP codes.

Table 2-1. List of HTTP codes

Code	Definition	Returned by
200	OK—The request succeeded.	GET, DELETE, PATCH, PUT
201	Created—A new resource or object in a collection was created.	POST
400	Bad Request—The request could not be performed by the server due to bad syntax or other reason in the request.	ALL
401	Unauthorized—Authorization credentials are required or the user does not have access to the resource/method they are requesting.	ALL
404	Resource not found—The URI is not recognized by the server.	ALL
500	Server error—Generic; something went wrong on the server side.	ALL

REST is more flexible than SOAP when it comes to data formats because SOAP is limited to XML. REST follows widely accepted standards such as HTTP and JSON, which makes it easier to use compared to SOAP, and it has its own standards like Web Services Description Language (WSDL) and WS-Security which can be complicated. Both protocols support security, but SOAP has built-in standards for authentication, encryption, and digital signatures. REST relies on external security mechanisms like OAuth or API keys for security. This makes REST protocol more popular for the development of web services.

Efficient, scalable, and maintainable RESTful APIs can be achieved by following best practices. Here are some REST best practices we will use in this book:

Resource-oriented URIs

Using nouns instead of verbs in URIs to represent resources. For example, use /users instead of /getUsers. Our goal is to transfer representations back and forth and not methods or states.

Correct HTTP method usage

Use HTTP methods (GET, POST, PUT, DELETE, PATCH) according to their intended purpose: GET for retrieval, POST for creation, PUT for replacement, DELETE for removal, and PATCH for partial updates. It is important to follow this to maintain consistency in the API spec.

Plural nouns for collections

Use plural nouns when representing collections of resources. For example, instead of using /user, it is better to use /users. This ensures consistency and clarity in your API design.

Consistent resource naming

Maintain consistent naming conventions for all your resources. Doing so can not only increase understanding but also make it easier for developers to use your API to its full potential.

Proper HTTP status codes

Use the appropriate HTTP status codes to represent the outcome of requests. For instance, use 200 to indicate success, 201 for successful creation, 404 for resource not found, and 400 for bad requests.

Versioning

Include a version number in URIs or headers to ensure backward compatibility when making changes to the API.

Query parameters for filtering, sorting, and pagination

Use query parameters to enable clients to filter, sort, and paginate large collections of resources effectively.

Consistent response structure

Maintain consistency in the structure of API responses, including data format (e.g., JSON) and the layout of success and error responses. Where possible, we will achieve this by using specification fragments to promote consistency and asset reuse.

Graceful error handling

Provide clear and concise error messages along with appropriate HTTP status codes to assist in troubleshooting. These error messages should offer meaningful information about what went wrong and how to resolve the problem. For instance, if a client requests a resource that does not exist, the error message should read something like "User with ID 123 not found".

Security measures

> Add authentication and authorization to secure the API from unauthorized access and attacks by creating and using security schemas.

Documentation

> Document the API so users know what resource endpoints, request/response formats, and authentication methods to use, and provide usage examples to assist developers in effectively utilizing the API.

To design and document REST APIs, you can utilize API specification languages. A variety of popular languages are available, such as OAS, RAML, API Blueprint, and GraphQL Schema Definition Language (SDL). The next sections will explore OpenAPI Specification (OAS) and REST. However, for the remainder of this book, REST will be our preferred language for design and development.

RAML

RAML is a language used to describe RESTful APIs. It has a concise syntax, supports data types, security definitions, and resource hierarchies, and allows easy generation of API documentation. Example 2-10 shows a simple RAML file for the /GET users endpoint.

Example 2-10. /GET users endpoint

```
#%RAML 1.0
title: My API
version: v1
/users:
  get:
    description: Get a list of users
    responses:
      200:
        body:
          application/json:
            example: |
              [{"id": 1, "name": "Alice"}]
```

API documentation can be generated easily from RAML files with the use of tools such as api-console or raml2html. RAML files can be used by API Gateways like MuleSoft Anypoint Platform or Apigee to configure routing, security, and transformations. All of these features make RAML a better fit for creating APIs to build application networks when compared to other API modeling languages. RAML syntax is based on YAML and JSON, which makes it lightweight and human-readable. The syntax uses indentation to specify data hierarchy. Figure 2-1 shows a sample RAML file written using YAML; note the data hierarchy specified by indentation.

```
1    #%RAML 1.0
2    title: Google Maps SAPI Integration
3    version: v1
4    baseUri: https://maps.google.sapi.com/maps/api
5    mediaType: application/json
6
7    /geocode:
8      get:
9        description: Retrieve geolocation information
     based on an address
10       displayName: get geocode
11       queryParameters:
12         address: string
```

Figure 2-1. Sample RAML file showing lines to indicate indentation

Although not all components are necessary for every API, it is important to understand how an API is designed and constructed. The following components cover particular aspects of RAML API design:

Basic structure

RAML documents start with the RAML tag followed by the version number and other metadata, as shown in Example 2-11.

Example 2-11. RAML documents start with RAML tag

```
#%RAML 1.0
title: Example API
version: v1
```

Resource definition

Using the resource keyword followed by the path and a nested block, methods and parameters are defined for resources. In Example 2-12, a nested block is shown for the resource /users.

Example 2-12. Resources are defined using resource keywords

```
/users:
  get:
    description: Retrieve all users
    responses:
      200:
        body:
          application/json:
            example: |
```

```
  [
    {"id": 1, "name": "Olive"},
    {"id": 2, "name": "Summer"}
  ]
```

Methods

Resource blocks define methods (GET, POST, PUT, PATCH, DELETE) and their properties, like description, query parameters, and request/response bodies.

Parameters

Parameters can be defined at the API or resource level using the parameters
keyword. They can include query parameters, URI parameters, headers, and so
forth. Example 2-13 shows that the */users/{userId}* resource path includes a URI
parameter {userId}. URI parameters are enclosed in { }.

Example 2-13. RAML with URI parameters

```
#%RAML 1.0
title: Users API
version: v1

/users/{userId}:
  uriParameters:
    userId:
      description: The ID of the user
      type: integer
      required: true
  get:
    description: Retrieve a user by ID
    responses:
      200:
        body:
          application/json:
            example: |
              {
                "id": 123,
                "name": "Olive A",
                "email": "olive@example.com"
              }
      404:
        description: User not found
  put:
    description: Update a user by ID
    body:
      application/json:
        example: |
          {
            "name": "Summer Autumn",
            "email": "summer@example.com"
          }
```

```
responses:
  200:
    description: User updated successfully
  404:
    description: User not found
```

Responses

Method blocks use the `responses` keyword to define responses, each with a status code, headers, and body.

Data types

In RAML, the `types` keyword allows for the definition of custom data types that can be used throughout an API. By defining these types, you can ensure consistency in data structures and avoid repetition of code. Custom data types can be used to represent anything from basic types, such as numbers or strings, to more complex structures like arrays or objects. Additionally, these data types can be reused throughout an API, making it easier to maintain and scale the API over time.

Includes and libraries

RAML enables extracting part of large API definitions into smaller, reusable components by utilizing includes and libraries. This makes it easy to reuse part of the API code. For example, error objects can be extracted into separate fragments and then reused throughout the organization.

Security schemes

API-level security schemes can specify authentication methods such as OAuth or API keys. This helps make APIs more secure.

Annotations

Annotations can be added to different elements of the RAML file to provide additional metadata and documentation.

Remember the Google Maps system API we discussed in our use case in Chapter 1? Now, let's apply all our learning to write Google Maps system API specifications for interacting and integrating with Google Maps. We will use Design Center on Anypoint Platform to create the API specification.

> The system API called *google-maps-sapi* is an API that will represent the system layer in our integration.

To start, click Design Center and click the Create button (see Figure 2-2).

Figure 2-2. Create button for creating API specification

Anytime you want to create a new API specification, you click Create and choose New API Specification from the drop-down menu, as shown in Figure 2-3, and begin.

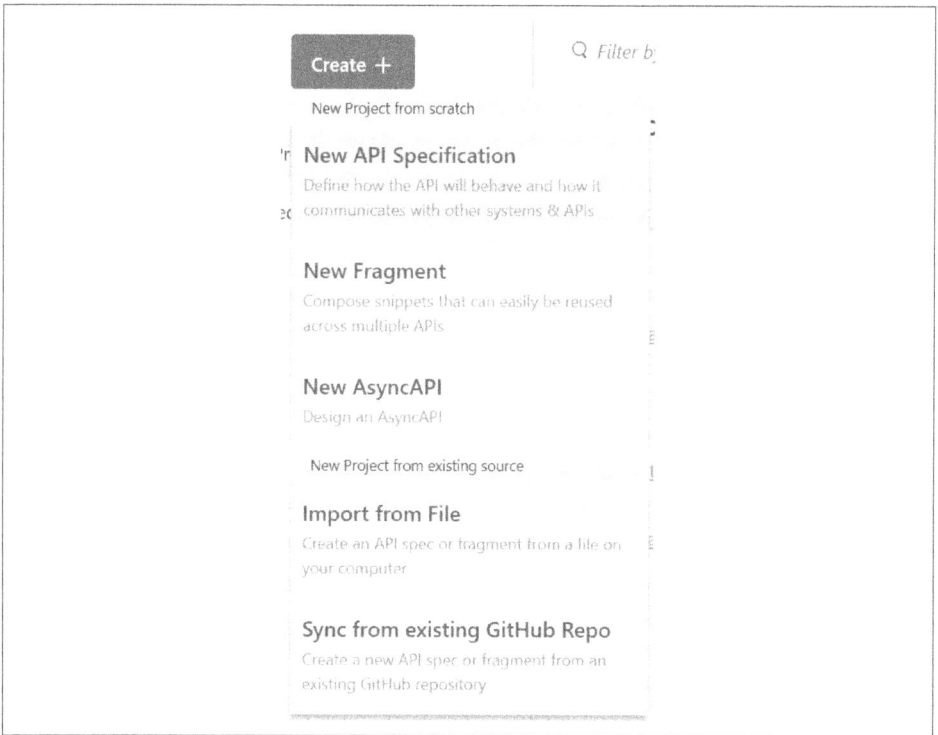

Figure 2-3. Drop-down options for Design Center asset creation

Next, you will see a pop-up, and you can choose to design the specification using either the text editor or visual editor. In Figure 2-4, you see two options. If you choose the first one, "I am comfortable designing it on my own," the text editor opens; if you choose "Guide me through it," the visual editor for specification design will open. Let's first design using the text editor.

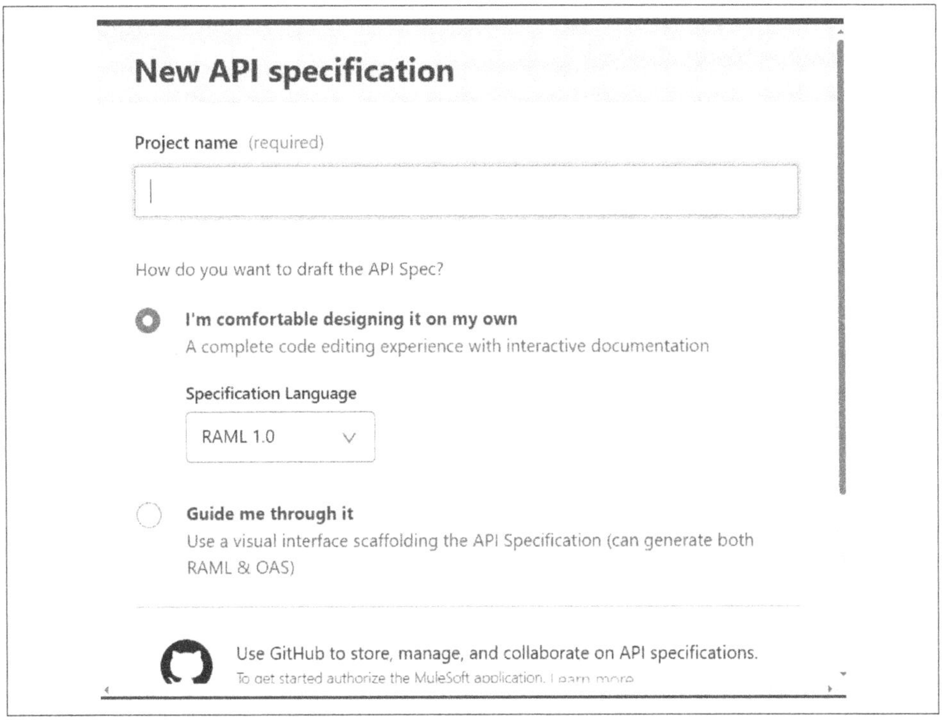

Figure 2-4. Choose the specification design options

Design Center: Text Editor

When you select option one in Figure 2-4, it opens the text editor. Figure 2-5 shows the Design Center text editor option. It has a file browser, editor, API console, and shelf.

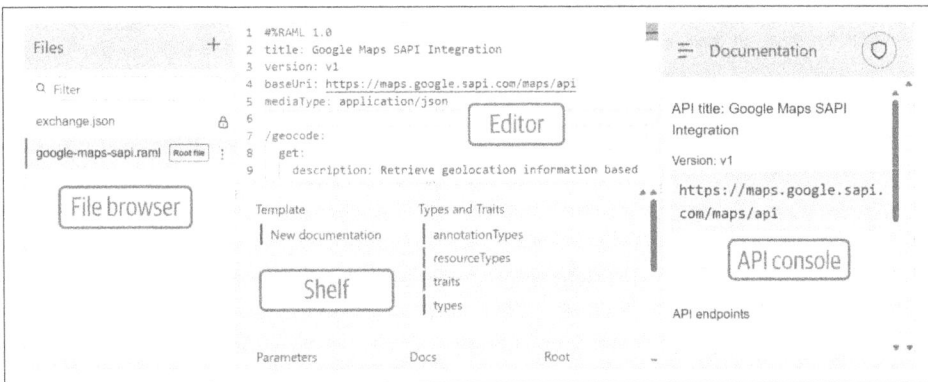

Figure 2-5. Design Center text editor with a sample API specification

Begin by adding the basic tags and title, and then start adding the resources. Example 2-14 shows a resource added.

Example 2-14. RAML with resource/geocode added

```
#%RAML 1.0
title: Google Maps SAPI Integration

/geocode:
```

Next, you define the methods. In our case, we are using the GET method to retrieve the geocode, shown in Example 2-15. It's best practice to write the description, and if you want to use your API spec as a connector you'll need to specify the displayName.

Example 2-15. GET method with display name

```
#%RAML 1.0
title: Google Maps SAPI Integration

/geocode:
  get:
    description: Retrieve geolocation information based on an address
    displayName: get geocode
```

Start by adding any necessary query parameters for the method you're working on. Note the indentations in the specifications, as shown in Example 2-16.

Example 2-16. Query parameters for HTTP method

```
/geocode:
  get:
    description: Retrieve geolocation information based on an address
    displayName: get geocode
    queryParameters:
      address: string
```

Now you can interact with the API using API Console. Example 2-17 shows a RAML for *google-maps-sapi* with methods, responses, and examples. When we talk about responses, we're laying out a map. This map shows what could happen with different HTTP status codes. For each status code, we'll explain what kind of data might come back, describe it a bit, and throw in some examples to make it clear.

Example 2-17. RAML for google-maps-sapi

```
#%RAML 1.0
title: Google Maps SAPI Integration
version: v1
baseUri: https://maps.google.sapi.com/maps/api
mediaType: application/json

/geocode:
  get:
    description: Retrieve geolocation information based on an address
    displayName: get geocode
    queryParameters:
      address: string
    responses:
      200:
        body:
          application/json:
            example: |
              {
                "latitude": 34.0522,
                "longitude": -118.2437
              }

/directions:
  get:
    description: Get directions between two locations
    displayName: get directions
    queryParameters:
      origin: string
      destination: string
    responses:
      200:
        body:
          application/json:
            example: |
              {
                "route": "Take I-405 S",
                "duration": "30 mins"
              }

/places:
  get:
    description: Search for places near a specific location
    displayName: get nearby locale
    queryParameters:
      location: string
      type: string
    responses:
      200:
        body:
          application/json:
```

```
example: |
  {
    "results": [
      {
        "name": "Central Park",
        "type": "Park"
      }
    ]
  }
```

When it comes to showing examples of data, there are two options: `example` and `examples`. If we use `example`, it's for showing just one example of what the data might look like. But if we go with `examples`, that's for when we want to show multiple examples. We'll organize these examples like a map, with key-value pairs, as shown in Example 2-18.

Example 2-18. Examples in RAML

```
responses:
    200:
      body:
        application/json:
          examples:
            example1: |
              {
                "status": "success",
                "results": [
                  {
                    "address": "221B Baker Street, London, UK",
                    "latitude": 51.523767,
                    "longitude": -0.158371
                  }
                ]
              }
            example2: |
              {
                "status": "success",
                "results": [
                  {
                    "address": "12 Grimmauld Place, London, UK",
                    "latitude": 51.530297,
                    "longitude": -0.123735
                  }
                ]
              }
```

Design Center: Visual Editor

To create API specifications in RAML 1.0 or OAS 2.0/3.0 (JSON) using the visual API editor in API Designer, you simply fill out straightforward forms that aren't tied to any specific programming language. Select the option "Guide me through it" to utilize the visual API editor and click Create API Spec to complete the process.

Figure 2-6 shows how the visual editor is organized. In the left panel, you'll find your API spec's name displayed along with buttons for creating resources, data types, and security schemes. Everything you generate here becomes part of the specification and remains within the same file. The middle panel is where you input details about your API components. Upon opening the editor, you'll encounter a form for the primary properties of your spec. Click items in the left panel to view their respective forms here. The right panel provides read-only views: the RAML viewer and the OAS viewer. You can toggle between them using tabs. They present your spec in either RAML 1.0 or OAS 3.0 format. As you fill out forms in the middle panel, the draft updates accordingly in the right panel. Additionally, you can initiate a mocking service from the panel to test the endpoints you've configured in your spec.

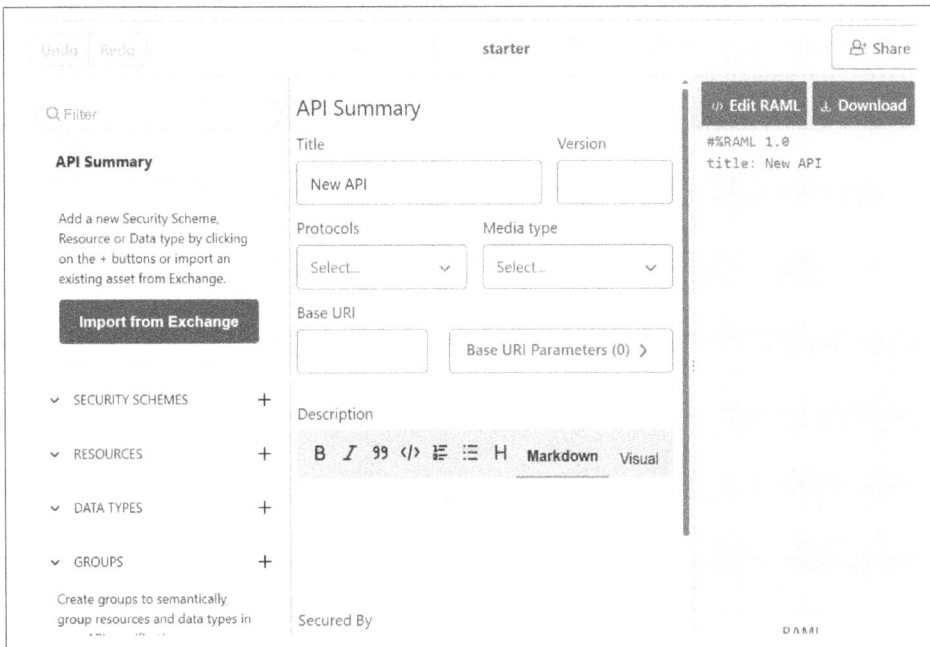

Figure 2-6. Visual editor

OpenAPI Specification

Now that you've been introduced to RAML, let's look into the second specification language used in Anypoint Design Center, OpenAPI Specification (OAS). Example 2-19 shows a simple OAS file for the /GET users endpoint.

Example 2-19. /GET users endpoint

```json
{
  "openapi": "3.0.0",
  "info": {
    "title": "My API",
    "version": "v1"
  },
  "servers": [],
  "paths": {
    "/users": {
      "get": {
        "responses": {
          "200": {
            "description": " ",
            "content": {
              "application/json": {
                "schema": {
                  "example": [
                    {
                      "id": 1,
                      "name": "Alice"
                    }
                  ]
                }
              }
            }
          }
        },
        "description": "Get a list of users",
        "operationId": "GET_users"
      }
    }
  },
  "components": {
    "schemas": {},
    "responses": {},
    "parameters": {},
    "examples": {},
    "requestBodies": {},
    "headers": {},
    "securitySchemes": {},
    "links": {},
    "callbacks": {}
  }
}
```

RAML Versus OAS

Both RAML and OAS are API specification languages that allow developers to define their APIs. However, they differ in some aspects. RAML comes with its data modeling language called Data Types, which makes it easy to define reusable data structures. On the other hand, OAS relies on JSON Schema for data modeling, which offers more advanced validation capabilities.

RAML allows for the creation of resource types, traits, and libraries within the API specification, providing flexibility and organization. OAS introduced components like schemas, parameters, and responses in version 3.0 to promote reuse, but it's not as flexible as RAML.

RAML has a smaller ecosystem than OAS, but it's supported by tools like API consoles, mocking services, and code generators. In contrast, OAS has a larger ecosystem with extensive support, including editors, validators, documentation generators, and code generators. This comparison is shown in Table 2-2.

Table 2-2. Compare RAML and OAS

Aspect	RAML	OAS
Data modeling	Data Types for reusable data structures	JSON Schema for advanced validation
Resource types and traits	Supports resource types, traits, and libraries	Components like schemas, parameters, responses
Flexibility and organization	High flexibility and organization	Less flexible compared to RAML
Ecosystem	Smaller ecosystem, supported by API consoles, mocking services, code generators	Larger ecosystem, extensive support including editors, validators, documentation generators, code generators

> Ultimately, it's your decision whether to use RAML or OAS, and the decision will depend on factors such as business factors, personal and project preferences, existing infrastructure, and community support.

Anypoint Code Builder

It is possible to create API specifications using ACB. To create an API spec project in ACB, click the Ⓜ button (Anypoint Code Builder) and choose "Design an API" from the Quick Actions menu, as shown in Figure 2-7.

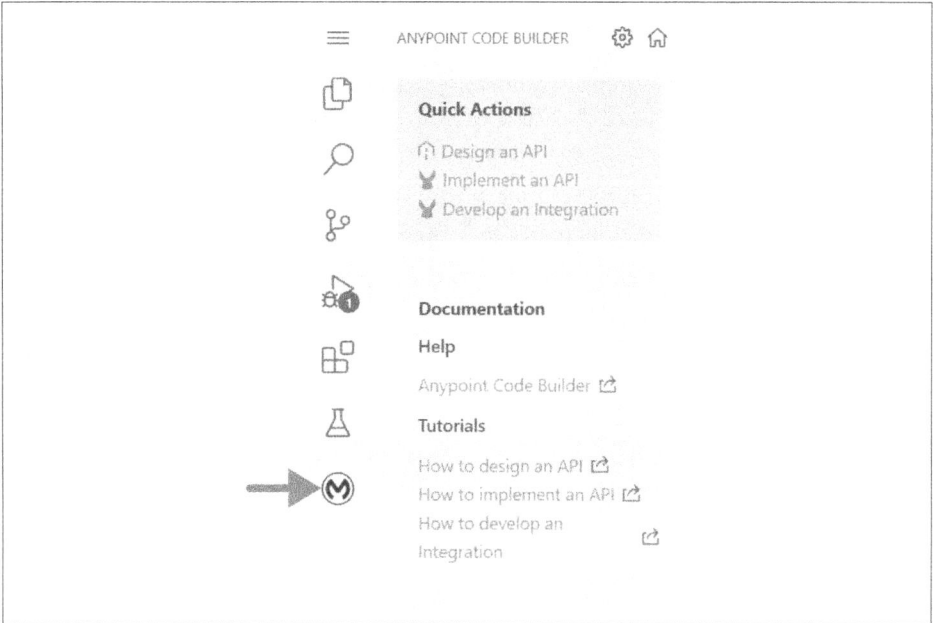

Figure 2-7. Anypoint Code Builder menu items

Fill in the API specification form in the dialog box shown in Figure 2-8. The project name is the unique name for your project—for example, *google-maps-sapi*. The project location must be a local directory or another directory you want to store the project in. It is not a best practice to create a project directory inside another project directory. API specification language can be RAML or OAS 3.0.

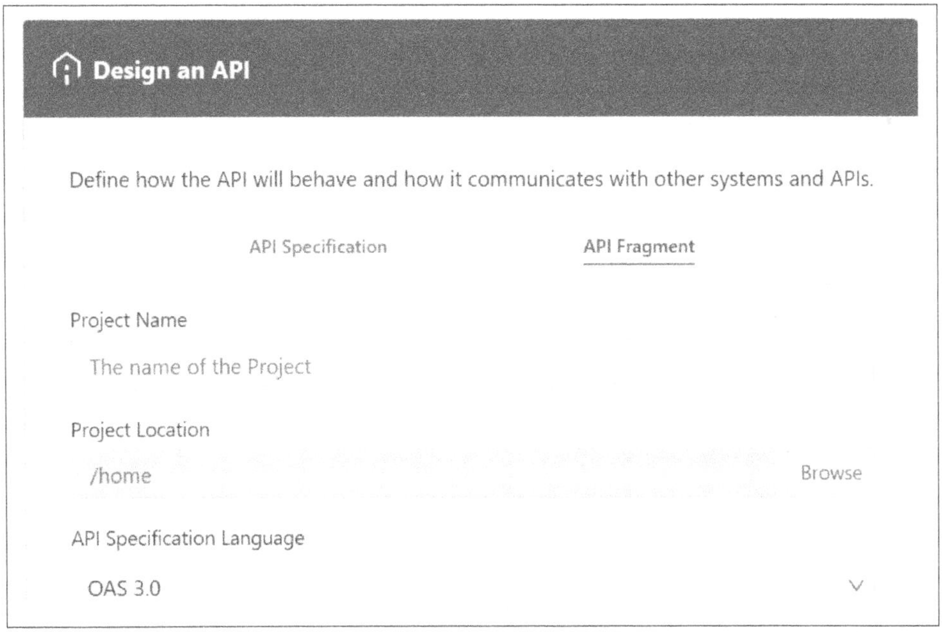

Figure 2-8. Form to create an API specification

To get started, click the Create Project button. If you are prompted to trust the authors of the files in the folder, go ahead and do so. Once the project is ready for editing, the API project will open the specification in the Editor view (Figure 2-9). This may include an OAS 3.0 (YAML) spec, for example.

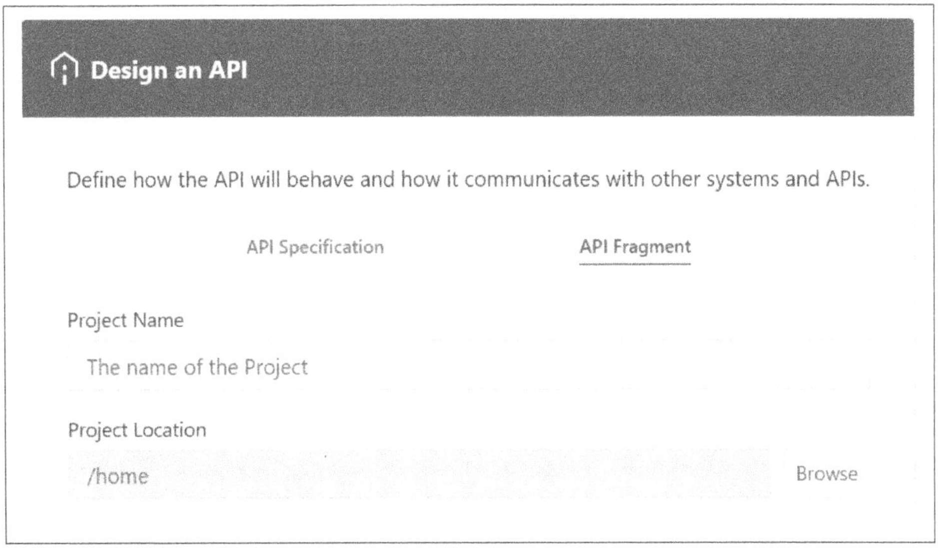

Figure 2-9. Form to create a fragment

When designing your API fragment, remember to use autocomplete (Ctrl + space bar) to view available options within the context. If you have created an OAS 3.0 (YAML) fragment project, you can test adding fragments to a spec by replacing the initial API fragment with the example code (see Figure 2-10).

```
 s3-impl.xml          !  queryparameter.yaml  ✕

queryParameter  >  !  queryparameter.yaml
    1    openapi: "3.0.0"
    2    info:
    3      version: 1.0.0
    4      title: queryparameter
    5    paths: {}
    6    components:
    7      parameters:
    8        MyQueryParameter:
    9          name: address
   10          in: query
   11          description: The address parameter for querying.
   12          required: true
   13          schema:
   14            type: string
   15
```

Figure 2-10. A fragment being edited

Next, to publish the asset, select View > Command Palette (Ctrl+Shift+P), as shown in Figure 2-11.

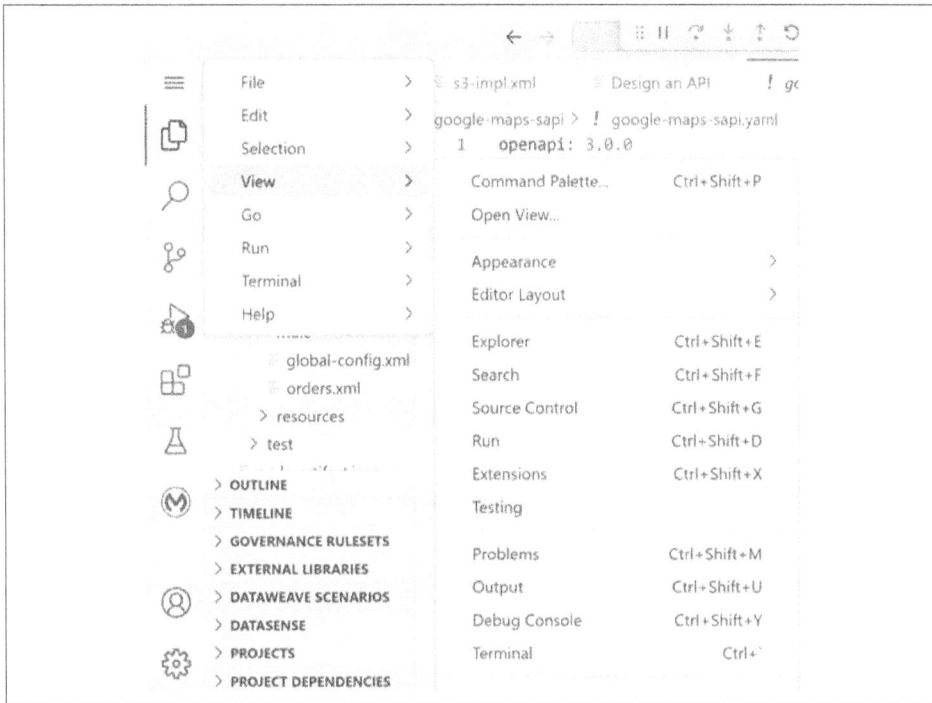

Figure 2-11. Select View > Command Palette to execute commands

Type the following command to publish the specification (see Figure 2-12):

```
Mulesoft: Publish API Specification to Exchange
```

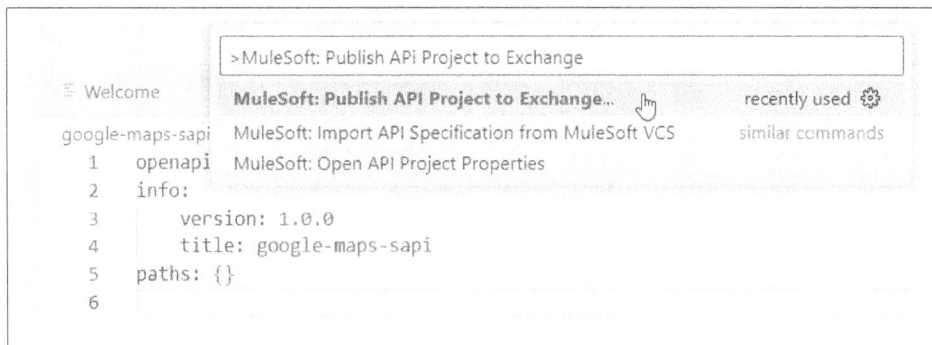

Figure 2-12. The command to publish assets using ACB

To select and import an asset from Exchange, use the command `Mulesoft: Add Fragment dependency from Exchange` and then verify that the fragment dependency was added by checking the dependencies section of the *exchange.json* file.

If prompted, click the Allow button and follow the prompts to sign in to Anypoint Platform. In the "Select a Business Group" section, search and choose your business group for the project. Next, in the Set Project Name section, confirm or type the project name and press Enter. After that, confirm or make changes to each item (Artifact ID, Asset version, and API version) and press Enter. To cancel publishing, press the Escape (Esc) button. The status bar will display the progress. Once it is complete, you will receive a message saying that the API specification has been successfully published to Exchange.

> If your API specification appears on Exchange as a REST API rather than an API spec fragment, ensure that the `classifier` attribute in the *exchange.json* file in your project folder in your IDE is set to one of the following values, depending on the language used:
>
> - For OAS, set the classifier attribute to `oas-components`.
> - For RAML, set the classifier attribute to `raml-fragment`.
> - For JSON Schema, set the classifier attribute to `json-schema`.
>
> If the classifier attribute is set to one of the following values, the project is considered an API specification rather than a fragment:
>
> - For OAS, the classifier attribute should be set to `oas`.
> - For RAML, the classifier attribute should be set to `raml`.

Summary

After completing this chapter, you should now know how to create API specifications. The main goal was for you to learn how to design APIs with consistency and clarity. However, the ultimate goal is to use these API specifications to create an application network that promotes the reuse of assets. It's important to note that you can use your own source control management (SCM) system when designing APIs in ACB. This allows for greater flexibility and control over your API specifications.

In Chapter 3, we will create API fragments that will let you reuse APIs and parts of the API and apply them to the use case and existing specifications. We will also explore how to apply security schemes to API specifications, publish APIs, and enable mocking. This will allow you to share the APIs you have created with others to try out and provide you with feedback.

Designing and Publishing APIs

When you're working with APIs, there's a lot to keep in mind. One of the first things you should think about is API readiness. *Readiness* refers to the process of ensuring that an API is fully prepared for deployment and integration into applications. The ultimate goal of any business organization is to create valuable assets that can be integrated into application networks while maintaining high levels of reliability, security, and performance. Without proper planning and structure, things can quickly become disorganized and chaotic. Therefore, it is important to follow standards from the beginning of the development process to ensure that APIs are cost-effectively developed and utilized.

In Chapter 2, you learned how to create RAML and explored its key concepts. You learned how to define RESTful APIs and to structure your documentation for clarity. But there's a special piece of the puzzle that we haven't explored in depth yet: RAML fragments, which are pivotal for efficient API design and maintenance.

In this chapter, you will learn about RAML fragments and their importance in developing scalable APIs. We will guide you through the process of creating and organizing fragments, making them reusable across various projects, and sharing and using them in APIs. Additionally, you'll learn to enable mocking service for your APIs, as well as how to share APIs internally and on public portals for external access and consumption of API assets. By the end of this chapter, you will have a strong grasp of RAML fragments and be able to use them to optimize your API design process.

> Before you dive into creating complex fragments, start simple. Build a basic fragment, incorporate it into your project, and ensure that it aligns with your API's structure and functionality. This initial step can save you a lot of reworking down the line.

API Fragments

RAML is a modular API specification language that promotes reusability. Its modular design makes it easy to read and maintain API specifications. One of the unique features of RAML is its support for various fragment types, including data types, examples, traits, resource types, overlays, extensions, security schemes, documentation, annotations, and libraries. Each fragment type serves a specific purpose, contributing to a more organized and flexible API design process.

You can store these fragment files in project folders, ensuring consistency throughout your API. Additionally, you can share your work across multiple projects by publishing them to Anypoint Exchange. Others can then include them as dependencies, fostering collaboration and speeding up development. This approach allows you to reuse existing fragments instead of starting from scratch every time. Table 3-1 provides an overview of various RAML fragment types, the folder names where they are stored, and the local library names used for easy reference.

Table 3-1. Example folders and file naming for RAML fragments

Fragment type	Folder name	Local library name
Trait	*traits*	`traitsLibrary`
Resource type	*resourceTypes*	`resourceTypesLibrary`
Library	*libraries*	`N/A`
Overlay	*overlays*	`overlaysLibrary`
Extension	*extensions*	`extensionsLibrary`
Data types	*datatypes*	`dataTypesLibrary`
User documentation	*documentation*	`documentationLibrary`
Example	*examples*	`N/A`
Annotation type	*annotationTypes*	`annotationTypesLibrary`
Security scheme	*securitySchemes*	`securitySchemesLibrary`

To see how these conventions play out in practice, consider the following example project structure:

```
/api_project/
    ├── api.raml  # Main API specification file
    ├── traits/  # Trait fragments
    │   ├── logging.raml # Logging trait
    │   └── authentication.raml  # Authentication trait
    ├── resourceTypes/  # Resource type fragments
    │   └── user_resource.raml  # User resource type
    ├── libraries/  # Libraries holding various fragments
    │   ├── traitsLib/  # Collection of traits
    │   ├── resourceTypesLib/  # Collection of resource types
    │   ├── dataTypesLib/  # Collection of data types
    ├── overlays/  # Overlay fragments
```

```
|   └── v2_overlay.raml  # Version 2 overlay
├── extensions/  # Extension fragments
|   └── extra_features.raml  # Extra features extension
├── datatypes/  # Data type fragments
|   ├── user.json  # Data type for user
|   └── product.json  # Data type for product
├── documentation/  # User documentation fragments
|   ├── overview.md  # Overview document
|   └── api_guide.md  # API guide
├── examples/  # Example data
|   ├── user_example.json  # Example of user data
|   └── product_example.json  # Example of product data
├── annotationTypes/  # Annotation type fragments
|   ├── custom_annotation.raml  # Custom annotation
├── securitySchemes/  # Security scheme fragments
|   ├── oauth2_scheme.raml  # OAuth 2 security scheme
|   └── basic_auth_scheme.raml  # Basic authentication scheme
```

Here's how you might reference these fragments and local libraries in your main API file:

```
#%RAML 1.0
title: My API
baseUri: http://api.example.com
version: v1

uses:
  Traits: libraries/traitsLib/authentication.raml
  ResourceTypes: libraries/resourceTypesLib/user_resource.raml
  DataTypes: libraries/dataTypesLib/user.json
  SecuritySchemes: securitySchemes/oauth2_scheme.raml
```

With this structure, each fragment type is stored in its designated folder and is accessible through its local library name. This consistent approach makes it easy to maintain and update the project as it evolves.

Let's see how to create common RAML fragments such as resource types, traits, data types, security schemes, and examples. In this process, we'll examine the structure of each fragment type and apply our knowledge to the RAML we built in Chapter 2.

Resource Type Fragments

Resource type fragments define the structure and behavior of API resources. There are two types of resource type fragments: collection resource type and member resource type. The *collection* resource type represents a list of items and includes operations to retrieve or add to the collection.

Following is an example collection resource type fragment for the Google Maps SAPI:

```
#%RAML 1.0 ResourceType
usage: "Defines a common structure for collection resources."
get:
  description: "Retrieve a list of items."
  queryParameters:
    limit:
      type: integer
      description: "The maximum number of items to retrieve."
      default: 10
    offset:
      type: integer
      description: "The starting point for retrieval."
      default: 0
  responses:
    200:
      body:
        application/json:
          example: |
            {
              "items": [
                { "id": 1, "name": "Place A" },
                { "id": 2, "name": "Place B" }
              ],
              "total": 2
            }

post:
  description: "Add a new item to the collection."
  body:
    application/json:
      example: |
        {
          "name": "Place C"
        }
  responses:
    201:
      description: "Item added successfully."
      body:
        application/json:
          example: |
            {
              "id": 3,
              "name": "Place C"
            }
```

The *member* resource type represents a specific item within a collection, such as an individual place or a geocode result. The typical operations for a member resource include retrieving, updating, and deleting that specific item.

The following fragment outlines a common structure for member resources, including operations like GET, PUT, and DELETE:

```
#%RAML 1.0 ResourceType
usage: "Defines common operations for a member resource."
get:
  description: "Retrieve a specific item by its ID."
  responses:
    200:
      body:
        application/json:
          example: |
            {
              "id": 1,
              "name": "Place A"
            }

put:
  description: "Update a specific item by its ID."
  body:
    application/json:
      example: |
        {
          "name": "Updated Place"
        }
  responses:
    200:
      body:
        application/json:
          example: |
            {
              "id": 1,
              "name": "Updated Place"
            }

delete:
  description: "Delete a specific item by its ID."
  responses:
    204:
      description: "Item deleted successfully."
```

Now, let's apply these resource types to the main RAML for the Google Maps SAPI. We'll create collection resources for places and member resources for a specific place based on its ID, and then reference it using the type keyword in the main API:

```
#%RAML 1.0
title: Google Maps SAPI Integration
version: v1
baseUri: https://maps.google.sapi.com/maps/api
mediaType: application/json

resourceTypes:
```

```
    Collection: !include resourceTypes/collection.raml
    Member: !include resourceTypes/member.raml

/places:
  type: Collection
  get:
    queryParameters:
      limit:
        description: "The number of places to return."
        default: 5
      offset:
        description: "The offset to start returning places."
        default: 0
  post:
    description: "Add a new place."

/places/{placeId}:
  type: Member
  uriParameters:
    placeId:
      description: "The ID of the place."
      type: integer
  put:
    description: "Update a place by ID."
  delete:
    description: "Delete a place by ID."
```

Traits

Traits in RAML are used for defining reusable attributes for resources or methods. These attributes may include common query parameters, response headers, or other behaviors. Using traits, you can apply shared functionality across different resources without duplicating code. For instance, some useful traits for the Google Maps SAPI Integration API may include the following:

Rate limiting
> Adds a rate-limiting header to the responses

Authentication
> Indicates that a resource requires an authentication token in the headers

Logging
> Logs the request for auditing or monitoring purposes

Let's create these traits and define their behavior:

```
#%RAML 1.0 Trait
usage: "Adds rate limiting headers to the response."
headers:
  X-Rate-Limit-Limit:
    description: "The maximum number of requests allowed in a given period."
```

```
      type: integer
    X-Rate-Limit-Remaining:
      description: "The number of requests remaining in the current period."
      type: integer
    X-Rate-Limit-Reset:
      description: "The time at which the rate limit resets."
      type: string


  #%RAML 1.0 Trait
  usage: "Requires an authentication token in the request headers."
  headers:
    Authorization:
      description: "Authentication token to access the API."
      type: string



  #%RAML 1.0 Trait
  usage: "Indicates that the request will be logged."
  queryParameters:
    log:
      description: "Whether to log this request for auditing or monitoring."
      type: boolean
      default: true
```

With the traits defined, let's update the original RAML with these traits. Example 3-1 adds the traits section to import the created traits and applies them to the relevant resources.

Example 3-1. A RAML with authentication, rate limiting, and authentication traits

```
#%RAML 1.0
title: Google Maps SAPI Integration
version: v1
baseUri: https://maps.google.sapi.com/maps/api
mediaType: application/json

resourceTypes:
  Geocode: !include resourceTypes/geocode.raml
  Directions: !include resourceTypes/directions.raml
  Places: !include resourceTypes/places.raml

traits:
  RateLimiting: !include traits/rate_limiting.raml
  Authentication: !include traits/authentication.raml
  Logging: !include traits/logging.raml

/geocode:
  type: Geocode
  is: [RateLimiting, Authentication]

/directions:
```

```
  type: Directions
  is: [Authentication, Logging]

/places:
  type: Places
  is: [Authentication, RateLimiting]
```

In this updated RAML, we've added the `traits` section to import the created traits and applied them to the relevant resources. Make a note of all endpoints and the traits applied to them. With these traits in place, next we can check out security schemes and see how to apply them to the Google Maps SAPI.

Security Schemes

Security schemes in RAML define the authentication and authorization methods used to secure an API. Common schemes include OAuth 2.0, API key-based authentication, and basic authentication. Using security schemes, you can establish consistent security practices across an API.

Example 3-1 introduced an authentication trait. This example specifically focuses on how clients authenticate to access protected resources. Additionally, security schemes cover a broader range of security measures and protocols implemented by the API to ensure comprehensive security.

The following code defines an OAuth 2.0 security scheme with authorization and access token endpoints. It can be used to secure the API with OAuth 2.0:

```
#%RAML 1.0 SecurityScheme
description: "OAuth 2.0 security scheme for authentication."
type: OAuth 2.0
settings:
  authorizationUri: https://auth.example.com/authorize
  accessTokenUri: https://auth.example.com/token
  authorizationGrants: [ authorization_code, client_credentials ]
  scopes:
    - read:geocode
    - read:directions
    - read:places
```

To apply this security scheme to the existing RAML, you need to import the security scheme and assign it to relevant resources or methods:

```
#%RAML 1.0
title: Google Maps SAPI Integration
version: v1
baseUri: https://maps.google.sapi.com/maps/api
mediaType: application/json

resourceTypes:
  Geocode: !include resourceTypes/geocode.raml
```

```
  Directions: !include resourceTypes/directions.raml
  Places: !include resourceTypes/places.raml

traits:
  RateLimiting: !include traits/rate_limiting.raml
  Authentication: !include traits/authentication.raml
  Logging: !include traits/logging.raml

securitySchemes:
  OAuth2: !include securitySchemes/oauth2.raml

securedBy: [ OAuth2 ]

/geocode:
  type: Geocode
  is: [RateLimiting, Authentication]

/directions:
  type: Directions
  is: [Authentication, Logging]

/places:
  type: Places
  is: [Authentication, RateLimiting]
```

The securitySchemes section in the preceding code imports the OAuth 2.0 security scheme from the corresponding fragment, and the securedBy attribute at the root level specifies that all resources in this API are secured by OAuth 2.0. In this setup, the OAuth 2.0 security scheme is applied to the entire API, ensuring that all requests must be authenticated.

The preceding are just recommendations. You can use the basic principles but create assets according to your business needs.

Creating Fragments on Exchange

Fragments can be stored in different locations, such as files and folders within a project. Additionally, they can be stored in a separate API fragment project in Design Center or a separate RAML fragment in Exchange. So you can see how it works, we will create a sample fragment in Design Center and then publish it to Exchange.

Log in to the Anypoint Platform to create fragments on Exchange and follow these steps:

1. Navigate to Design Center's Projects page and click Create to begin a new project. From the menu, choose New Fragment, as shown in Figure 3-1.

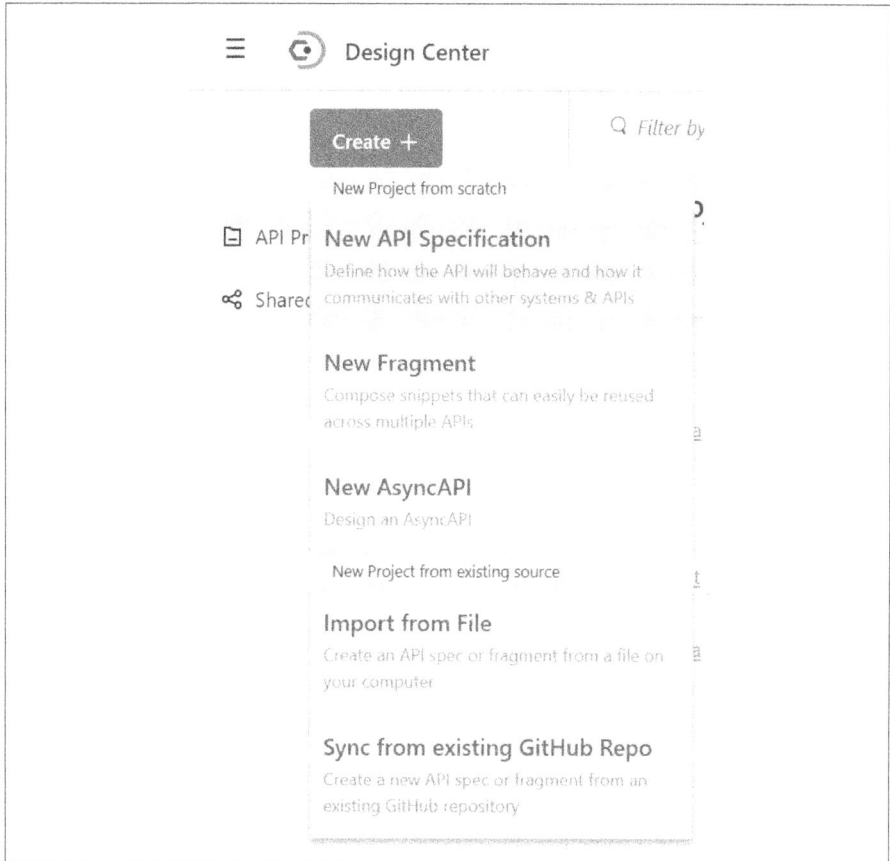

Figure 3-1. Creating a fragment in Design Center

2. Enter a name in the pop-up dialog, as shown in Figure 3-2, and fill out the form. "Project name" means the name of the fragment. In our example, we are calling the fragment *geocode*. Now choose the specification for the fragment. Options include RAML 1.0, OAS 3.0, and JSON Schema. If you decide on RAML 1.0, you'll be prompted to specify the fragment type, which can be changed later.

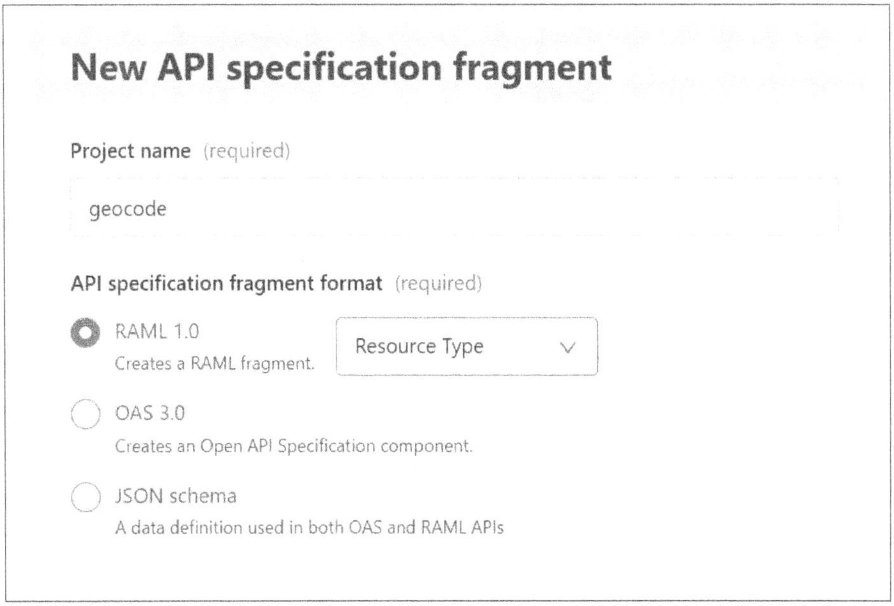

Figure 3-2. Filling out the form to create a fragment in Design Center

3. Once you've chosen the fragment type, click Create Fragment. This opens the text editor with a three-panel layout, as shown in Figure 3-3.

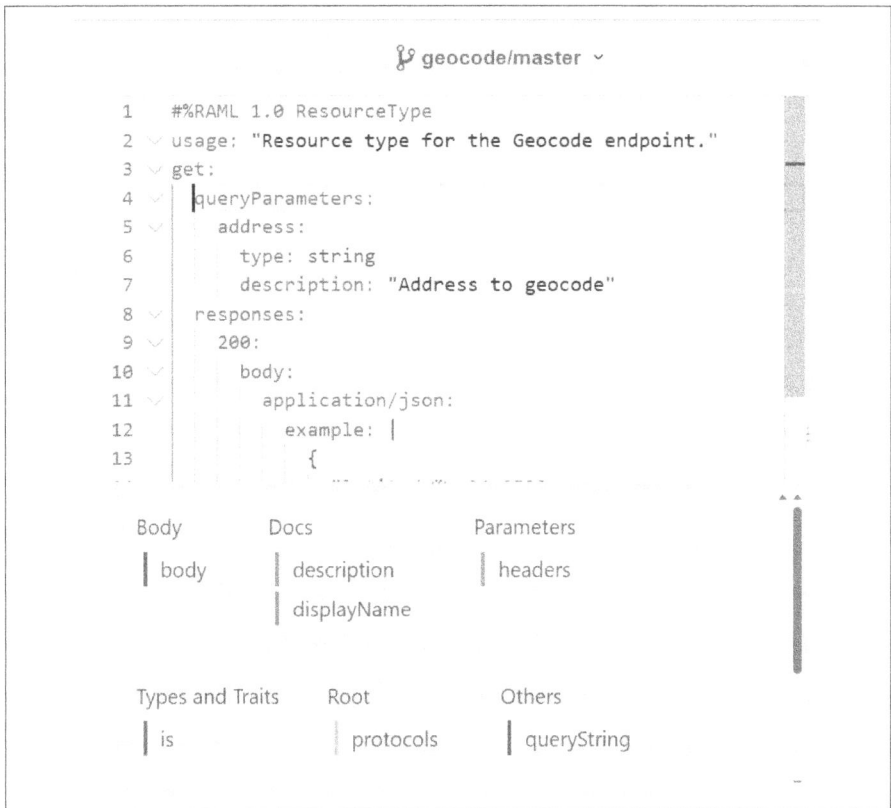

```
                        ᛘ geocode/master ˅

     1    #%RAML 1.0 ResourceType
     2  ˅ usage: "Resource type for the Geocode endpoint."
     3  ˅ get:
     4  ˅   queryParameters:
     5  ˅     address:
     6           type: string
     7           description: "Address to geocode"
     8  ˅   responses:
     9  ˅     200:
    10  ˅       body:
    11  ˅         application/json:
    12             example: |
    13               {
```

Body	Docs	Parameters
body	description	headers
	displayName	

Types and Traits	Root	Others
is	protocols	queryString

Figure 3-3. The space where fragments are edited in Design Center

In the left panel is the list of files in your project. To add new files, click the "+" icon and select New File. You can choose the format for the new file, such as RAML 1.0, OAS 3.0, or JSON Schema. Give your new file a name and click Create. By default, the editor creates a file with the same name as your project and sets it as the root file.

The middle panel is the main editing area where you can work on your API fragment. The editor suggests RAML nodes, methods, and other elements to help you with the design process. The right panel displays the types and resources related to the API fragment you're editing in the middle panel.

The left panel also includes a read-only file named *exchange.json* containing metadata for Anypoint Exchange, which is useful for when you publish your project.

To add content to your API fragment, start editing the middle panel. You can create and import various types of files, either individually or as a compressed (*.zip*) bundle. Supported formats for import include RAML 1.0, JSON, OAS 2.0, and OAS 3.0. You can import from local storage or through a URL if the files are hosted online.

MuleSoft APIs are developed incrementally, incorporating feedback from developers at each step and implementing necessary changes accordingly. The aim is to maintain functionality while ensuring continuous improvement. Figure 3-4 illustrates the approach behind MuleSoft development: sharing assets to get feedback.

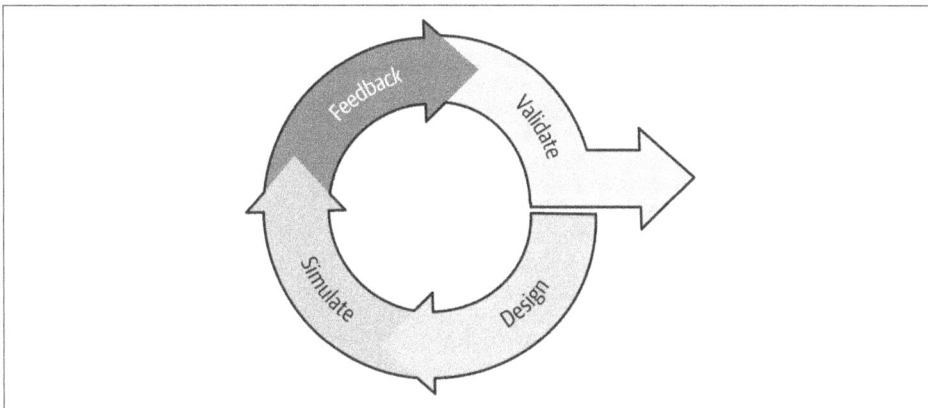

Figure 3-4. The iterative design approach to MuleSoft development

Our next topic is enabling mocking services for API testing.

Mocking APIs

Now that the assets are created, it's time to test the design, and for that, you must invoke the mocking service provided by the Anypoint platform. *Mocking service* is used to test API calls and the main and nested fragments within the API specification. The mocking service allows developers to simulate API responses without connecting to a real backend or service. This is particularly useful during development and testing, when the actual backend might not be available, or if you want to test different scenarios (like error handling, edge cases, or specific datasets) without affecting a live system.

With live simulation, developers can create sample API responses that represent what the API would return under different conditions. This allows them to test their code against mocked responses, ensuring that it works as expected. Shareable links can be given to clients, partners, or testers to try out the API without requiring authentication or setup. These links can be used to get feedback, demonstrate functionality, or validate use cases with nontechnical stakeholders. The ability to set an expiration date/time for these links adds a layer of security. Once expired, the links no longer work, which helps control access and reduce risk.

Follow these steps to configure the service settings of the mocking service:

1. Open your API project and click the right-hand Mocking Service Configuration button, as shown in Figure 3-5.

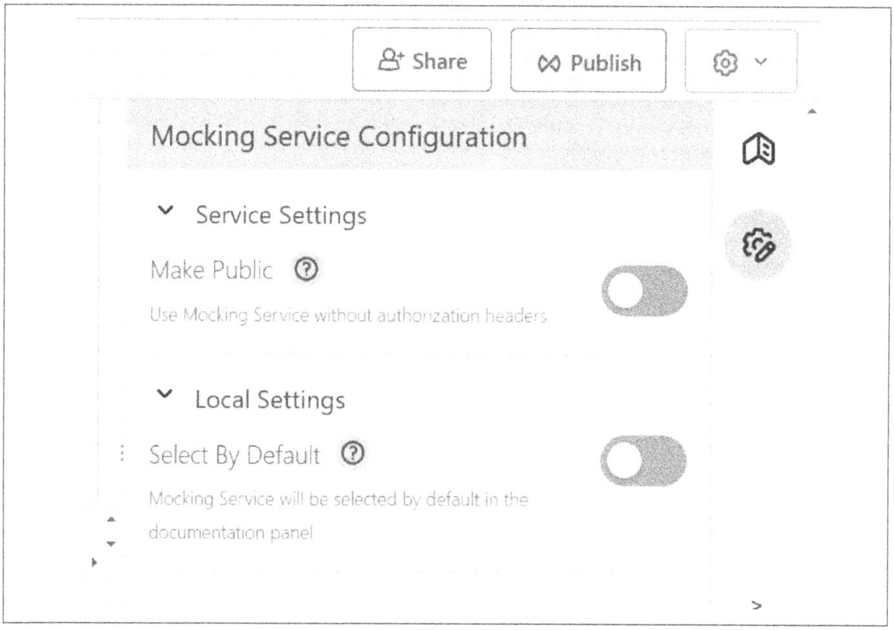

Figure 3-5. The mocking service configuration options

2. Choose to set the mocking service as public or private. If set as private, the mocking service will need to be requested using authentication.

3. Choose to have the mocking service selected by default in the documentation panel or not.

Now you need to request tokens for authentication to access the mocked API. For access with the Anypoint access token, the procedure depends on your system.

On macOS, replace **\<USERNAME\>** and **\<PASSWORD\>**:

```
curl -H "Content-Type: application/json" -X POST -d
'{"username":"<USERNAME>","password":"
<PASSWORD>"}'
"https://anypoint.mulesoft.com/accounts/login"
```

On Linux, replace **my-user** and **my-pass** with your actual username and password for your Anypoint Platform account and then run it:

```
curl -d 'username=my-user&password=my-pass'
https://anypoint.mulesoft.com/accounts/login
```

On Windows, run the following code to request a token:

```
curl -sq 'https://anypoint.mulesoft.com/accounts/login' \
    -H "Content-Type: application/json" \
    -d '{"username": "my-user", "password": "my-password"}'
```

You can optionally get the organization ID to use in other CloudHub API calls. In the following command, replace **my-token** with the bearer token from the previous command and run:

```
curl -sq
'https://anypoint.mulesoft.com/accounts/api/me' \
    -H 'Authorization: Bearer my-token'
```

Access the mocking service with the access token obtained previously. Be sure to add the ms2-authorization header:

```
curl -X GET \
    -H "Content-Type: application/json" \
    -H "authorization: bearer 2eef0ee4-737b-4306-b94a-f0001049c6e5" \
    -H "ms2-authorization: bearer 2eef0ee4-737b-4306-b94a-f0001049c6e5" \

"https://anypoint.mulesoft.com/mocking/api/v1/sources
/exchange/assets/b2ee7923-e6c7-4ca3-86a0-
6304559b935d/google-maps-sapi/1.0.0/m/products"
```

You can also get the token from the Anypoint Platform directly.

Now that you have learned how to invoke the mocking services for the APIs we create, "Publishing APIs" on page 76 shows how to publish the APIs.

Publishing APIs

Anypoint Exchange provides a structured space for developers to access your API and collaborate. If the API is intended for internal use, it is published to a private exchange so internal teams can work with the API securely. This method supports internal collaboration without exposing sensitive data to external users. If you are targeting a broader audience, a public exchange is ideal. It provides a platform for external developers to interact with your API, encouraging community feedback and wider adoption.

To publish API specifications and other assets to Exchange, you can use API Designer and click the Publish button located on the upper-right side of the interface, as shown in Figure 3-6.

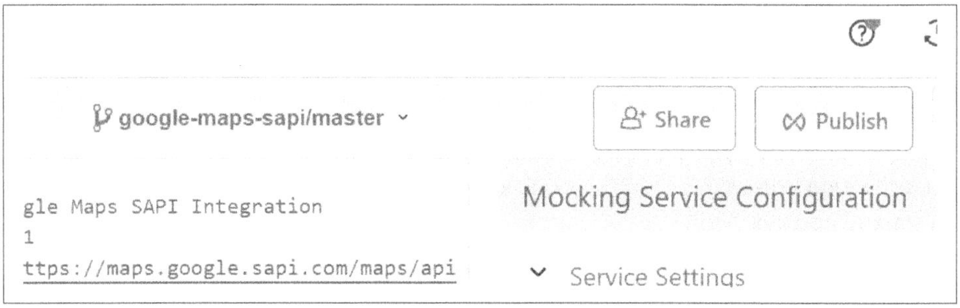

Figure 3-6. The Publish and Share buttons on the API design page, at the upper right area of the window

When publishing an asset, you will need to specify its lifecycle state and version on the "Publishing to Exchange" dialog box that pops up (see Figure 3-7). The LifeCycle State in the dialog indicates the developmental stage of the asset. *Development* means the asset is still in the iterative design process. *Stable* means the asset is finalized and ready to be used. It's important to note that API assets require a Stable state to be consumed by Anypoint Platform tools such as Studio and API Manager.

Figure 3-7. The "Publishing to Exchange" dialog box is where you can add the Asset version

When you publish a REST API specification, it creates the API portal, which has an API console and a mocking service instance to enable testing of the API. API portals can be shared both internally and with external parties for testing.

> There are some OAS 3.0 limitations you must consider when writing your API Fragments. At the document root level, the only valid fields are: openapi, info, components, and paths. The info object must contain a title and a version field, and the paths field must be an empty object.

When assets are published to Exchange, they are accessible exclusively to users within the Business Groups where the assets were posted, but only if those users have been assigned an Exchange role. The Share button (see Figure 3-8) allows you to extend access to these assets to other users within your organization or even to external users.

There are two ways to delete assets after creation:

Hard delete
> An asset deleted within the first seven days of creation.

Soft delete
> An asset deleted after seven days. After seven days, if you want to reuse the asset name, choose a new version number or put the asset in a different Business Group.

After a hard delete or a soft delete, an asset cannot be recovered or undeleted.

Additionally, if your organization has acquired the Anypoint API Community Manager or Anypoint API Experience Hub, both provide tools to create customized developer API portals. These portals not only help to promote API products but also enhance engagement within your API ecosystem by offering features like developer forums, chat, and case management. This makes it easier for developers and other stakeholders to interact, share knowledge, and resolve issues.

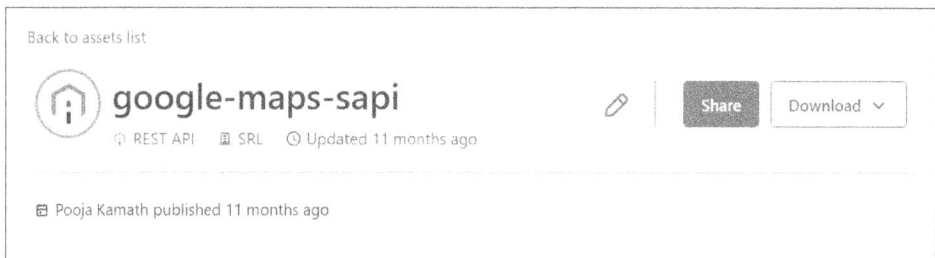

Figure 3-8. The Share button on the API design page

Summary

In this chapter, you've learned to create API fragments, enabling the reuse of assets and enhancing application development efficiency. We've investigated applying security schemes to API specifications, publishing APIs, and enabling mocking. Building a successful API hinges on incremental development, gathering consistent developer feedback, and providing easy exploration and testing options for users. It's important to become familiar with all the tools MuleSoft provides to make API design, development, and validation easy.

In the upcoming chapters, we will utilize the API specification that we formulated in Chapters 2 and 3 to create APIs. This process will help you understand the various connectors, flows, and components that MuleSoft offers out of the box, which will help you develop APIs quickly and efficiently.

CHAPTER 4

Build Essentials

MuleSoft's true power is evident when it connects your Mule application with other systems. This is where MuleSoft demonstrates its strength as an integration platform. It serves as the conductor of data, harmonizing different systems and enabling seamless communication between them.

There are various ways to use MuleSoft for system integration. This chapter walks you through the process of creating integrations. Before we proceed, it's important to establish a foundational understanding of the structure and elements that make up a Mule project. To do this, we will focus on configuring primary components, setting up trigger flows, and enabling logging and debugging in Mule flows. Understanding Mule development begins with comprehending the Mule event.

Mule Events

A *Mule event* is the fundamental unit of data that carries information throughout your application. A Mule event, as shown in Figure 4-1, holds all the core elements needed for processing within a Mule flow.

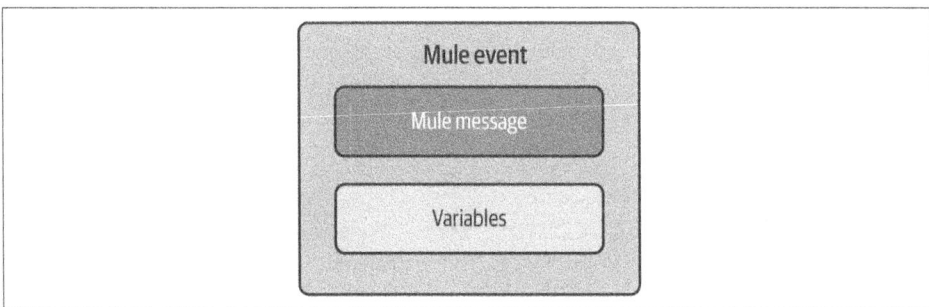

Figure 4-1. Mule event

When triggered, the application generates a Mule event at the source. This event contains the Mule message and variables. The Mule message, as shown in Figure 4-2, is filled with data and metadata passed by the application trigger. The variables are created and managed by processors within the flow. The attributes are the metadata contained in the message headers. Figure 4-3 shows a Mule event that was generated in a flow in ACB.

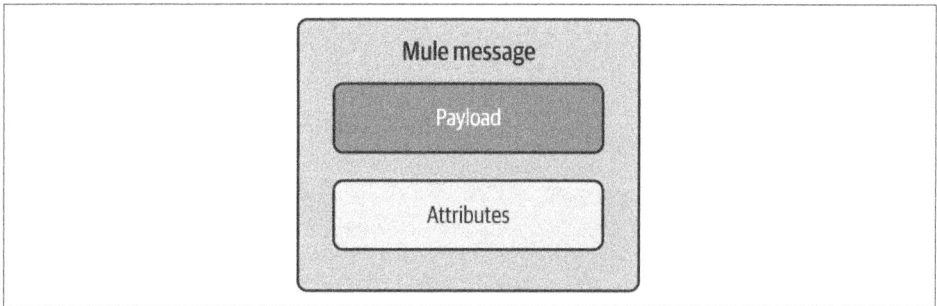

Figure 4-2. Mule message

Figure 4-3. Mule event flowing through the application

It's possible to view Mule events during design time and runtime. During design time, a Mule event is viewed with the help of Data Sense in the input/output section of the connector settings, as shown in Figure 4-4. Using Data Sense, you can understand the format and content of the data flowing through your Mule events. For runtime viewing of events, logging and studio Logger components are utilized.

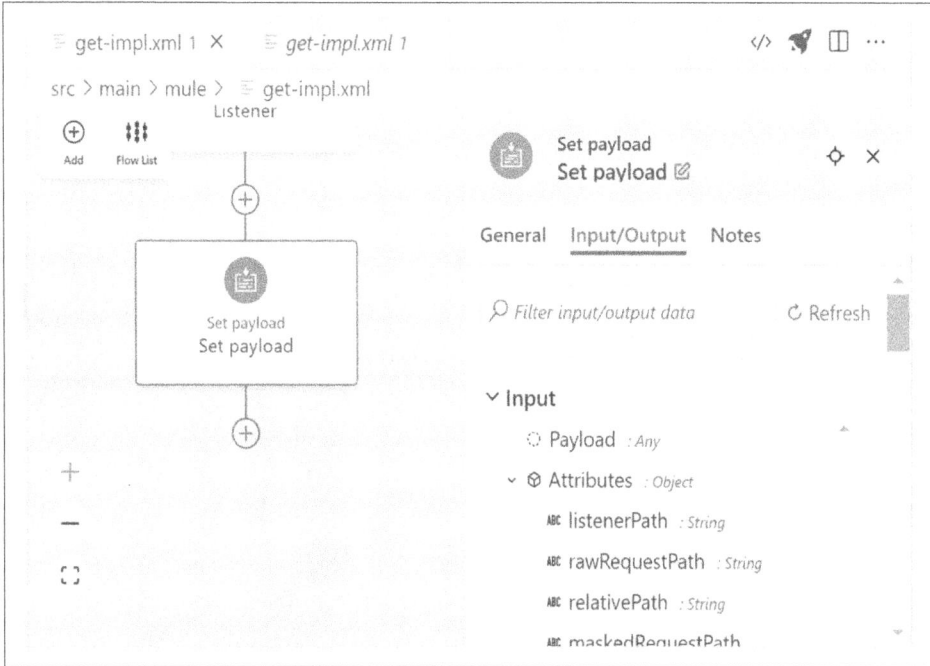

Figure 4-4. Mule event data visible during flow design

Mule automatically generates a correlation ID for every Mule event (see Figure 4-3). This ID is like a tracking number, helping you trace an event's path through the processing steps in your Mule flow. It's important to manage correlation IDs because they can help trace requests across APIs. Imagine a scenario where your Mule flow might need to make multiple calls to different backend services to fulfill the request. In that case, the correlation ID helps you track the entire processing chain for that single client request. By correlating logs across different backend calls using the same correlation ID, you can understand the overall flow and identify any potential issues.

Before setting a correlation ID, Mule checks whether the source already generates one. If there is one, it propagates that throughout the API. It is best to not change the correlation ID, although there might be business-specific or implementation-specific use cases. For example, when your Mule flow interacts with external systems, those systems might have their respective correlation mechanisms. For instance, you might receive a message from a Java Message Service (JMS) queue with a JMS correlation ID and then call a web service that uses a separate correlation ID header. In that case, you would need to manage both correlation IDs to trace the entire processing chain across different systems.

Before we look at a Mule event in action, let's first create an example integration on ACB.

Creating Projects from Scratch

To start building integrations, click the ACB icon in the IDE sidebar. Then choose "Develop an Integration" from the Quick Actions menu, as shown in Figure 4-5.

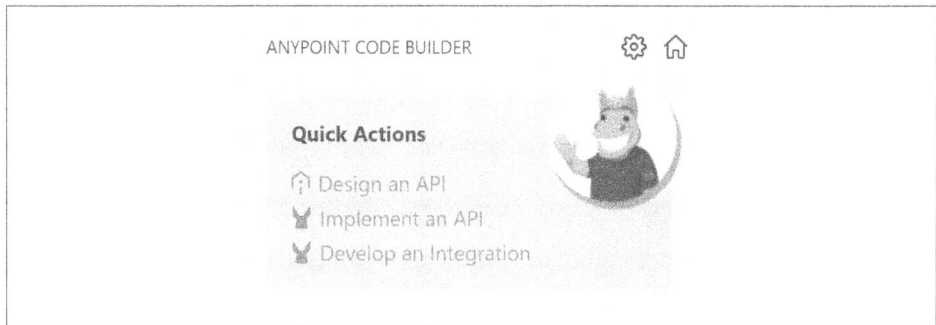

Figure 4-5. Code Builder Quick Actions menu

This opens the "Develop an Integration" dialog box, as shown in Figure 4-6. Here, you type in the project name and choose a Create option. In our case, we have chosen to create an empty project. Before creating a new Mule project, you'll need to select compatible Mule runtime and Java versions. The IDE provides a list of supported options. Your choices are saved for future reference. If the required versions aren't installed, the IDE will automatically download them to specific directories on your computer.

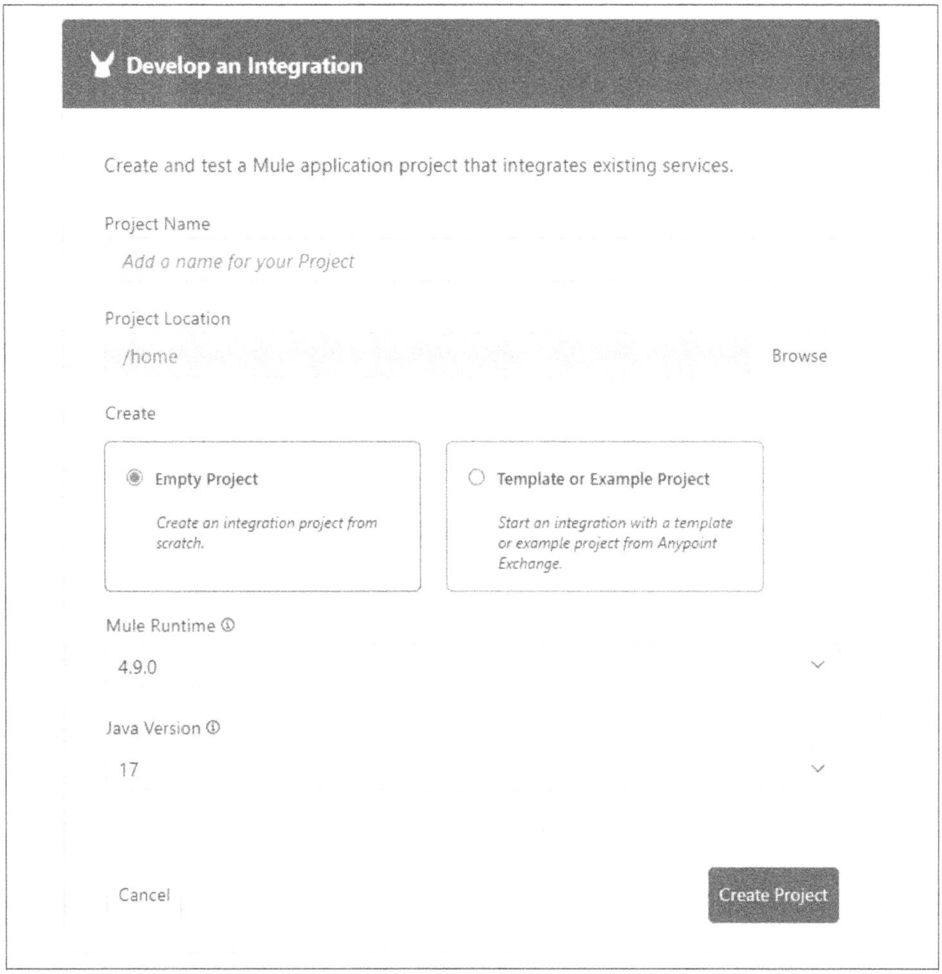

Develop an Integration

Create and test a Mule application project that integrates existing services.

Project Name

Add a name for your Project

Project Location

/home   Browse

Create

◉ Empty Project

Create an integration project from scratch.

○ Template or Example Project

Start an integration with a template or example project from Anypoint Exchange.

Mule Runtime ⓘ

4.9.0

Java Version ⓘ

17

Cancel   **Create Project**

Figure 4-6. Dialog box to develop an integration from scratch

When you click the Create Project button, the canvas UI appears on screen, as shown in Figure 4-7. This page shows a blank canvas without a predefined flow structure, which gives you the flexibility to design your flow from the ground up using the canvas UI. However, if the imported asset already contains flow components like flows, subflows, or error handlers, the canvas will automatically generate a visual representation of these elements, allowing you to start customizing and building upon the existing structure.

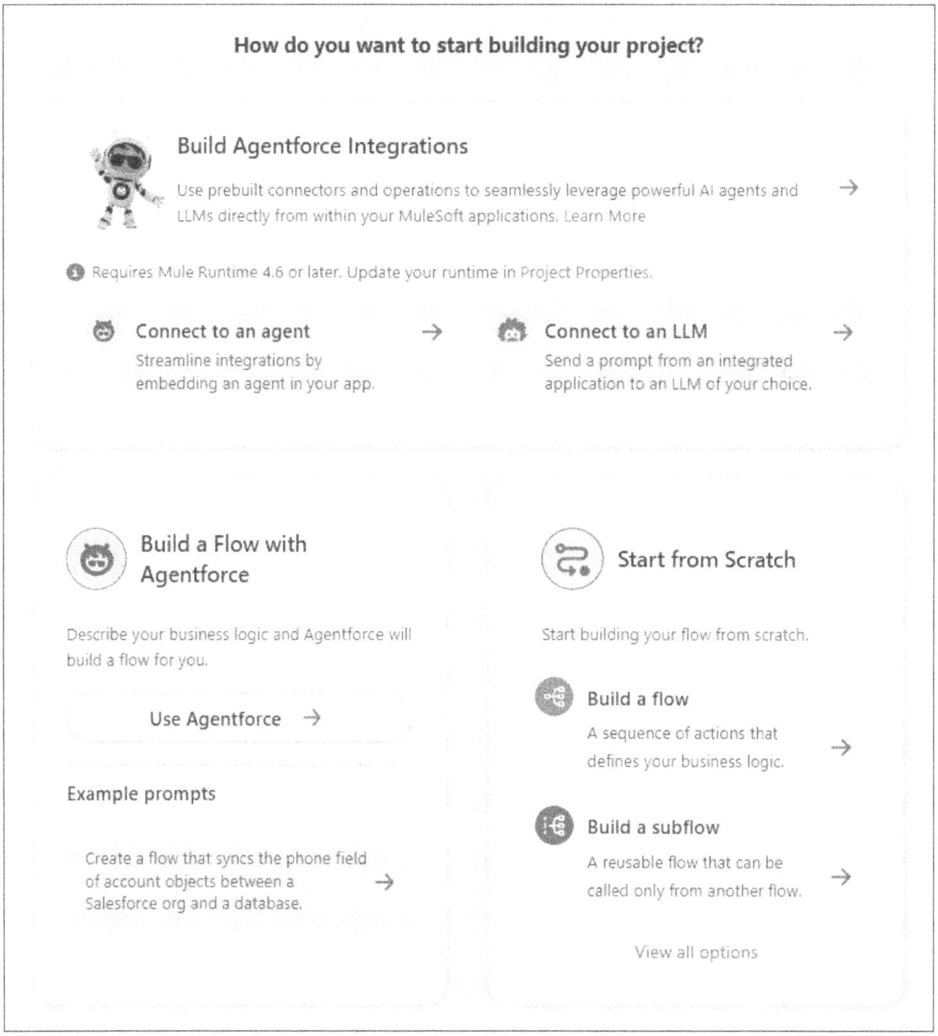

Figure 4-7. UI canvas for a new project

Next, click "Build a flow." This adds a new flow to the UI canvas, as shown in Figure 4-8. You can then customize the flow's name either directly on the canvas or by editing the configuration XML.

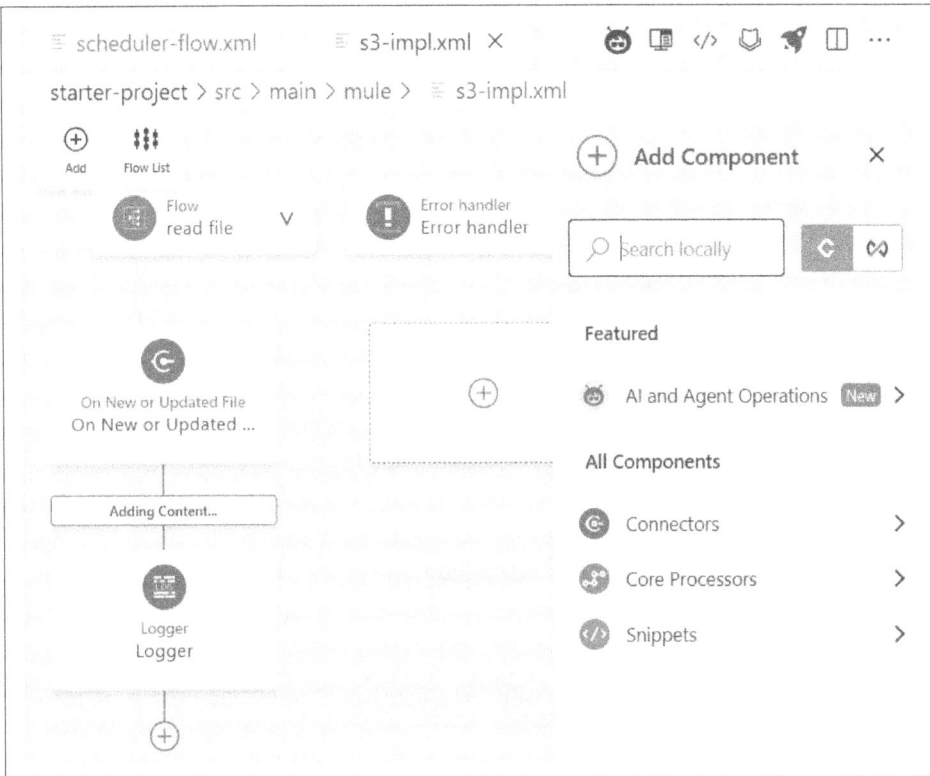

Figure 4-8. New flow

Adding Connectors

To add a connector to your integration, access your project's XML file and switch to the visual interface. Click the "Add component" button, select Connectors, and choose the desired connector and operation, as shown in Figure 4-9. If the connector isn't readily available, utilize the "Search in Exchange" function to locate and add it to your project. This process seamlessly integrates the connector into your integration flow.

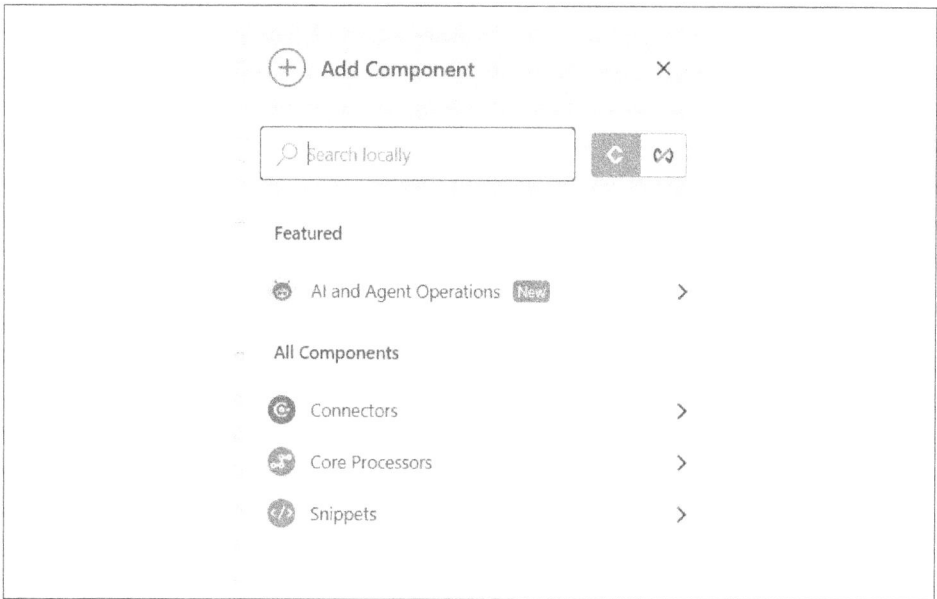

Figure 4-9. Adding a connector

To use the Command Palette, go to Command View and select the following command:

```
MuleSoft: Import Asset from Exchange
```

Select Connector, then choose the connector you want, and follow prompts to pick the version (see Figure 4-10).

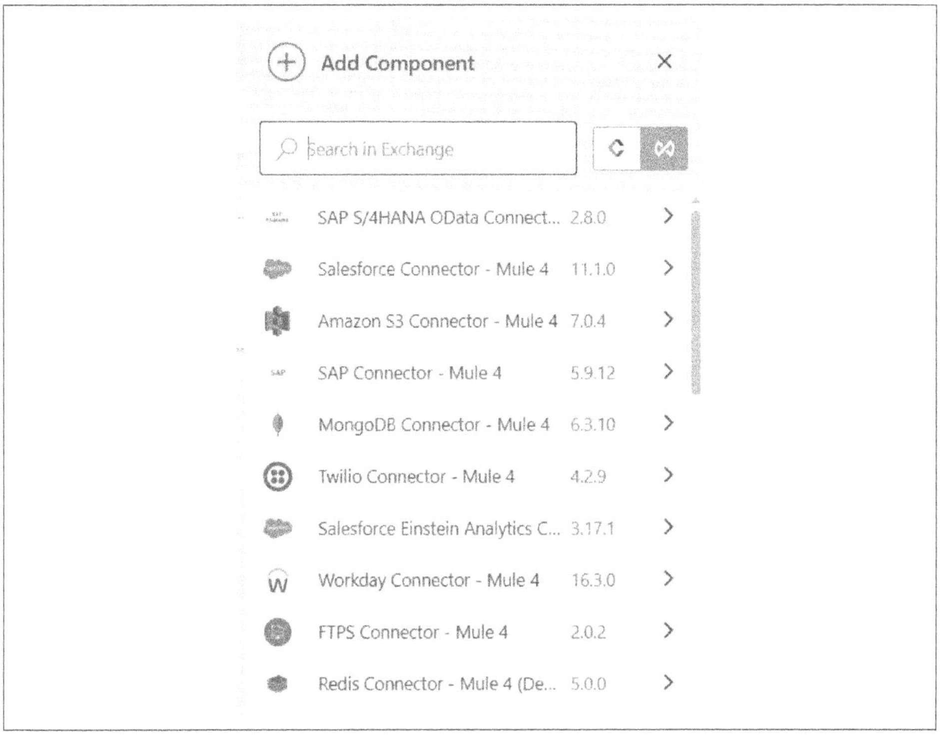

Figure 4-10. Adding an asset from Exchange

To see your component in action, do the following:

1. Find the component in your XML code.

2. Right-click it.

3. Choose "Show Component in Canvas UI."

This will open a visual view of your component where you can customize its settings, as shown in Figure 4-11.

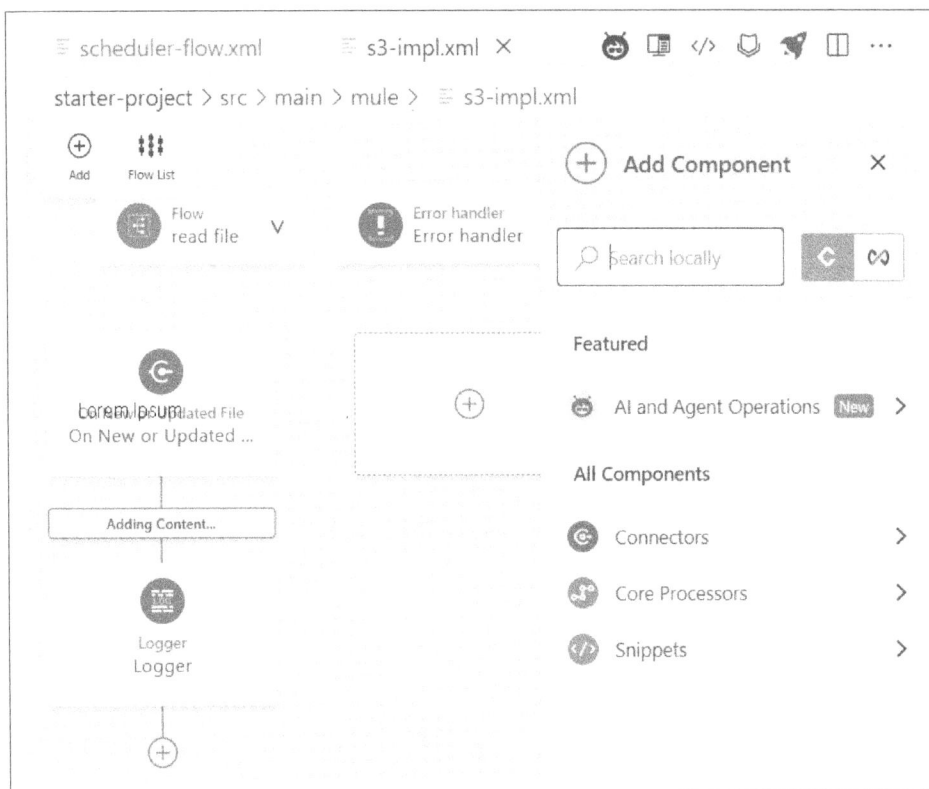

Figure 4-11. Adding a component in canvas UI

> Adding a connector to an integration project does not make that connector available to other projects in your ACB workspace.

Code Snippets: A Coding Shortcut

In application programming, there are often situations where you need to quickly add connector configurations or other commonly used pieces of code. Since projects can be quite large during development, you can use code snippets to streamline this process. *Code snippets* are prewritten chunks of code that you can quickly insert into your Mule application. Think of them as handy templates for common tasks. Snippets save time, reduce errors, and improve efficiency. Snippets are stored in a special JSON file. When you insert one into your Mule application, it's automatically converted into XML code, as shown in Figure 4-12.

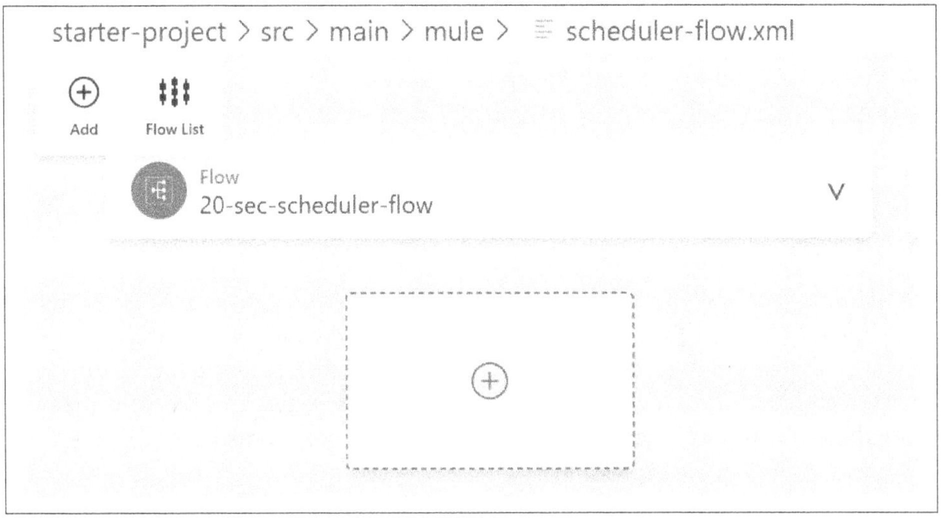

starter-project > src > main > mule > ≡ scheduler-flow.xml

⊕ ⫶⫶⫶
Add   Flow List

Flow
20-sec-scheduler-flow   ∨

⊕

Figure 4-12. Add component to UI

There are two types of code snippets you can add: User Snippets and Built-in Snippets, as shown in Figure 4-13.

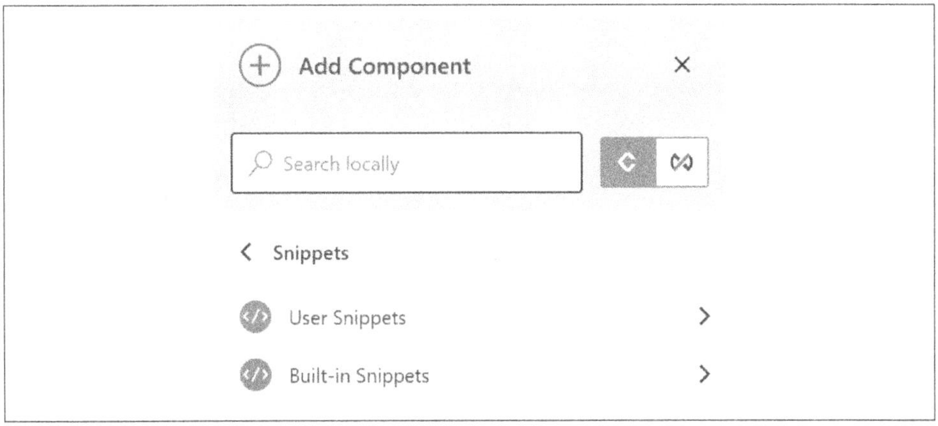

⊕ **Add Component**   ✕

🔍 Search locally   ↻ ∽

‹ Snippets

</> User Snippets   ›

</> Built-in Snippets   ›

Figure 4-13. User snippets menu

To add a prebuilt code snippet, do this:

1. Click the "+" button on your integration canvas where you want to add the snippet.

2. Select Snippets and then Built-in Snippets.

3. Choose the snippet you need. The code will automatically be added to your integration.

To use a code snippet you created:

1. Click the "+" button on your integration canvas.

2. Choose Snippets and then User Snippets.

3. Select the snippet you want to add.

Variables

Variables are essential for managing dynamic data in Mule flows. The "Set variable" component (shown in Figure 4-14) is used to create new variables or update existing ones with dynamic values. Think of it as a designated storage space for data that can be accessed later. The variables created are referenced in the DataWeave expression using the `vars` object. For example, if you create a variable named `oreilly`, then you can reference it with the expression `#[vars.oreilly]`.

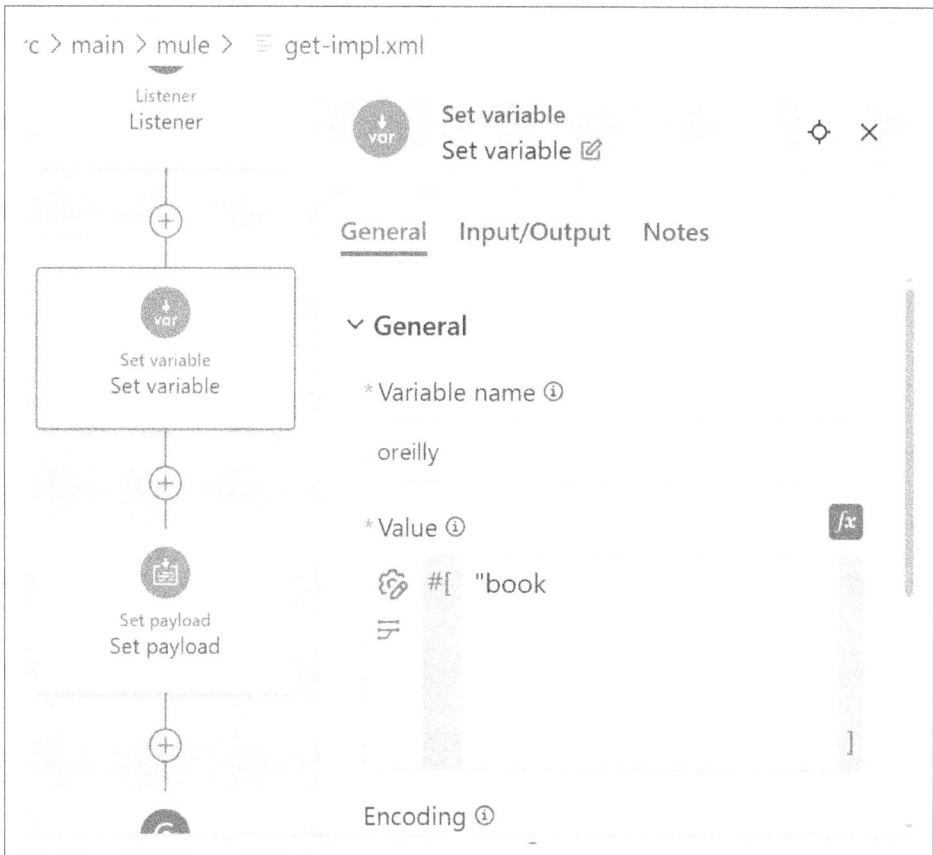

Figure 4-14. Set variable configuration

DataWeave

DataWeave is a Mule-specific transformation language. DataWeave adheres to a strict case-sensitive syntax. This means that variable names, property names, and function calls must be spelled with precise capitalization. This characteristic ensures clarity and prevents unintended errors due to typos.

DataWeave expressions excel in providing direct access to the rich tapestry of data contained within a Mule event. This event acts as a central hub, encompassing the following key components:

Payload
> The core data that your flow is processing, often represented in formats like JSON, XML, or plain text. DataWeave empowers you to transform, extract, and manipulate this data with precision.

Attributes
> Additional metadata associated with the event, often used to store contextual information relevant to the processing task. DataWeave expressions provide a gateway to access and leverage these attributes within your flow logic.

Variables
> As previously discussed, variables serve as dynamic data storage units within your flow. DataWeave expressions act as keys that unlock the information stored within these variables, allowing you to integrate them seamlessly into your processing steps.

DataWeave expressions are highly flexible in how they can be used. There are two main ways to use them:

Standalone scripts
> For complex transformations or reusable logic, you can use the Transform Message processor. This allows you to treat a DataWeave script as a standalone entity, providing a dedicated space for intricate data manipulation tasks.

Inline integration
> For simpler transformations or direct property manipulation, DataWeave expressions can be embedded directly within properties. These inline expressions start with a single hash (#) and are enclosed in square brackets ([ ]). This method offers a concise and efficient way to integrate data manipulation steps within your flow configuration.

Debugging

Effective debugging is very important for building robust Mule applications, helping to pinpoint issues and improve code performance. This section focuses on the core concepts of debugging.

The debugger operates as a distinct entity, communicating with your Mule runtime through a designated port (default: 6666). This separation offers greater flexibility and control during the debugging session. If port 6666 conflicts with other applications on your system, fret not—the port can be conveniently reconfigured to a free and suitable alternative, ensuring seamless communication.

Imagine your application flow as a road map. *Breakpoints* act as waypoints along the road, allowing you to pause execution at specific points of interest. These breakpoints can be strategically placed anywhere within your flow, including processing steps and error-handling sections. Once a breakpoint is hit, the application execution comes to a halt. This empowers you to embark on an interactive debugging journey. You can meticulously step through each application processor, one by one. While stepping through the flow, you gain valuable insights. You can inspect the properties and values associated with events, gaining a clear understanding of data manipulation throughout the process. During debugging, you can directly evaluate DataWeave expressions, ensuring they produce the expected results. Both Anypoint Studio and ACB provide a dedicated breakpoints list within the debug perspective. This list offers a centralized view for managing your breakpoints, allowing you to effortlessly add, remove, and edit them as needed.

Here are steps you can follow to perform debugging in ACB.

To set breakpoints:

1. Begin by opening your configuration file. In the Explorer view, locate and open the XML file that defines your Mule application flow, such as *my-project-name.xml*.

2. Access the Run and Debug panel by clicking the RUN AND DEBUG icon in the activity bar or using keyboard shortcuts (Mac: Cmd+Shift+D, Windows: Ctrl+Shift+D), as shown in Figure 4-15.

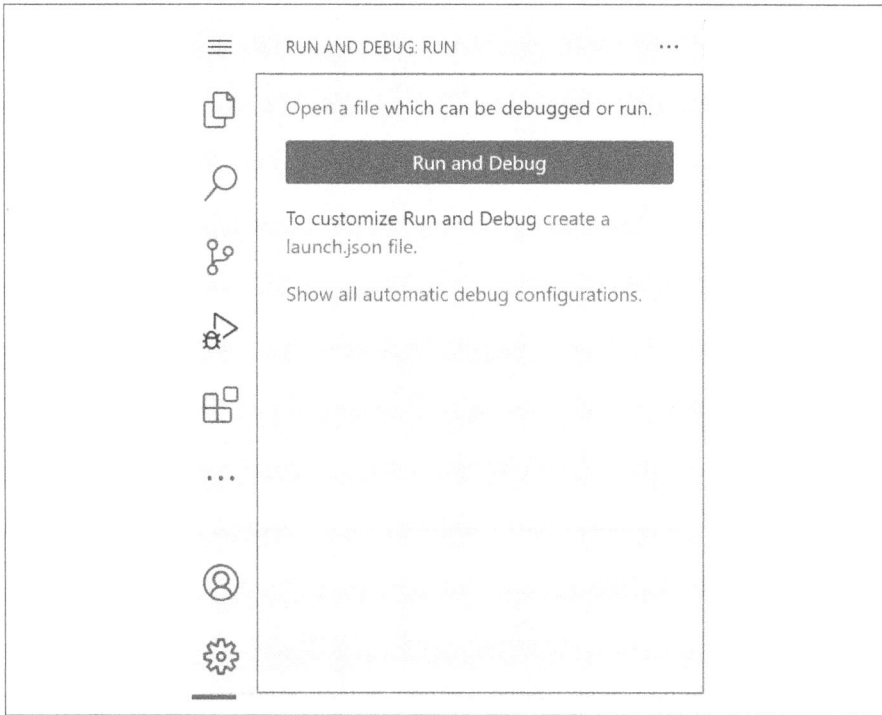

Figure 4-15. Run and Debug panel

To start a debug session:

1. Select the appropriate debug configuration for your project in the Run and Debug panel.

2. Initiate debugging by clicking the green Run button (play icon) or by pressing F5 to start the application in debug mode, as shown in Figure 4-16.

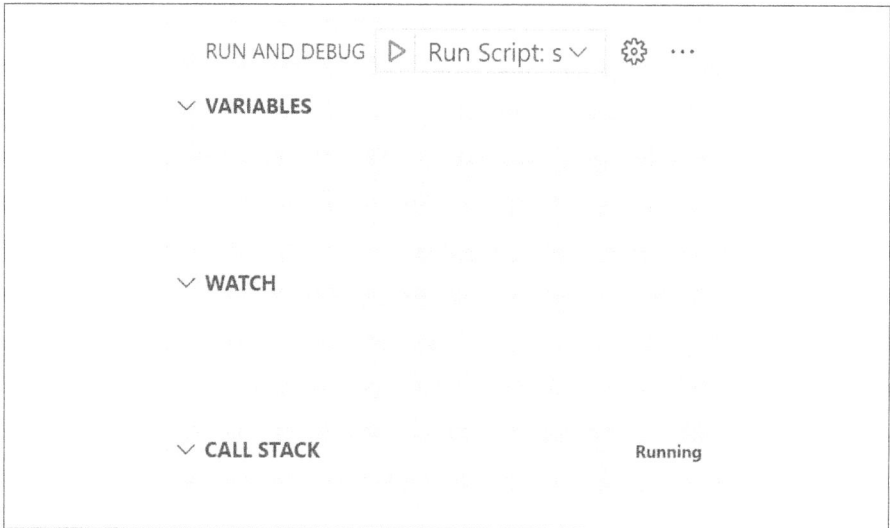

Figure 4-16. Debug options

To interact with breakpoints (for the breakpoint shown in Figure 4-17):

1. When the execution reaches a breakpoint, the application pauses.

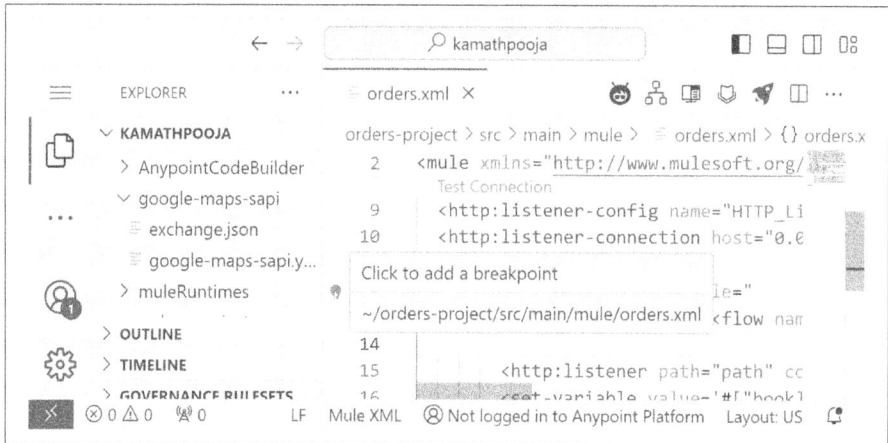

Figure 4-17. Breakpoint is shown with a dot

2. Use the debug toolbar buttons such as Step Over to execute line by line, Step Into to delve into method calls, or Step Out to exit functions, as shown in Figure 4-18.

Figure 4-18. Debug breakpoint options

3. The Variables panel provides details about the current Mule event, including properties and their values.

> During a breakpoint, you can evaluate DataWeave expressions directly within the debug view to verify their output. Also, the Run and Debug panel allows you to manage breakpoints by providing a list of breakpoints, enabling you to add, remove, and enable/disable breakpoints throughout your flow.

Managing Properties

Properties allow you to manage sensitive information, use dynamic values in your Mule applications, and tailor configurations for different environments. By encrypting sensitive data, employing variables, and selecting specific property files, you can enhance security, improve code maintainability, and adapt your application to various deployment scenarios.

Mule allows you to store configuration values in external files; to do this, create YAML or properties files and place them in your project's *src/main/resources* folder. These files hold key-value pairs that can be referenced in your Mule configuration XML for both sensitive and nonsensitive data. An example YAML file is shown here:

```
S3:
  bucketname: mybucket
  accesskey: "![NmERTT]BBBB"
  secretkey: "![==]!!n2LDIe456BBDTgHTfdsFQDR"
```

Referencing Properties

To reference nonencrypted properties, use the syntax ${property-key} within your Mule configuration XML. Employ the <configuration-properties/> element to specify the property file location. For instance, if the s3. accesskey property is set to "![NmERTT]BBBB" in *dev.yaml*, you can reference it as ${accesskey} within the accesskey attribute of an < s3:config /> element, as shown here:

```
<configuration-properties file="dev.yaml"/>

<s3:config name="Amazon_S3_Configuration"
doc:name="Amazon S3 Configuration"
doc:id="7f692dd">
  <s3:connection accessKey="${s3.accesskey}"
secretKey="${s3.secretkey}" region="us-west-2"/>
</s3:config>

<http:listener-config name="HTTP_Listener_config">
  <http:listener-connection host="0.0.0.0" port="8091"/>
</http:listener-config>

<flow name="get-impl">
  <http:listener path="path" config-
ref="HTTP_Listener_config" doc:name="Listener"
doc:id="pusplp"/>
  <set-variable value='#["book]' variableName='orielly'
doc:name="Set variable" doc:id="haqabd"/>
  <set-payload value='#["test"]' doc:name="Set
payload" doc:id="wzjejh"/>
  <s3:put-object bucketName="${bucketname}"
key="ID1" config-ref="Amazon_S3_Configuration"
doc:name="Put Object" doc:id="wtkyoy"/>
</flow>
```

Encrypting Properties

Protecting sensitive data, like passwords or API keys, is crucial for any Mule application. For best practices purposes, it's best to store secure properties in files that denote the properties are secure (for example, *dev.secure.yaml* or *statging.secure.yaml*). MuleSoft offers the Secure Properties Tool (download (*https://oreil.ly/Xm3TD*)) to encrypt these values before adding them to your properties files. This is an executable jar; after downloading, run the following command to get encrypted values. In our case, we are encrypting the accesskey value using my-key-value:

```
$ java -cp secure-properties-tool.jar com.mulesoft.tools.SecurePropertiesTool \
string \
encrypt \
Blowfish \
CBC \
my-key-value \
"![NmERTT]BBBB"
```

Upon running this command, an encrypted value is generated that may look something like the following string:

```
/MU0/xB/zoMPjxBA7/9X44Ad2H808AY54h5kjwr
```

Next, update the *dev.secure.yaml* with the encrypted value:

```
S3:
  bucketname: mybucket
  accesskey: "/MU0/xB/zoMPjxBA7/9X44Ad2H808AY54h5kjwr"
  secretkey: "![==]!!n2LDIe456BBDTgHTfdsFQDR"
```

Here is the secure configuration properties snippet, which you need to add to use the secure properties you just created:

```
<secure-properties:config name="Secure_Properties_Config"
  doc:name="Secure Properties Config" doc:id="ukvpll"
  file="${env}.secure.yaml" key="${encryption.key}" >
      <secure-properties:encrypt algorithm="Blowfish" />
</secure-properties:config>

<flow name=" " >
...
```

Now that you know how to create property files, securely encrypt properties, and use them in your project, let's learn about different ways to trigger flows.

Other Ways to Trigger Flows

So far, our focus has been on triggering flows using HTTP listeners for web services. In this section, we'll explore alternative flow initiation methods, including file system monitoring, database event detection, scheduled execution, and JMS message consumption.

File System Monitoring

A File Connector is very commonly used in industries like retail and transportation to move daily pricing files and transport manifests. The File Connector continually scans designated directories for newly created or modified files. On discovering such files, it generates corresponding messages to initiate subsequent flow processing. To implement this, begin by creating a new project in ACB and selecting the "New or Updated File" component from the Mule Palette. Configure essential parameters such as the directory path, file filtering criteria using matchers, and file processing frequency. To manage processed files, you can enable automatic deletion, relocation to a specific directory, or renaming. This versatile connector empowers you to seamlessly integrate file-based events into your integration workflows.

Mule offers four different connectors for working with files and folders: File, FTP, FTPS, and SFTP. While they have different ways of connecting to files (like using a local drive or a remote server), they all work similarly and offer features such as searching for specific files, locking files, and creating new files.

To add the File Connector, follow the directions to add a connector described in "Adding Connectors" on page 85. After adding the connector, select "On New or Updated" operation from the Add Component panel and add it to the UI. It's a best practice to create a global configuration element to specify the working directory.

When utilizing the File Connector on the platform, be mindful that it's exclusively compatible with the */tmp* folder. For deployments on customer-hosted Mule runtimes, ensure the Mule account possesses necessary read and write privileges for designated directories. To prevent data loss, exercise caution when deleting or overwriting files, opting instead for moving or renaming them postprocessing. To avoid processing the same file twice, you can either move, rename, or delete files after using them. Or you can use the watermarking feature to keep track of new files and only process files that were changed after the last read. This way, you can be sure you're always working on the latest files.

Watermarking

Watermarking is a technique used to keep track of the progress of a process, especially when dealing with large datasets or continuous data feeds. To add the watermarking feature, you have to enable watermarking mode in the connector configuration, as shown in Figure 4-19.

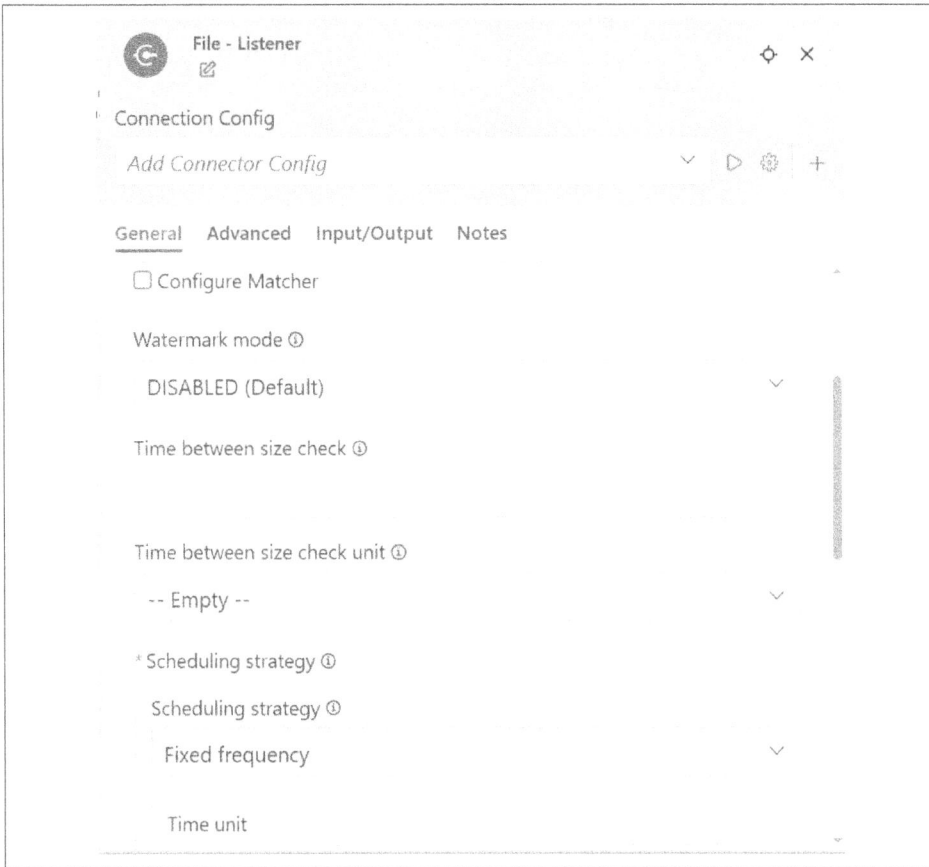

Figure 4-19. Watermarking options selected

The File and Database Connectors make watermarking more efficient by automating the retrieval, comparison, and storage of identifiers to locate new data for processing. As demonstrated in the figure, you can easily set up these connectors to utilize file creation or modification dates or specific database column values. In more complex data identification scenarios, manual watermarking can be used, which involves custom logic to regularly check for new data, manage identifiers, and update the watermark accordingly. Now, let's examine how we can use the Database Connector to trigger flows.

Database Event Detection

The Database Connector's On Table Row operation processes each table row, handling query generation, watermarking, and idempotency. You can designate a watermark column or an ID column, or both, to manage data processing efficiency and prevent duplicate processing.

The Database Connector automatically generates a query like `SELECT * FROM table WHERE table_column > :watermark` when a watermark column is specified. For each poll, it processes all retrieved rows and updates the watermark with the highest value found.

> Potential issues with watermarking are that if the polling interval is short, the dataset is large, or individual record processing is time-consuming, subsequent polls might start before the watermark is updated, leading to potential duplicate processing.
>
> The solution is to ensure that each record is processed exactly once, specifying a unique ID column. The listener will track processed records based on this ID, preventing reprocessing even if the record is fetched multiple times.

Schedulers

Mule's Scheduler component allows you to automate flow execution based on predefined time intervals. You can set up flows to run every few seconds, minutes, hours, or even at specific times of the day. For instance, you could schedule a flow to process daily sales reports at midnight or update inventory levels every five minutes.

The Scheduler offers flexible scheduling options, including fixed intervals and cron expressions for intricate timing patterns. When configuring the Scheduler, it's essential to consider time zones. While Mule typically uses the local machine's time zone, Anypoint Platform environments adhere to UTC. You can specify a different time zone using the time zone attribute.

To prevent overlapping executions, the `disallowConcurrentExecution` property can be used. Additionally, if system resources are unavailable at a scheduled time, the Scheduler will skip that execution and try again later.

It's important to note that in clustered environments, the Scheduler runs on only one node (the primary node) to avoid duplicate executions. Figure 4-20 shows the Scheduler added to the canvas.

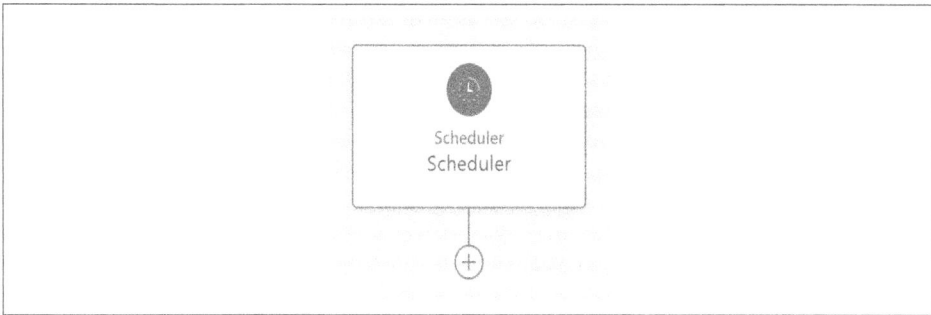

Figure 4-20. Scheduler component

In the following example, the Scheduler runs every 20 seconds:

```
<flow name="20-sec-scheduler-flow">
      <scheduler doc:name="Scheduler" doc:id="ativtx" >
         <scheduling-strategy>
      <fixed-frequency frequency="20" timeUnit="SECONDS" />
    </scheduling-strategy>
        </scheduler></flow>
```

In the following example, the execution skips if the Scheduler does not complete its run within 20 minutes:

```
<flow name="20-sec-scheduler-flow">
        <scheduler doc:name="Scheduler" doc:id="ativtx"
disallowConcurrentExecution="true">
          <scheduling-strategy>
              <fixed-frequency frequency="20"
timeUnit="SECONDS"/>
          </scheduling-strategy>
        </scheduler>
</flow>
```

When this happens, Mule logs an "Execution skipped" message, for example (edited for readability):

```
INFO 2022-11-09 15:15:43,082 ...
...scheduler.DefaultSchedulerMessageSource:
Flow 'scheduler-disallowConcurrentExecution-ex' is already running and
'disallowConcurrentExecution' is set to 'true'. Execution skipped.
INFO 2022-11-09 15:15:43,083 ...
...scheduler.DefaultSchedulerMessageSource:
Flow 'scheduler-disallowConcurrentExecution-ex' is already running and
'disallowConcurrentExecution' is set to 'true'. Execution skipped.
```

Mule provides two main ways to schedule flow execution:

Fixed frequency
> This method runs a flow at regular intervals, like every minute or every hour. It's simple to set up and ideal for routine tasks.

Cron expression
> For more complex schedules, cron expressions offer precise control. You can define schedules like "every Tuesday at 2 P.M." or "on the first day of every month."

By using these methods, you can effectively automate your Mule flows based on specific time requirements.

Cron expressions provide a powerful and flexible way to define complex scheduling patterns. They consist of six fields representing:

> Second (0–59)
> Minute (0–59)
> Hour (0–23)
> Day of month (1–31)
> Month (1–12 or JAN-DEC)
> Day of week (0–6 or SUN-SAT)

For example:

> 0 0 12 * * ?: runs at 12:00 PM every day
> 0 15 10 ? * MON–FRI: runs at 10:15 A.M. every weekday
> 0 0 0 1 * ?: runs at midnight on the first day of every month

By mastering cron expressions, you can create highly specific and tailored schedules for your Mule flows.

Cron Expressions

Here are some practical examples of cron expressions:

Daily jobs
> Running a backup at midnight: 0 0 0 * * ?
>
> Executing a report generation process at 3 P.M.: 0 0 15 * * ?

Weekly jobs
> Processing payroll on Fridays at 5 P.M.: 0 0 17 * * FRI
>
> Sending a weekly report on Monday mornings: 0 0 9 * * MON

Monthly jobs

Running a month-end report on the last day of every month: 0 0 0 L * ?

Executing a task on the second Tuesday of every month: 0 0 10 ? * 2#2 *

Yearly jobs

Running an annual audit at the start of the year: 0 0 0 1 1 ?

Remember that the "?" character is a wildcard that can be used for day-of-month or day-of-week fields when you don't care about the specific value. The "L" character in the day-of-month field represents the last day of the month. The "#" character in the day-of-week field specifies the *n*th occurrence of a day within a month.

Object Store

Object storage is a data storage architecture that treats data as distinct units called objects. Unlike traditional file systems, which organize data in a hierarchical structure, object storage stores data flat and unstructured. Each object includes the data, metadata (information about the data), and a unique identifier. Each Mule application has a built-in, persistent Object Store. If you plan to utilize the Object Store for watermarking, after adding the Object Store to the project, use the `Store` and `Retrieve` operations to compare and update the watermark values.

Application Structure

So far, we have explored various methods of triggering flows, adding components, understanding variables, and utilizing Mule events. Next, we will delve into the structure of Mule applications and the concepts of flows and subflows, and take a closer look at what a Mule project entails.

Flows

Flows represent a sequence of connected components that process data and events. Imagine a flow as a pipeline where data enters, undergoes transformations, and exits in a desired format. A Mule flow has the following components:

Inbound endpoint

This is the starting point, where the flow receives data (e.g., HTTP listener, file listener, JMS listener).

Processors

These components manipulate the data (e.g., data transformations, enrichments, error handling).

Outbound endpoint

This is the final destination where the processed data is sent (e.g., database, file system, JMS queue).

Flows can be of the following types:

Synchronous flows

These flows process messages sequentially.

Asynchronous flows

These flows process messages independently, allowing for better performance and scalability.

Subflows

Reusable flows that can be called from other flows; subflows do not have their own exception handling strategy. All error handling is inherited from the calling flow.

> When you design your integration, subflows act like placeholders. Once you build the application, these placeholders are replaced with the actual logic from the subflow. This improves performance compared to directly referencing another flow.
>
> Subflows can cause issues when used incorrectly. Because subflows are expanded into the main flow during deployment, components within the subflow can be duplicated multiple times if the subflow is referenced in several places. This is particularly problematic for components that rely on unique identifiers, like batch processors. Having multiple instances of the same Batch Job with the same ID can lead to application failures during deployment.

We have already looked at how to create a flow earlier in this chapter. You can send data from one flow to another using the Flow Reference component. This data, including metadata, is automatically passed along. However, variables might not be shared if the data is sent across different systems. This means that data you create in one flow might not be available in another flow if they're on different platforms.

For readability and best practices, it's best to split large flows into manageable chunks of smaller flows or subflows.

Configuration Files

Just as we've seen the benefits of breaking down our flows into smaller, more manageable units, we can apply the same principle to our configuration files. Instead of one large, complex file, we can create multiple focused configuration files. This approach significantly enhances readability, maintainability, and testability. By organizing settings logically, we improve code comprehension and reduce the chances of errors.

Global Elements

When global elements are scattered across multiple configuration files, it can hinder readability and maintainability. To streamline management, consider consolidating most global elements into a single configuration file. This centralized approach simplifies the process of locating and modifying these elements. However, if a global element is exclusively used within a specific file, keeping it within that file can improve the organization.

Mule domains provide a centralized location for sharing configuration elements across multiple applications. This ensures consistency, as changes are made in a single place. You can share resources like database connections, error handlers, and properties. Additionally, domains allow multiple services to share a port and facilitate communication between applications using VM Connector. While this feature is beneficial for on-premises deployments, it's currently unavailable for CloudHub or Runtime Fabric. To utilize domains, create a Mule domain project and associate your applications with it. Then define your shared configurations within the domain project.

Summary

This chapter explored various techniques for handling data and controlling flow execution in MuleSoft. It covered debugging with filesystem monitoring, using watermarking, and manipulating data with the Set Payload transformer and DataWeave expressions. Additionally, the chapter discussed the importance of watermarks for synchronizing data across different systems and components. It introduced connectors for database interactions, explaining how to trigger flows based on file changes or new database records. Finally, it covered the Scheduler component for time-based flow execution and the Object Store for persistent data storage. Next, we will focus our efforts on understanding the mechanisms of message orchestration so we can improve our flows with error handling and applying flow control tactics.

CHAPTER 5

Mechanics of Message Orchestration

Message orchestration is a crucial concept in integration environments. It involves coordinating and managing messages between different systems, services, or components. This process ensures that messages are properly routed, transformed, and delivered to the intended destinations based on predefined business logic and rules. Message orchestration plays a vital role in ensuring seamless communication and data flow within complex systems.

Chapter 4 covered the essentials of data flow. We identified data sources such as databases and APIs, imported data into the system, and transformed it into the required format. Then we stored the data in databases, processed it to extract insights, and delivered the processed data to users or systems. Additionally, Chapter 4 talked about logging. We will incorporate detailed logging for errors. By logging clear messages about where and why an error occurred, we can diagnose issues more quickly and efficiently. This practice not only helps in resolving current issues but also provides a valuable history that can inform future improvements and prevent similar problems from occurring again.

In this chapter, you will master error handling to ensure reliable message processing, learn to resolve errors confidently, and keep systems running smoothly. Next, you'll dive into advanced routing techniques like Scatter-Gather, Choice, First Successful, and Round Robin to ensure messages reach their destinations. You'll explore transaction management to complete operations successfully and consistently. And we'll look at For Each, Parallel For Each, and batch processing to handle large messages and datasets efficiently. By the end, you'll transform your understanding of message orchestration, making your integration solutions more robust and effective.

Think of message orchestration like Super Routes Logistics (SRL) operations. Their entire business depends on getting the right data (traffic, package load, driver status) to the right system at the right time. MuleSoft becomes their logistics coordinator, ensuring quotes are accurate, packages are prioritized, and customers stay informed—all orchestrated in real time. You need to ensure each package (message) reaches the correct address (endpoint), gets properly sorted and labeled (transformation), and doesn't get lost or damaged (error handling). Using tools such as MuleSoft is like having a highly efficient logistics manager who keeps everything running smoothly while you focus on growing your business.

Error Handling

Handling errors is a crucial aspect of application development. When errors occur within our applications, it can be frustrating for both developers and users. Therefore, it's essential to build applications with robust error-handling mechanisms. These mechanisms ensure that the system can gracefully manage issues and provide helpful feedback when something goes wrong. In SRL's real-time quote engine, a failed traffic data API call shouldn't crash the system or give a vague 500 error. Instead, an error-handling strategy could catch the failure, notify the customer of delayed quote availability, and log the event for review—keeping trust intact.

If you find error handling challenging, you're not alone. Many developers struggle with this aspect, especially when starting out. However, effective error handling is key to creating reliable and user-friendly applications. By anticipating potential problems and planning for them, you can significantly improve your application's overall stability and user experience.

To handle errors effectively, it's important to first understand the basics of error handling. This includes identifying different types of errors, understanding error handling scopes, and learning about the behavior of the HTTP default settings, including how to override them. To simplify error-handling topics, you can work with some basic flows to see these concepts in action and better understand how to handle errors in the Mule 4 runtime. Let's get started.

Error Types: System and Messaging Errors

Understanding the different types of errors is crucial to preventing future mishaps. There are two main types of errors: system errors and messaging errors. Let's dive deeper into these types of errors to ensure the smooth functioning of your processes.

System errors occur at the system level. They may happen during an application's startup or when a connection to an external system fails. These errors cannot be resolved within a Mule flow, but you can set a reconnection strategy to handle them.

Messaging errors occur within a Mule flow, such as when invalid data or bad requests are processed. These are the errors that can be handled in Mule applications. When an error occurs, the flow execution stops. If there is an error handler scope present, the Mule event is passed to it, and any processors within the error handler scope are executed according to the error-handling strategy. If there is no error handler scope present, the Mule default error handler is invoked, which does not allow any custom error-handling strategy to be executed. You might be wondering, what is an error handler scope? Don't worry, we will discuss that later in this chapter.

Family of Errors: Hierarchy

Errors come in different types and can be classified based on their type and relationship with other error types within each category. To understand this classification, imagine a parent/child hierarchy where the most general error type sits at the top. This top-level error type can catch all errors in your examples. As you move down the hierarchy, you encounter more specific error types that allow you to handle errors in a more targeted manner.

Figure 5-1 shows the broadest error type at the top, capable of catching any error. Below it, more specific error types branch out, each tailored to handle particular scenarios. This structure helps you manage errors more effectively by allowing you to address specific issues as they arise.

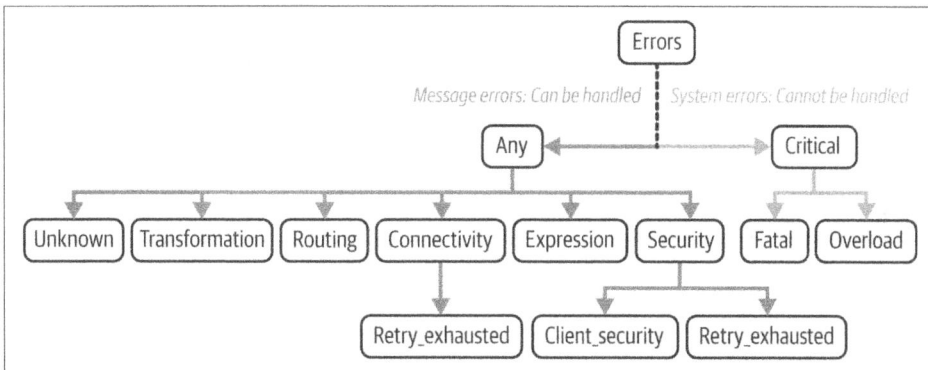

Figure 5-1. Error type hierarchy

In practice, you'll select specific error types to handle based on the situation at hand. By understanding this hierarchy and knowing when to apply each error type, you can ensure your Mule applications are robust and capable of dealing with a variety of error conditions.

Error Object Creation

An *error object* in MuleSoft is a structured representation of an error that occurs during the execution of a flow. It provides detailed information about the error, enabling you to diagnose and handle issues effectively. The error object typically contains two key pieces of information:

Error description
> A concise summary that describes what went wrong

Error type
> A categorization of the error into a predefined hierarchy of error types, which helps in identifying the nature and context of the error

The error object is crucial for implementing robust error handling in your Mule applications. By examining the error description and error type, you can determine the cause of the error and apply appropriate error-handling strategies to manage and resolve it, ensuring the smooth operation of your integrations.

Decoding HTTP Listener Default Settings

The *HTTP default settings* in MuleSoft's HTTP Listener configuration define how the listener responds to your incoming requests, particularly in terms of success and error handling. These settings are crucial for managing client interactions and ensuring that appropriate responses are sent based on the outcome of request processing. Figure 5-2 shows a breakdown:

Success response
> *HTTP status code*
>
> When a request is processed successfully, you will receive a 200 HTTP Success status code. This indicates that your request was handled correctly.
>
> *Payload*
>
> The response's payload will contain the data processed or generated by the Mule application, signifying successful execution.

Error response
> *HTTP status code*
>
> If there is an error during the processing of the request, you will receive a 500 Server Error status code. This indicates that the server encountered an issue while handling your request.

Error description

You will receive an error description along with the 500 status code. This provides details about the nature of the error, helping you diagnose and understand what went wrong.

These default settings ensure that you are informed about the outcome of your request, whether it is successful or encounters an error. By observing these default responses, you can better understand and manage how your Mule applications interact with clients and handle various scenarios.

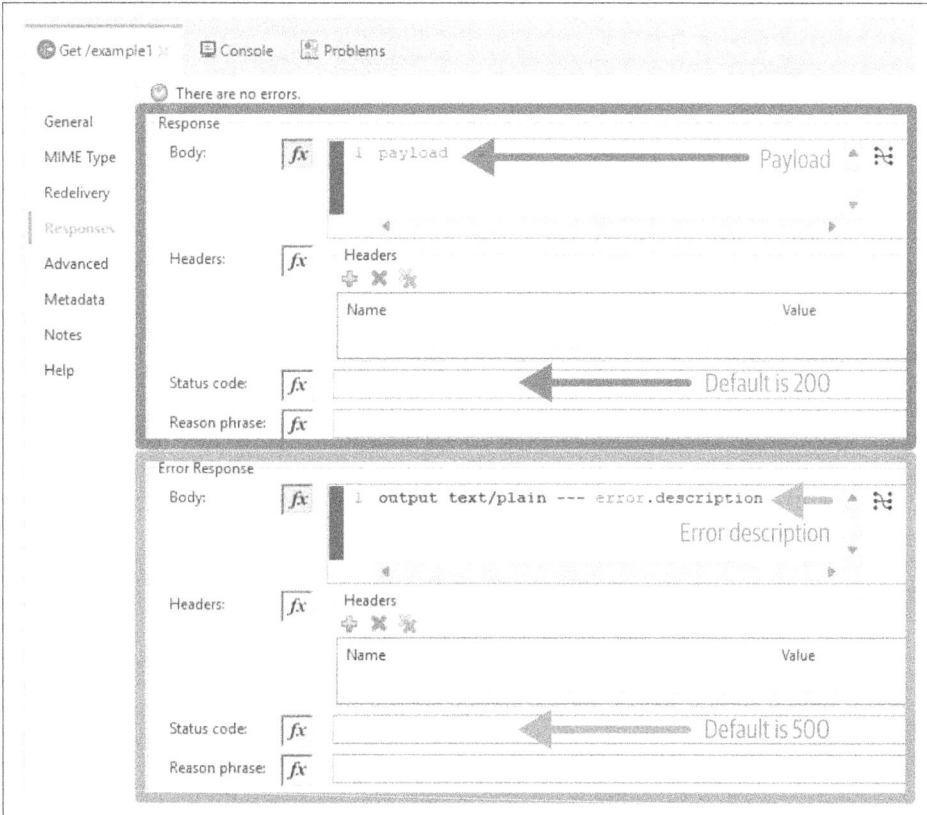

Figure 5-2. HTTP Listener default settings

Modifying HTTP Listener Default Settings

To enhance your error handling, you need to modify the HTTP Listener response configuration to ensure that error messages are clear and understandable and that responses include specific HTTP status codes. Figure 5-3 shows the modifications you will make.

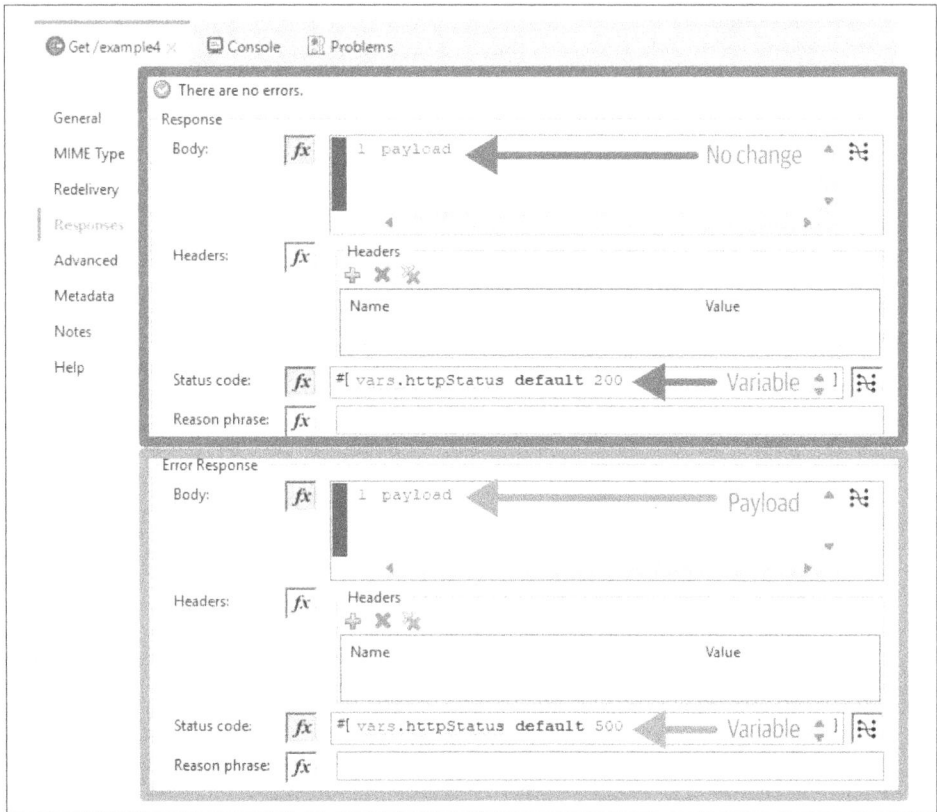

Figure 5-3. Modified HTTP Listener settings

Success response
> *HTTP status code*

Set a variable `httpStatus` with a default value of 200.

Error response
> *HTTP status code*

Set a variable `httpStatus` with a default value of 500.

Payload

The payload includes an error message that explains the issue, providing details about the nature of the error and helping you diagnose and understand what went wrong.

In these examples, the variable `httpStatus` is used, which is not a reserved variable name but is a name commonly used in the integration space. By making these changes, you will improve the clarity and usefulness of your responses, providing users with more helpful information and appropriate status codes based on the outcome of their requests.

Mule Default Error Handler

The *Mule default error handler* is a built-in mechanism in MuleSoft that handles errors you haven't explicitly managed with custom error handlers in your application. When an error occurs and there's no specific error handler configured, the Mule default error handler steps in, as shown in Figure 5-4.

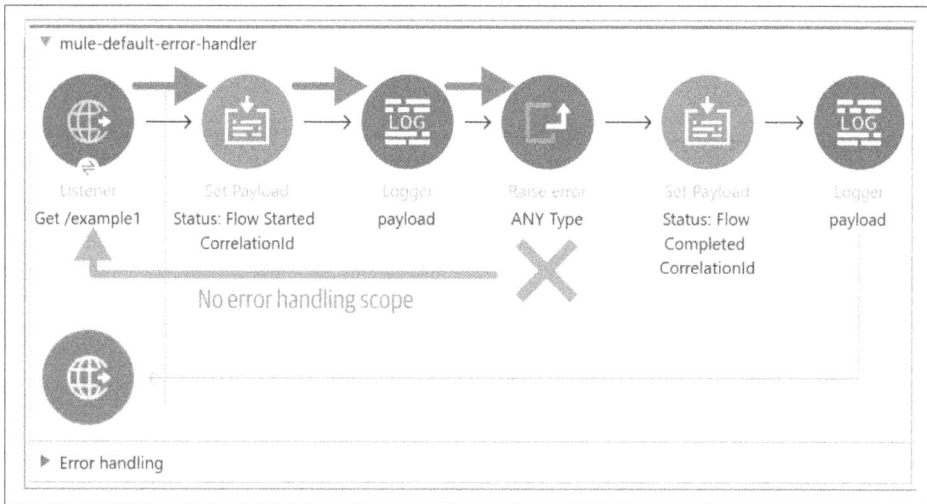

Figure 5-4. Mule flow with no error handler

Here are the key points for you to understand:

Handling unmanaged errors
> If an error happens within your Mule flow and you haven't defined a custom error handler to address that specific type of error, the default error handler takes over. This prevents your application from crashing abruptly and ensures some basic level of error management is in place.

Error propagation
> The default error handler typically propagates the error up the chain, escalating it to higher levels of the application. This can result in your application returning an HTTP 500 status code to the client if the error isn't caught and managed elsewhere.

No custom processing
> The default error handler doesn't perform any custom processing or logging. It simply allows the error to bubble up, providing minimal handling. This means it won't transform the error message, attempt retries, or perform any corrective actions.

Fallback mechanism
> The default error handler acts as a safety net to catch unhandled errors, ensuring they aren't ignored and that your application behaves predictably.

So remember: the Mule default error handler is a safety net that catches errors you haven't explicitly handled in your Mule application. Though it provides basic error management by propagating errors up the chain, it doesn't offer detailed logging or corrective actions. For more robust error handling, you should implement specific error-handling strategies using Mule's error handling scopes and components, which is our next topic.

Error Handling Scopes

When working with Mule, there are two *error handling scopes* you can use to manage errors, and each behaves in distinct ways. Understanding these scopes is crucial for effective error handling.

The On Error Propagate scope is one of the two error handling scopes available in Mule. When an error occurs within this scope, a Mule error object is passed along. This can be useful when you need to propagate the error to downstream components or services for further handling.

In contrast, the On Error Continue scope passes a normal Mule message when an error occurs. This allows you to handle errors in a specific way without propagating them further, which can be beneficial when you want to log errors or perform alternative processing without interrupting the flow.

SRL might use On Error Continue when Google Maps fails, logging the issue but continuing with the best-effort local quote. But if customer data is missing, On Error Propagate ensures the client is informed and no invalid quote goes out.

The error handling scopes are located in the Mule Palette, as shown in Figure 5-5. Depending on your error-handling strategy, you will add them to your Mule project in various locations. We will discuss those strategies later in this chapter.

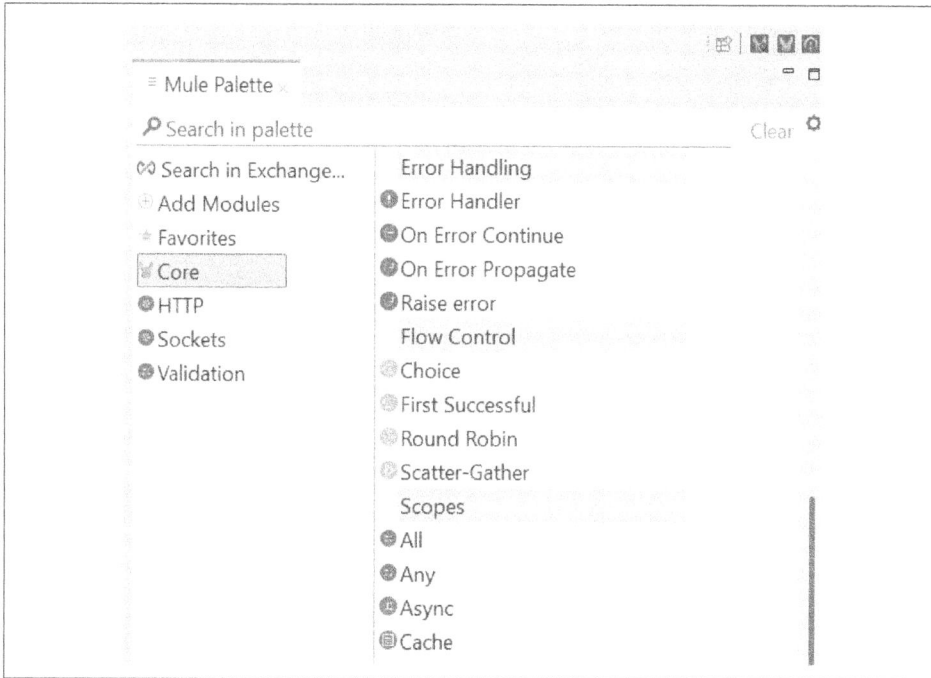

Figure 5-5. Error-handling processors in Mule Palette

After adding the error handling scope, you will configure it under the Settings tab. Here, you can specify the error types that the scope will catch, as shown in Figure 5-6. Alternatively, you can set a When condition using a Boolean expression to define more specific criteria for when the scope should handle an error.

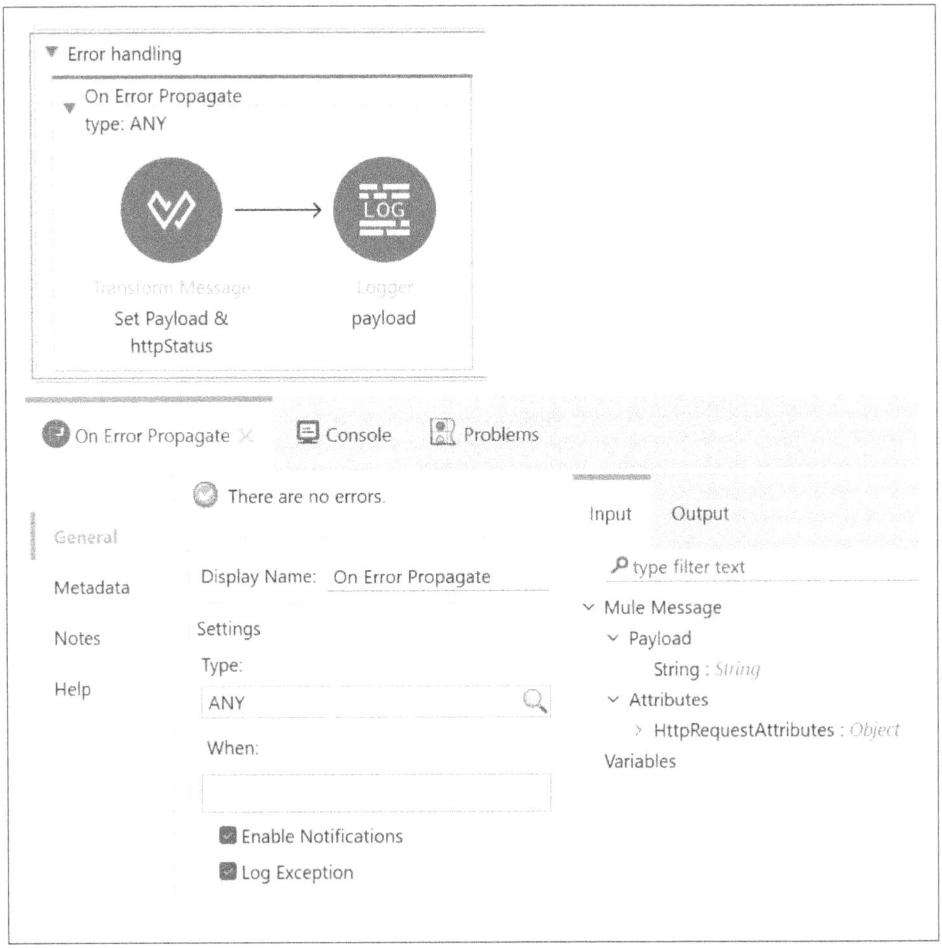

Figure 5-6. Error handling scope configuration options

Raise Error Processor

The Raise Error processor in MuleSoft is used to explicitly generate an error within a Mule flow. This can be useful in various scenarios where you need to trigger error-handling logic deliberately, based on specific conditions or validations. You configure the Raise Error component by specifying the error type and an optional error message, as shown in Figure 5-7. The error type should be part of the error hierarchy you have defined for your application.

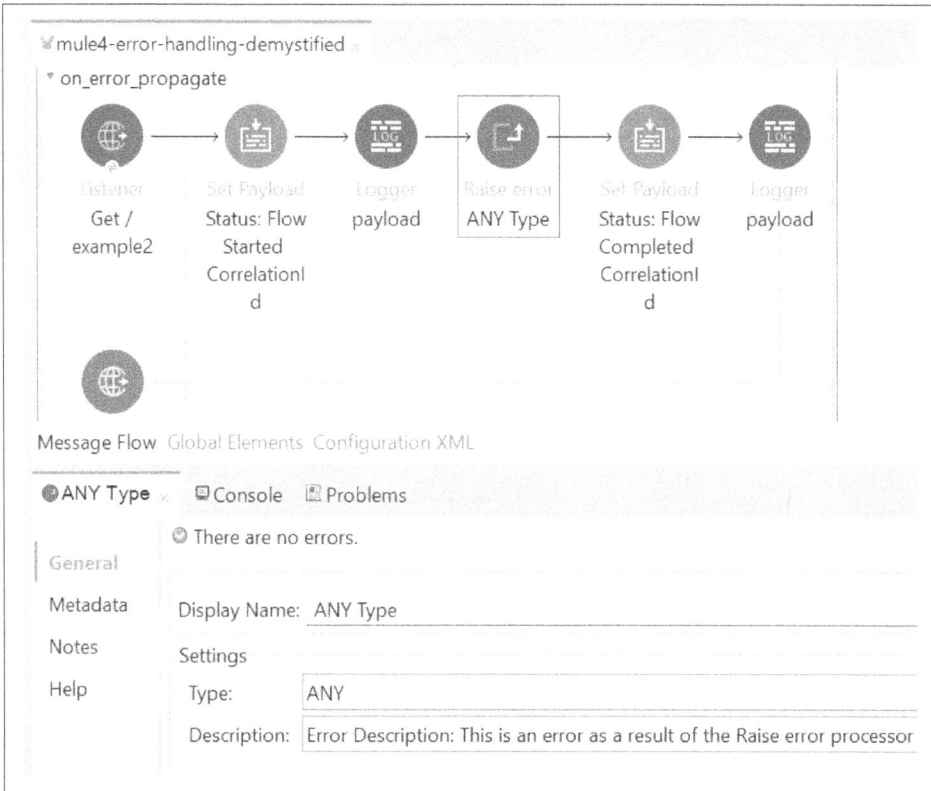

Figure 5-7. Raise Error configuration

On Error Propagate

When you add the On Error Propagate scope to a flow and an error is thrown, the processors inside this scope are executed, as shown in Figure 5-8.

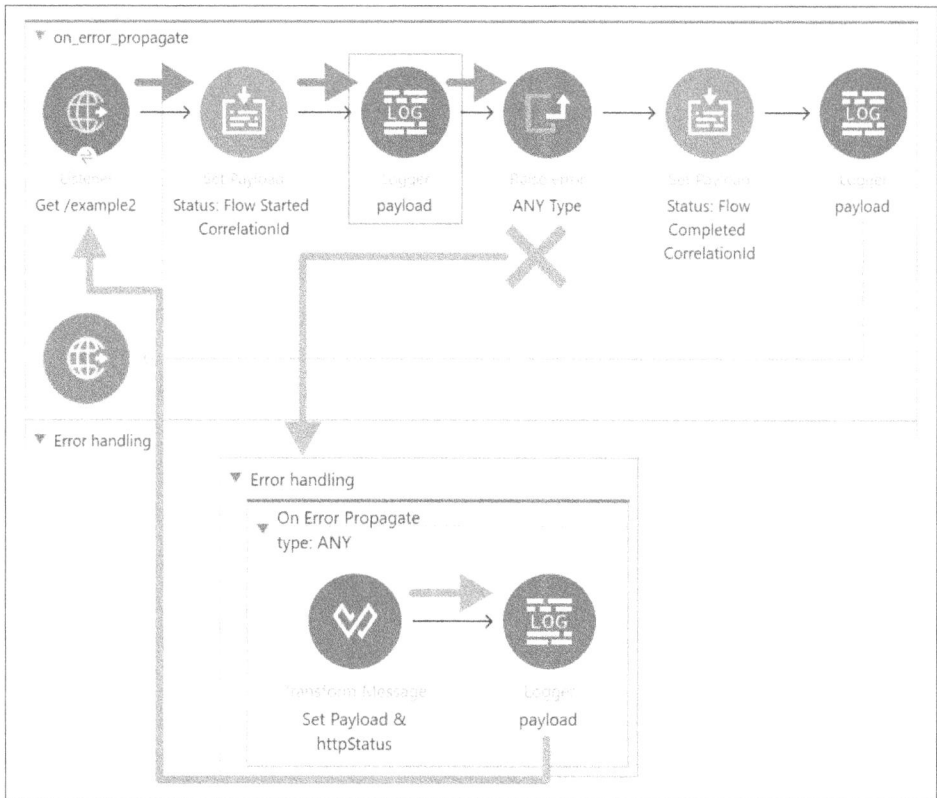

Figure 5-8. Mule flow with On Error Propagate scope

If you run the example in debug mode, you will see these processors being invoked. For instance, the Set Payload processor might set the payload to "Status: Error Occurred!," and a Logger would display this payload value in the console.

Since the scope is set to On Error Propagate, the Mule error object is passed to the HTTP error response. In this case, we did not set the httpStatus variable value, so it will use the default value of 500, sending the client a 500 Server Error. The response body will be the payload message "Status: Error Occurred!" Notice that the remaining two processors in this flow are not executed.

This approach is useful when you need to provide detailed error messages via the Set Payload to clients or downstream services, helping them understand what went wrong.

On Error Continue

When you add the *On Error Continue* scope to a flow and an error is thrown, the processors inside this scope are executed, as shown in Figure 5-9.

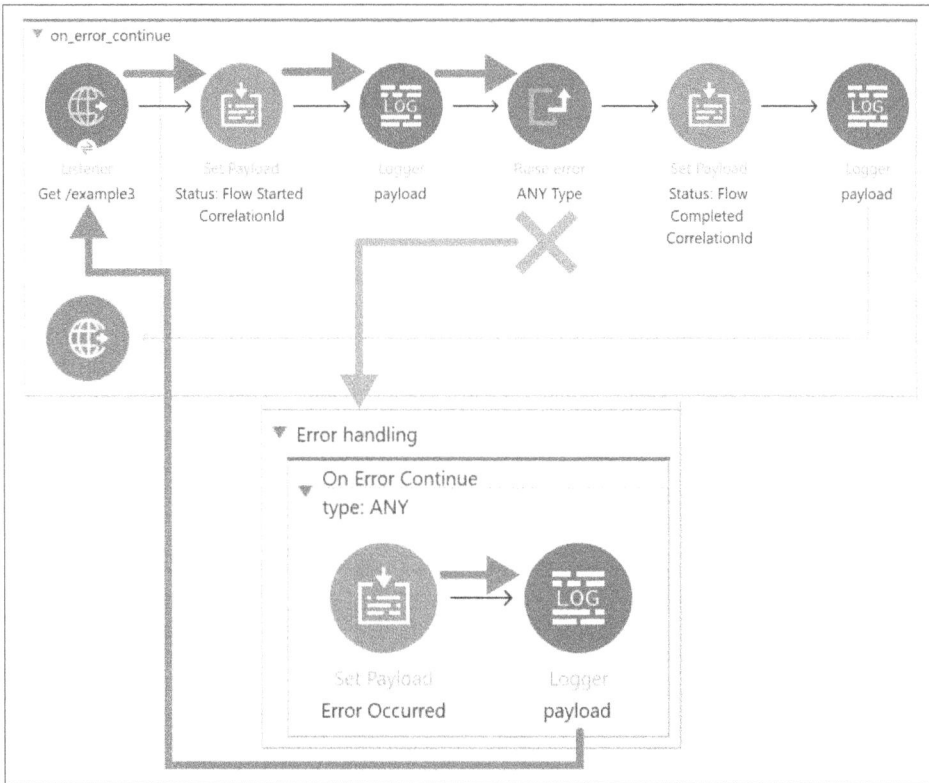

Figure 5-9. Mule flow with On Error Continue scope

In this case, the scope is set to On Error Continue, and a normal Mule message is passed to the HTTP response. As a result, the client receives a 200 HTTP Success status code, and the response body will be the payload message "Status: Error Occurred!" Notice that the remaining two processors in this flow are not executed.

Overriding HTTP Status Codes

Overriding an HTTP status code in a MuleSoft application provides clearer and more meaningful responses to clients, ensuring accurate communication about the outcome of their requests. Custom error handling allows you to convey specific error details beyond the default codes, making it easier for clients to understand and respond to issues. Ensuring adherence to RESTful API conventions, you can maintain compliance with API standards. This practice also enhances user experience by improving the clarity of feedback for users. Additionally, custom status codes simplify debugging and monitoring by making it easier to identify and address issues. Finally, controlling response behavior through specific status codes can influence client actions, such as retrying after rate limiting.

Imagine you have an API that tracks and manages shipments. If a user tries to track a package that's already delivered, instead of returning a default 500 Internal Server Error, you override it with a 409 Conflict status code. The custom message reads: "409 Conflict: This package has already been delivered. No need to track it again, it's safely at its destination!" This way, the issue is clearly communicated, and users get a friendly, engaging response that enhances their experience.

Set Variable processor

So, how do you override the status code? In the error handling scope, you can use the *Set Variable processor,* as shown in Figure 5-10. You name the variable and set the appropriate status code.

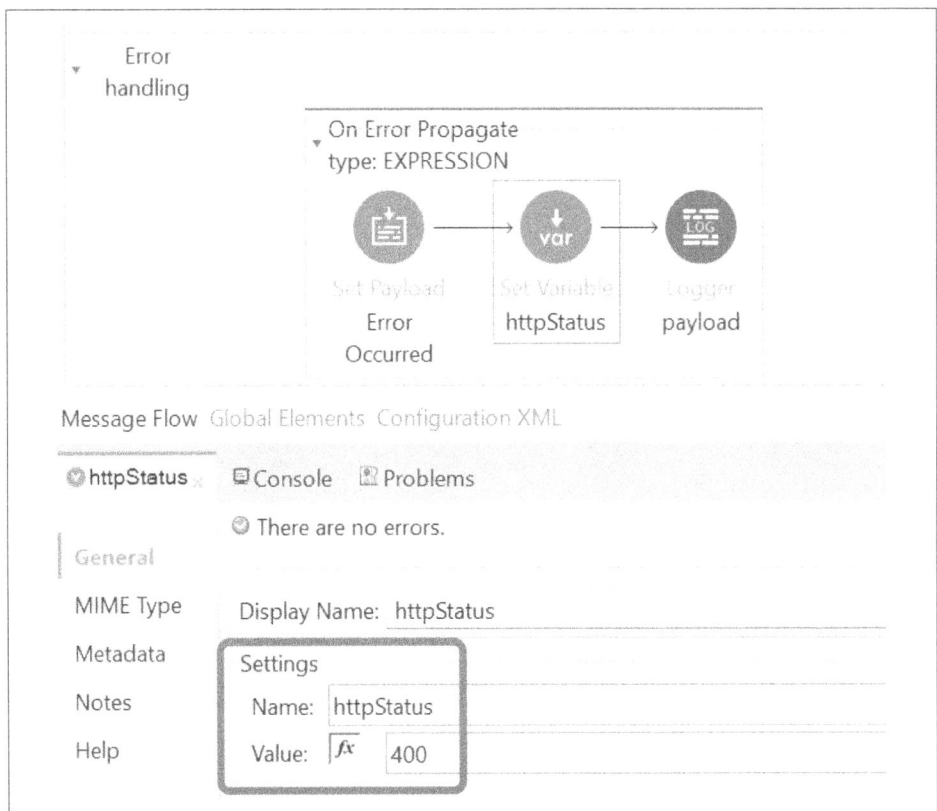

Figure 5-10. Use Set Variable to override the default HTTP status code

Transform Message processor

You can also use the *Transform Message processor* to set both the payload and the variable, as shown in Figure 5-11. First, set the value of the payload.

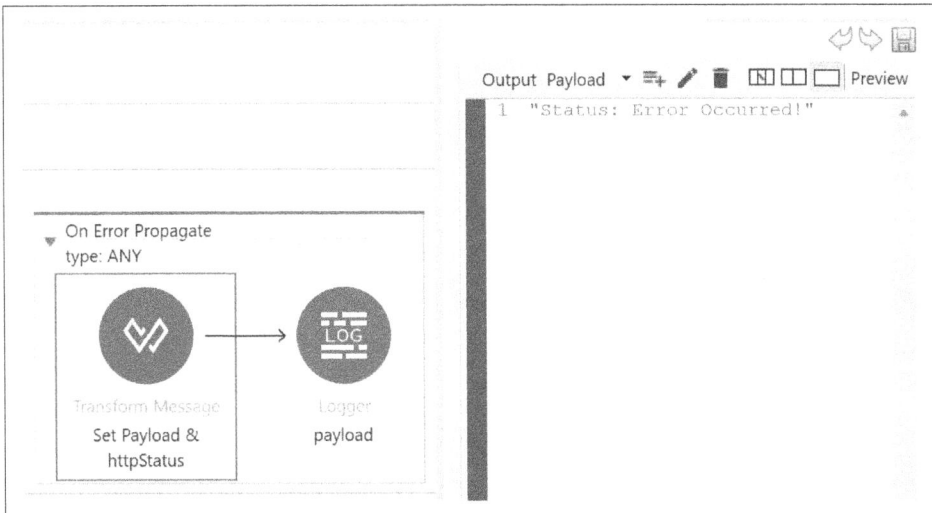

Figure 5-11. Transform Message: set output payload value

Next, you will click the add "+" icon, choose to add an Output variable, and name it "httpStatus," as shown in Figure 5-12.

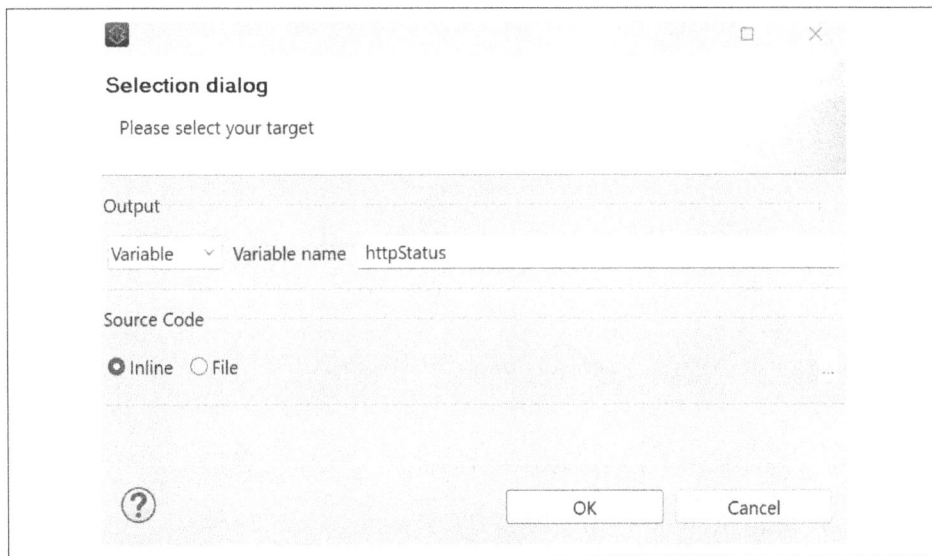

Figure 5-12. Transform Message: add a variable

Finally, as shown in Figure 5-13, set the variable's value to the desired HTTP status code.

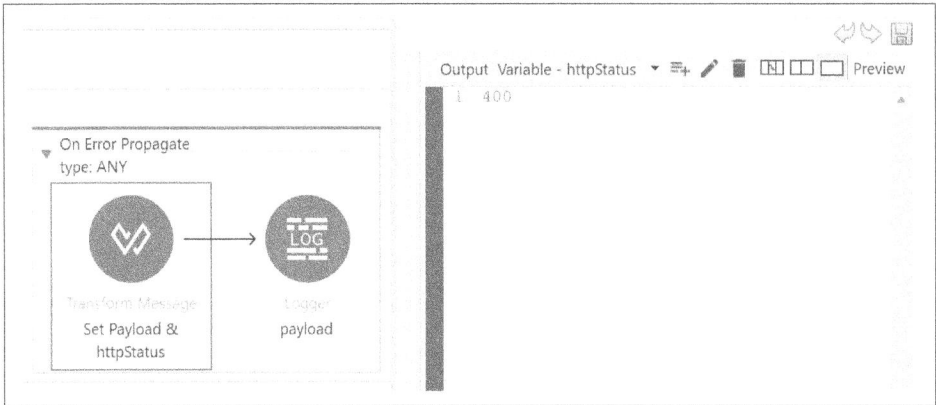

Figure 5-13. Transform Message: set value of `httpStatus` variable

Test the outcome, and you should see that your modified payload and `httpStatus` are reflected in the client application response, as shown in Figure 5-14.

Figure 5-14. Client response with modified HTTP status code and payload

Flow-Level Error Handling

Flow-level error handling works best for applications that require precise control over error management within specific parts of a flow. It is ideal when you need to address issues locally without impacting the entire application, provide context-specific error messages, simplify debugging, and maintain a smooth user experience. By offering granular control over error handling, such as retrying operations or logging errors, this strategy ensures your application remains robust and user-friendly even when encountering errors in specific flows.

The example flows observed in Figures 5-9 and 5-10 show how to use the error-handling section of a flow to add the On Error Continue and On Error Propagate scopes.

Application Level: Global Error Handler

You use a *global error handler* to ensure consistent and comprehensive error management across your entire application. This centralized approach simplifies maintenance by providing a single point for updating error-handling logic and ensures uniform handling of unhandled errors. It acts as a safety net, preventing unexpected application crashes and providing a consistent user experience with informative error messages. By establishing a baseline level of error handling, you can ensure that errors are managed efficiently even if specific flows do not have error handling. In addition, this prevents the Mule default error handler from being invoked.

Let's create a global error handler. The global error handler is often called an *application error handler* because it handles errors for the entire application. An application may consist of a single configuration file (XML) or multiple, as shown in Figure 5-15.

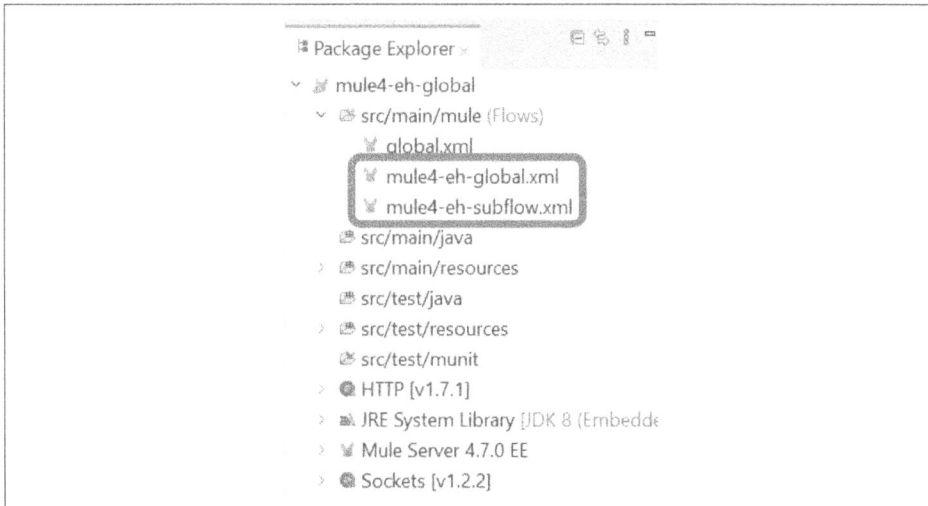

Figure 5-15. Multiple XML files and global.xml

Creating a global configuration file

You begin by creating a global configuration file (see Figure 5-16):

1. In the file structure of your Mule application, right-click the *src/main/mule* folder.

2. Select New > Mule Configuration File.

3. Name the file *global.xml*.

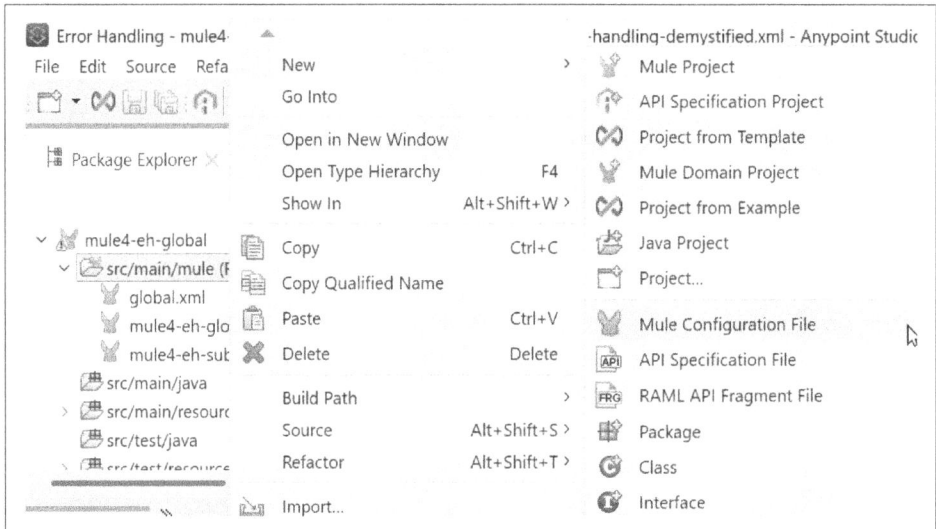

Figure 5-16. Create the global.xml *configuration file*

Adding the error handler scope to global.xml

Now you are ready to add the error handler to *global.xml* from the Mule Palette, as shown previously in Figure 5-5. Once it is placed in the Message Flow canvas, configure the name of the globalError_Handler, as shown in Figure 5-17.

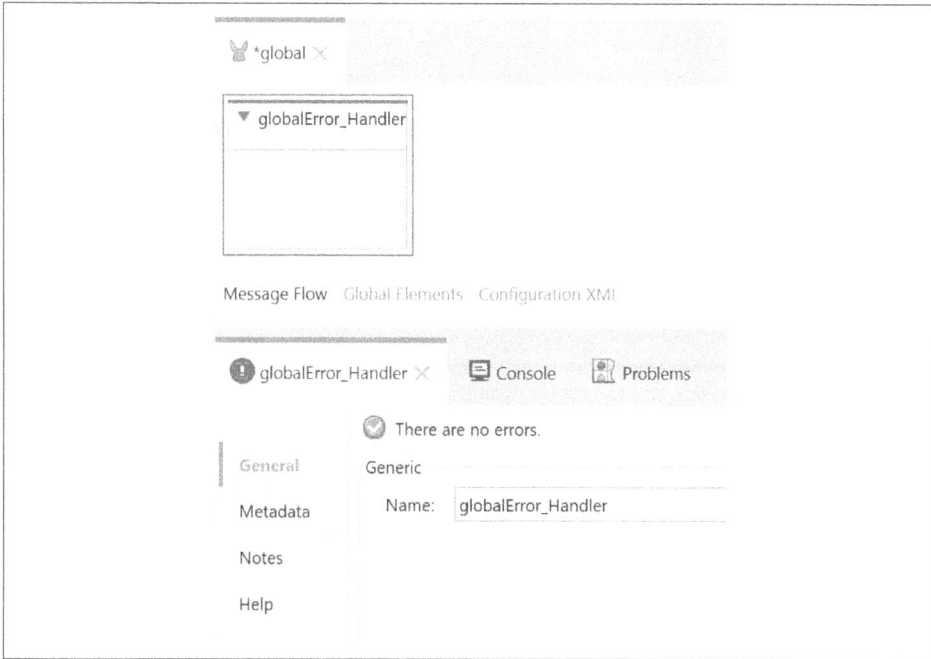

Figure 5-17. Global error handler added to global.xml

Creating a global element for the global error handler

Follow these steps:

1. Navigate to the Global Elements tab of the *global.xml* file.

2. Click Create and select Configuration in the *Global Configurations* folder, as shown in Figure 5-18.

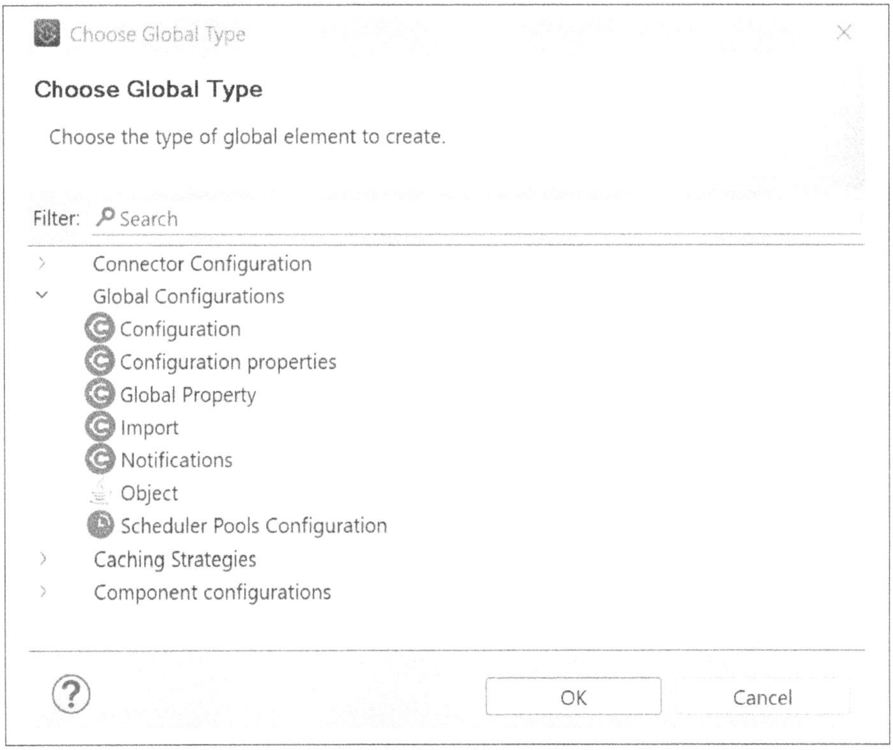

Figure 5-18. Choose Configuration in the Global Configurations *folder*

3. In Settings, under Default Error Handler, select the `globalError_Handler` and click OK, as shown in Figure 5-19.

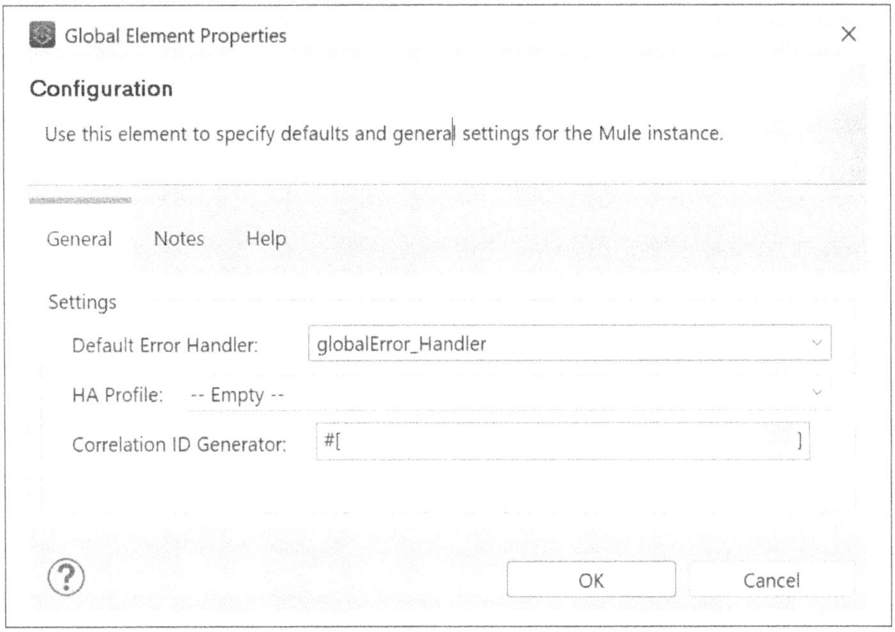

Figure 5-19. Set the default error handler

You are now ready to add either On Error Continue and/or On Error Propagate scopes to your global error handler. For an example, we will look at a flow that does not have an error handler but uses the global error handler with an On Error Propagate configured to catch *any* type of error, as shown in Figure 5-20.

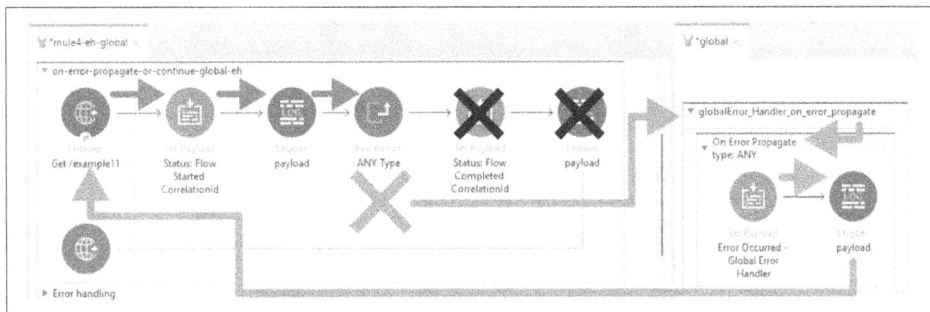

Figure 5-20. Behavior of the global error handler

If you change this scope to On Error Continue, the behavior will remain the same; however, it will return a 200 Success with the custom message in the payload.

To manage different errors effectively, you can stack error scopes in a specific order. By arranging error scopes hierarchically, you prioritize error handling logic, ensuring that specific error types are caught and processed first, followed by more general error handlers. This structured approach allows for granular error management, as shown in Figure 5-21.

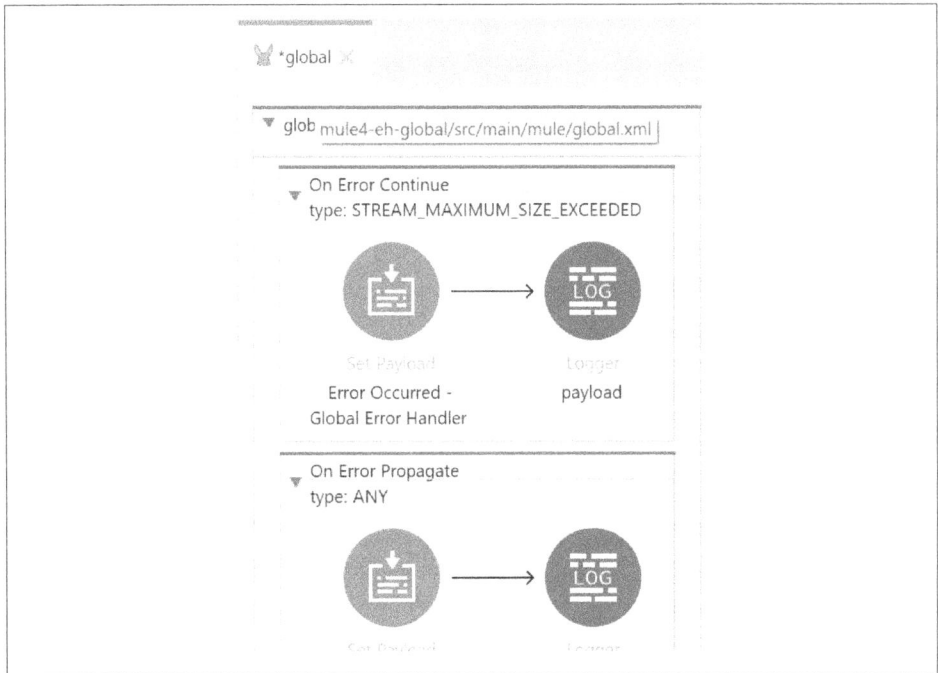

Figure 5-21. Multiple error scopes executed in top-down order

Process Level: Try Scope

You use a processor-level error handler like the Try scope in MuleSoft to gain granular control over error management in specific parts of your flow. The Try scope allows you to isolate error handling for critical sections, apply retry logic, and define custom error responses and fallback mechanisms. This level of control ensures that errors are managed independently without affecting other parts of the flow, providing meaningful feedback and corrective actions. Additionally, using the Try scope simplifies debugging by containing errors within a defined area, making it easier to identify and troubleshoot issues in specific sections of your flow.

Navigate to the Mule Palette and drag the Try scope onto your flow where you want to implement granular error handling (see Figure 5-22).

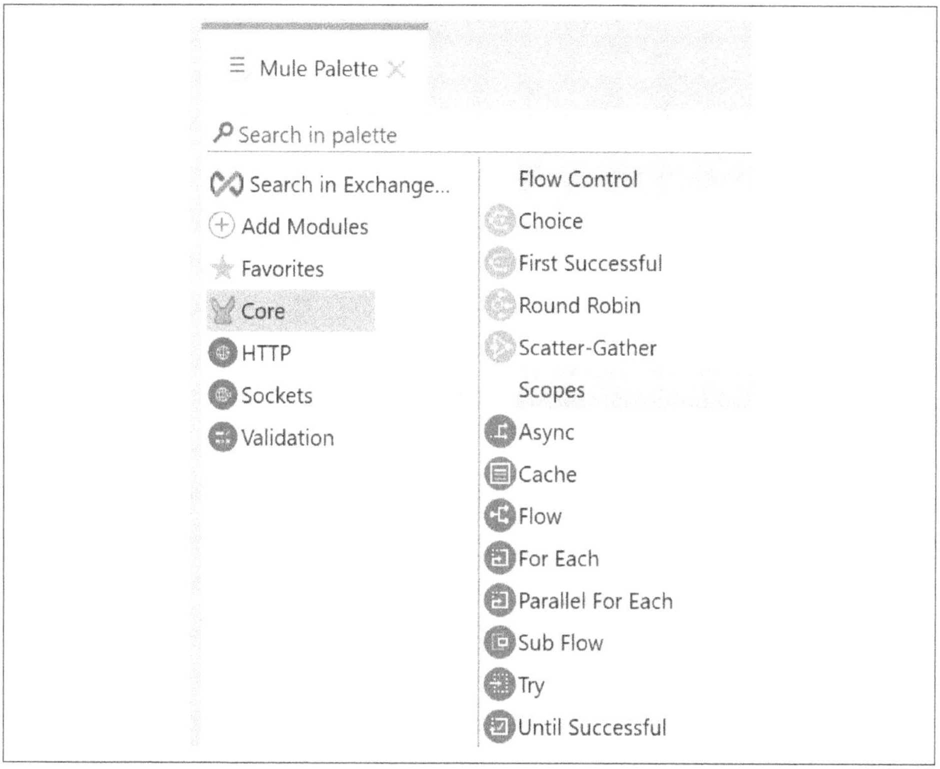

Figure 5-22. Select Try under the Scopes header in the Mule Palette

Place the processors or components that you want to monitor for errors inside the Try scope, as shown in Figure 5-23. These can be any operations that might potentially throw an error.

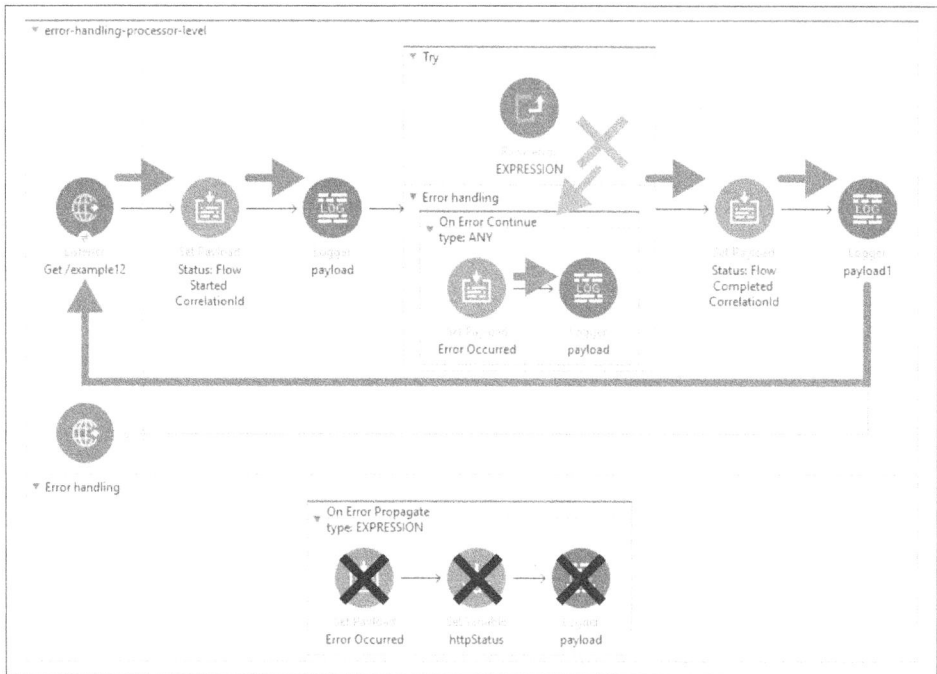

Figure 5-23. Try scope with On Error Continue scope

Next, configure error handling within the Try scope:

- Use the On Error Propagate scope in the Try scope's error handling section. Inside this scope, configure the processors to execute when an error occurs, such as setting an error payload or logging the error. This ensures the error propagates up the flow chain with detailed information.

- Use the On Error Continue scope if you want the flow to continue execution despite the error. Configure the processors within this scope to handle the error, such as sending a notification or performing a compensating action.

If you want to implement retry logic, configure the Try scope to retry certain operations upon failure. This can be set within the properties of the processors inside the Try scope.

Customize Error Types with Error Mapping

To customize error types with *Error Mapping* in MuleSoft, you'll define custom error categories tailored to your application's specific needs, such as `ValidationError` or `AuthorizationError`. By mapping these error types to specific responses or actions, you streamline error handling, making your integration applications more robust and reliable.

If your application throws the same error type in different flows or processors, customizing the error type to pinpoint the exact cause is crucial. The Error Mapping feature, available on specific processors, allows you to do this effectively. It involves configuring error handlers in Anypoint Studio and defining how each error type should be managed.

For example, if you're using the Is True validator in the Validation module, you can customize the error-handling process by selecting the Error Mapping tab, as shown in Figure 5-24.

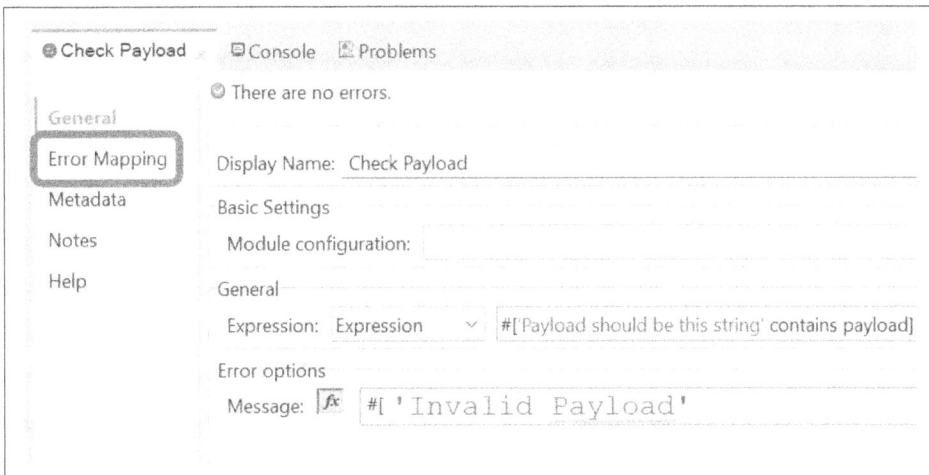

Figure 5-24. Error Mapping tab

Next, you can map the INVALID_BOOLEAN error type to a custom error type like PAYLOAD_INVALID. This way, when the error occurs, you can identify it specifically as a PAYLOAD_INVALID error instead of the more generalized INVALID_BOOLEAN error type, as shown in Figures 5-25 and 5-26.

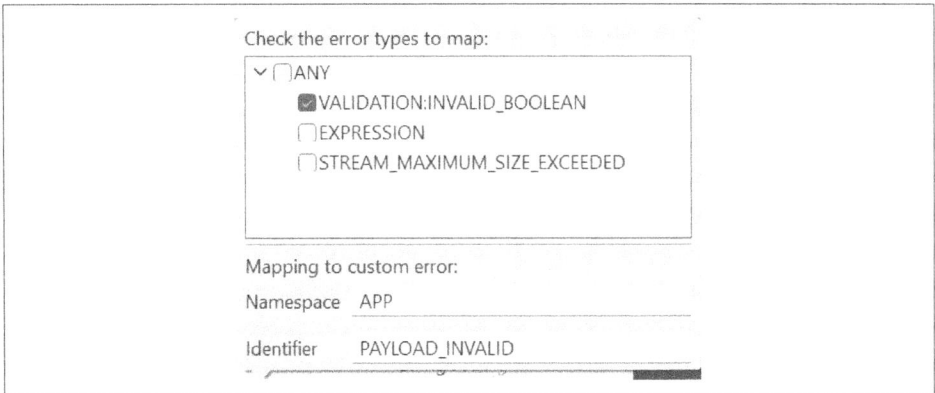

Figure 5-25. Configure the custom error type

Figure 5-26. Error types mapped to custom error type

In this flow, when the Check Payload error occurs, the custom error APP:PAYLOAD_INVALID is shown as the error type. We can catch that error with the ANY error type in the scope, as shown in Figure 5-27.

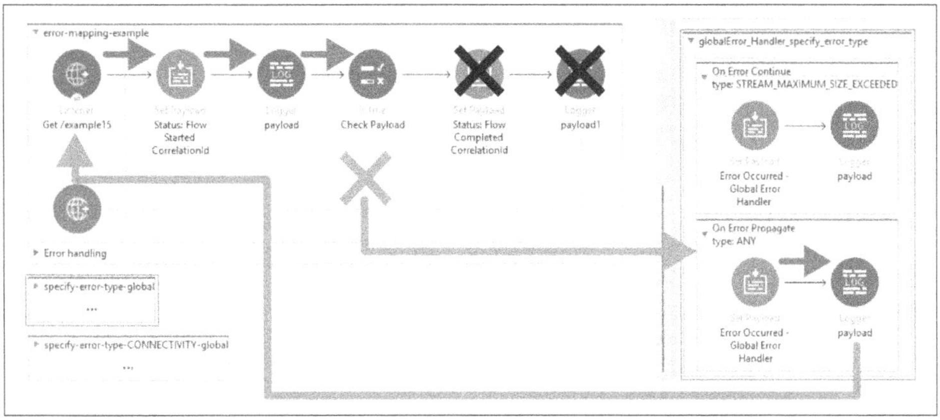

Figure 5-27. Example of custom error type

When this error occurs, you will see the actual mapping details in the logs, as illustrated in Figure 5-28. This logging provides you with valuable insight into the specific error mappings, allowing you to diagnose and resolve issues efficiently. By examining the log details, you can understand precisely why an error occurred and how it was categorized, helping you fine-tune your error-handling strategy and improve overall application reliability. This level of detail ensures that you can quickly identify and address any issues.

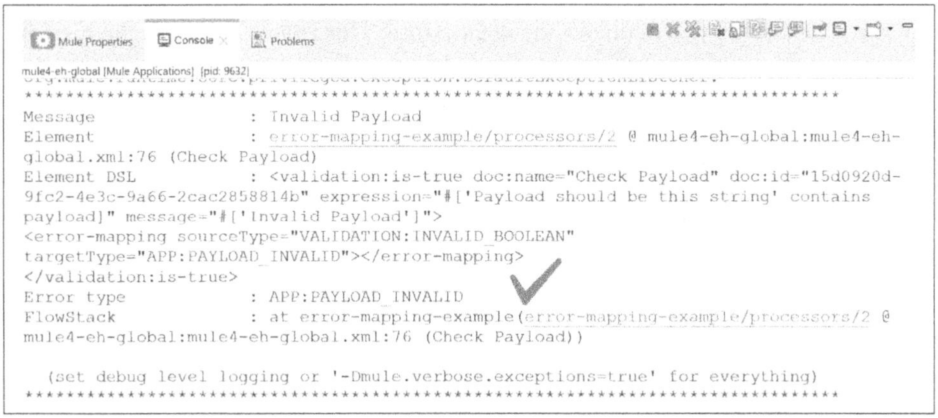

Figure 5-28. Logs reflecting the custom error mapping

Practical Error-Handling Use Cases

Now that we have a comprehensive understanding of error-handling concepts, default settings, and error scopes in MuleSoft, we will look at some practical error-handling use cases. These use cases will demonstrate how to apply the principles we've discussed to real-world scenarios, ensuring that your applications can effectively manage and respond to various error conditions. By exploring these examples, you'll gain valuable insights into designing robust error-handling strategies tailored to your specific integration needs, enhancing the reliability and user experience of your solutions.

Routers: Control the Flow

Routers are components that enable you to control the flow of messages within your application. By using routers, you can determine how and where messages should be directed based on specific conditions and business logic. Routers help you implement advanced routing strategies to ensure that each message reaches its correct destination, whether it's a different system, service, or application component. Let's look at the routers we have in MuleSoft.

Choice Router

The Choice router allows you to route messages to different paths based on conditions or expressions you define in the WHEN clause. This router evaluates the message content or other criteria at runtime and dynamically determines the appropriate route for each message. By configuring various conditions, you can create a flexible decision-making process that directs messages to specific flows or components tailored to handle those particular conditions. If none of the conditions are met, the default route is executed.

For example, you might use the Choice router to retrieve specific data, depending on the category that is sent in a request. If no category is defined, the default route is executed. SRL can use the Choice router to send the request to a different pricing model based on whether the request is from a Server Message Block (SMB) customer, a recurring client, or a new business. In this example, the default route is referencing the Scatter-Gather router, as shown in Figure 5-29.

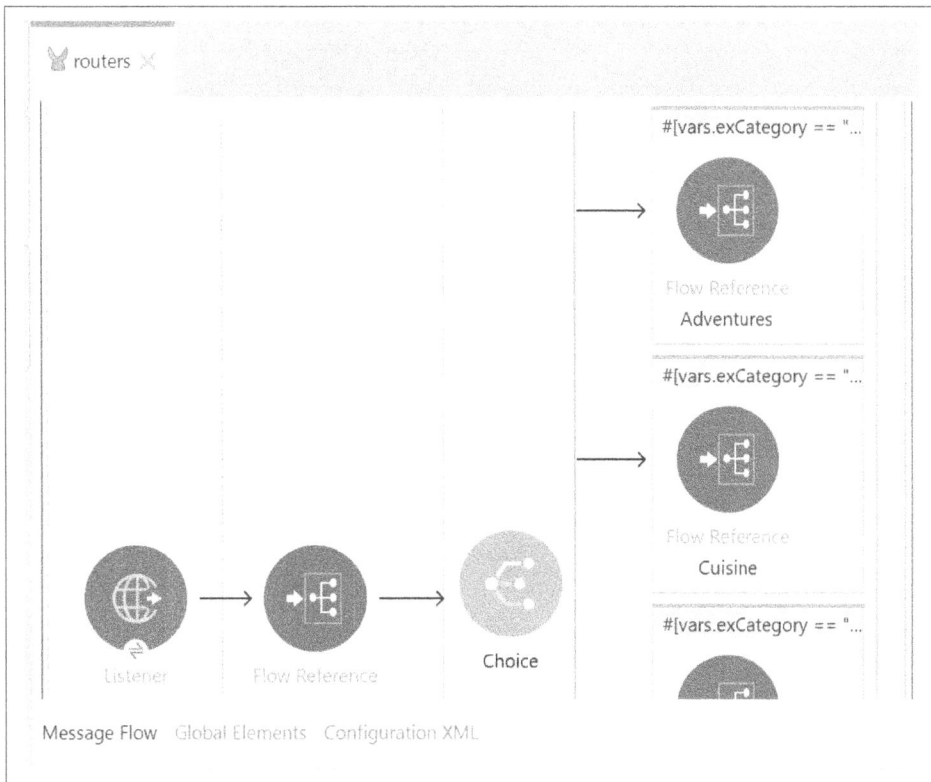

Figure 5-29. Choice router example

Scatter-Gather Router

When you use the Scatter-Gather router, you "scatter" the incoming message to various routes defined in the router configuration. Each route processes the message independently and in parallel. Once all the routes have processed the message, their responses are "gathered" back into a single aggregated response. You can then use this aggregated response for further processing or send it back to the requester.

The Scatter-Gather router offers several key benefits. It allows for parallel processing, significantly improving the efficiency and speed of your application by performing multiple tasks simultaneously. It also provides aggregated results, enabling you to collect and combine responses from different systems or services into a unified response, making it easier to manage and utilize the data. The router offers flexibility, as it can handle various types of processing tasks, from calling different APIs to performing different types of data transformations simultaneously. Additionally, it provides fault tolerance; if one route fails, the router can still gather and process responses from the other routes, allowing for partial success scenarios.

In our example, we are using the Scatter-Gather router to retrieve all excursion categories by referencing each child flow, as shown in Figure 5-30. You send the order information to three different services simultaneously: Adventures, Guided Tours, and Cuisine. Each service processes the request in parallel, and their responses are gathered and aggregated into a single response. This aggregated response provides the necessary details for a single payload of all excursions, ensuring that you get a comprehensive overview of all available excursion categories in one go. By using the Scatter-Gather router in this way, you streamline the process and enhance the efficiency and responsiveness of your application.

This is perfect for when SRL wants to parallel-call Google Maps, the Load System, and Driver Manager to enrich the quote. In SRL's integration, a Scatter-Gather router allows simultaneous API calls to external services—reducing the overall response time for quote delivery.

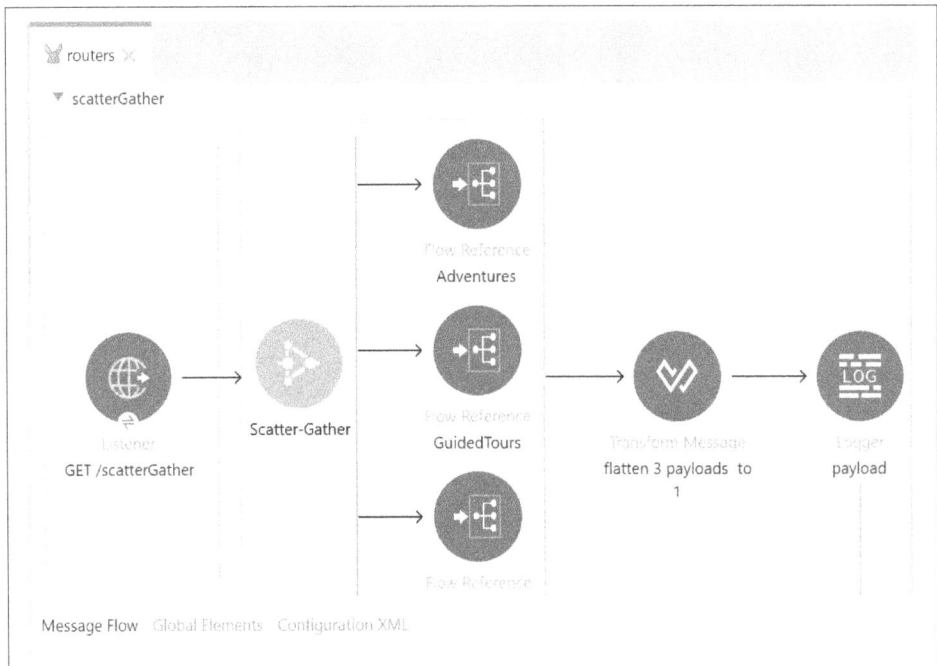

Figure 5-30. Scatter-Gather router example

Round Robin Router

When you use the Round Robin router, it cycles through the list of defined targets in a sequential manner. Each incoming message is sent to the next target in the sequence, effectively balancing the load across all targets. For instance, if you have three targets and four incoming messages, the first message goes to the first target, the second message to the second target, and the third message to the third target. The fourth message will then go back to the first target, and the cycle continues.

This router is beneficial when you need to distribute processing tasks evenly, such as in scenarios where you want to distribute requests evenly as they come in, as shown in Figure 5-31. SRL could use Round Robin to distribute quote requests across multiple instances based on geography, ensuring no single service is overwhelmed and all services share the workload equally, resulting in more efficient processing and a better overall user experience.

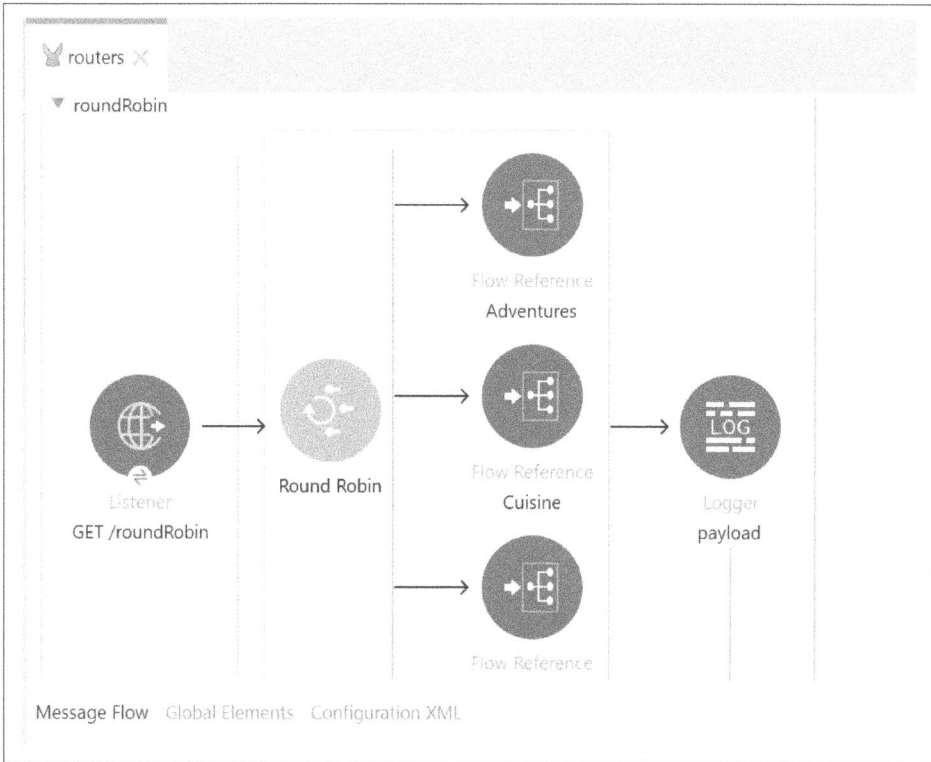

Figure 5-31. Round Robin router example

First Successful Router

When you use the First Successful router, you define a series of targets, and the router attempts to process the message with each target in the order they are listed. If the first target fails to process the message, the router moves on to the next target, and so on, until one target succeeds. Once a target successfully processes the message, the router stops and returns the successful result, ignoring the remaining targets, as shown in Figure 5-32.

This router is particularly beneficial in scenarios where you have redundancy built into your system. If SRL's primary route optimizer fails (due to an outage), the First Successful router can try a backup model—ensuring the quote engine remains functional. This approach increases the reliability and robustness of your application by ensuring that there is always a backup option available to handle the request.

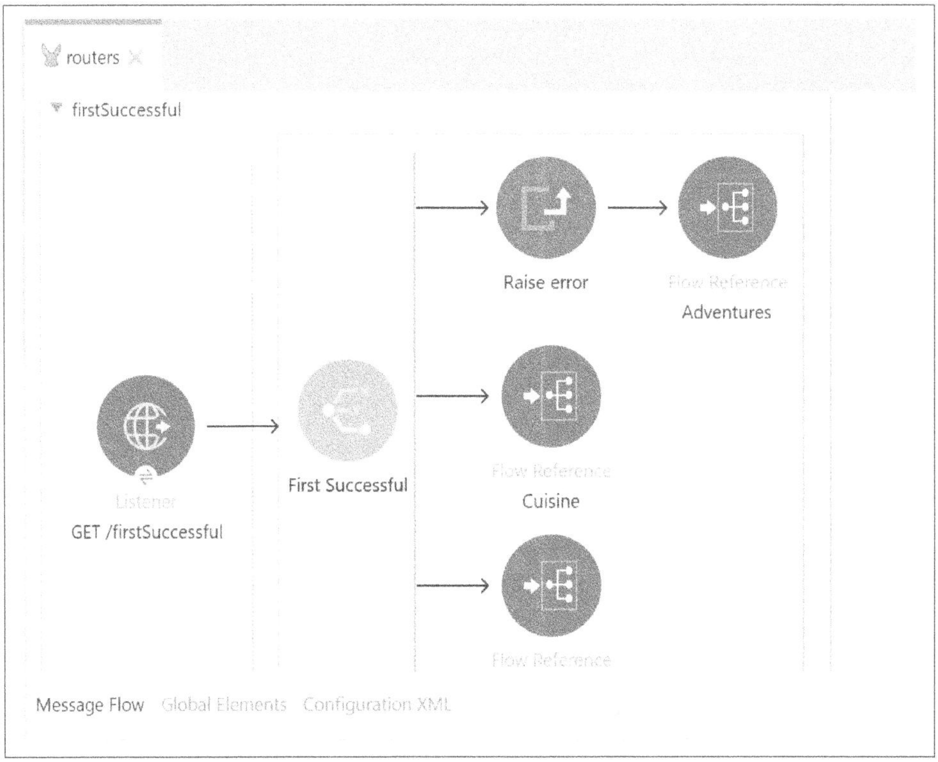

Figure 5-32. First Successful router example

Processing Records

Processing records in MuleSoft is like managing a busy shipping warehouse. You've got a long list of packages (data records), and you need to ensure each one reaches its destination. MuleSoft offers some fantastic tools—For Each, Parallel For Each, and batch processing—to ensure everything runs smoothly.

Imagine For Each as handling each package individually, ensuring it's correctly labeled and shipped. Parallel For Each is like having multiple workers, each processing a group of packages simultaneously, speeding up the workflow. Batch processing is your team sorting and preparing large batches of packages efficiently, ensuring every shipment is perfect.

By mastering these tools, you can manage your shipping operations smoothly, no matter how many packages you have or how complex their requirements are. Let's dive into how you can use MuleSoft's data processing tools to be the perfect manager for your shipping operations!

For Each

The *For Each* component helps you loop through a list of items, handling each one separately. You specify the collection you want to process, and it runs your specified logic for each item. Inside the For Each, you can add whatever operations you need, like transforming data or making API calls.

To use the For Each component, select it from the Mule Palette and place it into your flow where you need to process the collection. Then, inside the For Each scope, add the Mule components and logic you want to apply to each item. This could include transformations, data enrichment, or sending data to another system. After the For Each component finishes processing all items, the flow will continue beyond it without modifying the original values of the payload.

At SRL, customers often submit shipping requests with multiple packages—each with unique delivery priorities, weights, and destinations. To handle this, SRL uses the For Each component to loop through every package in the request. Within each iteration, the system validates the package data, calculates delivery options, and generates a quote. This ensures each package is treated independently while still following a structured, consistent process—similar to labeling and routing each item in a shipping warehouse.

Parallel For Each

The *Parallel For Each* component helps you handle a list of items by processing them concurrently. You specify the collection you want to work with, and it runs your specified logic for each item simultaneously. Inside the Parallel For Each, you can add various operations, like transforming data or making API calls.

To use the Parallel For Each component, select it from the Mule Palette and place it into your flow where you need to process the collection. Inside the Parallel For Each scope, add the Mule components and logic you want to apply to each item. This can include transformations, data enrichment, or sending data to another system. After the Parallel For Each component finishes processing all items, the flow will continue beyond it; however it does modify the original values of the payload.

Speed is critical for SRL, especially when dealing with time-sensitive quote generation. To optimize performance, SRL uses Parallel For Each to process multiple packages in a single request simultaneously. This enables real-time API calls to services like traffic data, driver availability, and load management for each package, all in parallel. By doing so, SRL shortens quote response time and enhances the customer experience—much like having multiple agents working at once to prepare deliveries faster.

Batch Processing

Imagine you're dealing with a massive dataset that needs to be processed quickly. Instead of handling each data item one by one, you divide the dataset into smaller chunks and process these chunks simultaneously. Each chunk is handled by different processing units at the same time, speeding up the overall process. Once all chunks are processed, you combine the results to ensure everything is complete and accurate.

This is exactly how a MuleSoft *Batch Job* works. It splits a large dataset into smaller pieces, processes each piece in parallel to optimize efficiency, and then aggregates the results for a final review. This method ensures that your data is processed quickly and accurately, making it ideal for handling large datasets efficiently.

To use a Batch Job in MuleSoft, you start by adding the Batch Job component to your flow. Define the source of your data in the Input phase, like a database query or file read. Inside the Batch Job, add Batch Steps to specify the processing logic for each chunk of data. Configure the size of each chunk and set the concurrency level to optimize performance. Include error handling within each Batch Step to manage issues for individual records without disrupting the entire process.

Within a Batch Step, you can use the Batch Aggregator to collect and process the results from the various Batch Steps. After the Batch Steps process each chunk of data, the Batch Aggregator gathers all these processed chunks back into a single dataset to be processed.

Once you have aggregated the results, you can apply additional processing or transformations as needed. This is useful for tasks that require the entire dataset, like summarizing data, generating reports, or further analysis. You can then perform final actions on this aggregated data, such as storing it in a database, sending it to another system, or creating an output file. The Batch Aggregator ensures these actions are executed only once, after all records have been processed.

Inside the Batch Aggregator, you can define custom logic to handle the aggregated data, including further transformations, validations, or integrations with other systems. It also includes error handling to manage any issues that might arise during the aggregation process.

Finally, use the On Complete phase to perform any necessary actions after all chunks have been processed. After all the records have gone through the Batch Steps and any aggregation, the On Complete phase kicks in. This phase is used to perform any final actions that need to be taken once the Batch Job is fully processed. This could include tasks such as logging the completion status, sending notifications, updating a database with the final status, or triggering downstream processes.

In this phase, you have access to Batch Job summary statistics, such as the number of records processed successfully, the number of failed records, and other relevant metrics. This information can be used to make decisions or perform actions based on the Batch Job's outcome.

For large-scale operations, such as recalculating pricing models across thousands of deliveries, SRL leverages Batch Jobs. Their system breaks massive datasets into smaller chunks and processes them concurrently through Batch Steps. For example, a nightly Batch Job might update route estimates using new fuel prices and delivery data. Once processed, the Batch Aggregator combines the results and feeds them into the cost-analysis engine. This approach ensures SRL can make timely, data-driven pricing updates without slowing down operations.

Anypoint Code Builder

Everything we've built in Anypoint Studio—flows, logic, transformations, and error-handling strategies—is executed the same way in Anypoint Code Builder (ACB). The Mule runtime doesn't change. What changes is how we interact with it. ACB offers a modern, code-centric interface where you configure components using a mix of lightweight visual panels and inline XML editing. While the processors and their behaviors are the same as in Studio, the layout and workflow feel more streamlined and transparent. Let's look at how error handling works in ACB, starting with how we define and manage On Error Propagate, On Error Continue, and custom error responses in this new environment.

Configuring error handler scopes like On Error Propagate and On Error Continue are defined directly in the flow using visual forms as shown in Figure 5-33, that instantly reflect in the XML. You can still set error types, add expressions, and customize payloads—just with more transparency.

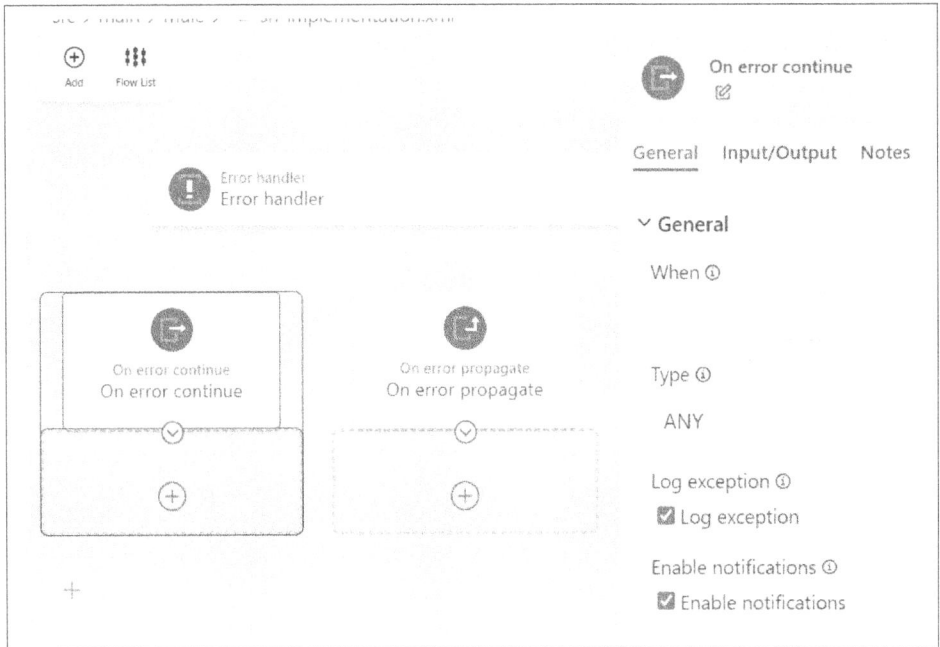

Figure 5-33. Error handler scopes

The Raise Error processor also gets a boost with a simplified panel for defining custom error types and messages, shown in Figure 5-34.

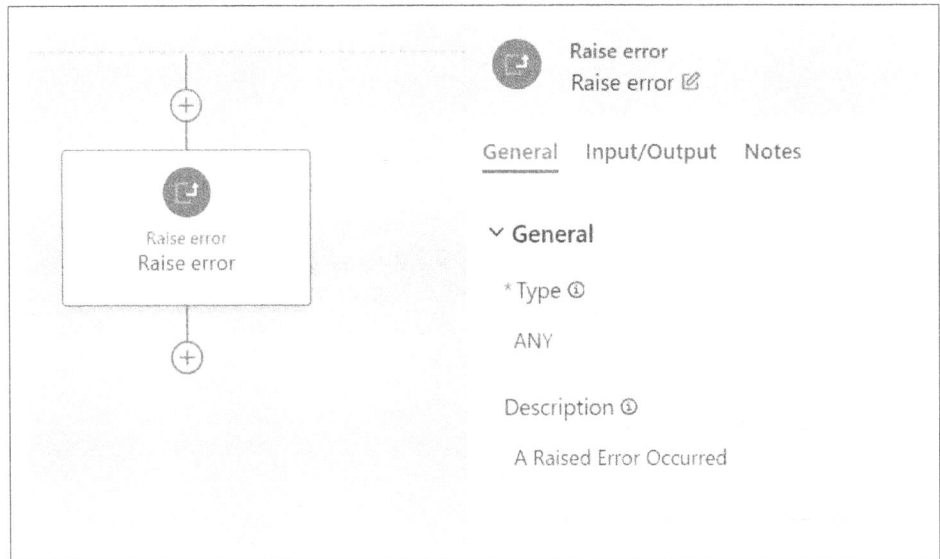

Figure 5-34. Raised Error

And when you're customizing HTTP responses, you'll use a combination of Set Variable and Transform Message inside your error scope—same logic, just a more modular layout as in Figure 5-35.

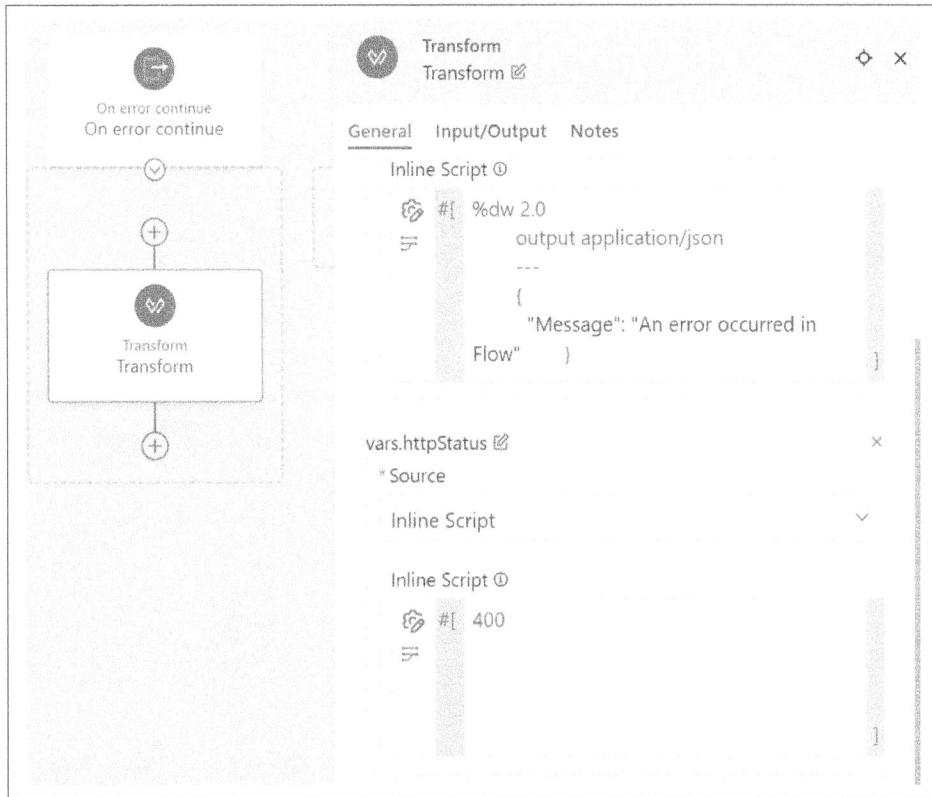

Figure 5-35. Transport Message Set Payload and Variable

Once your flows are built to handle errors gracefully, the next step is guiding messages down the right path—and that's where routers come in. In Anypoint Studio, routers like Choice, Scatter-Gather, and First Successful are configured visually on the canvas. In ACB, the logic is the same, but the structure is more declarative. You define routes directly in XML or with a lightweight configuration panel, and each routing condition is clearly mapped in your flow. Let's start with the Choice router, which evaluates conditions at runtime to determine where to send the message next.

Let's look at the Choice router in Figure 5-36 for an example in ACB.

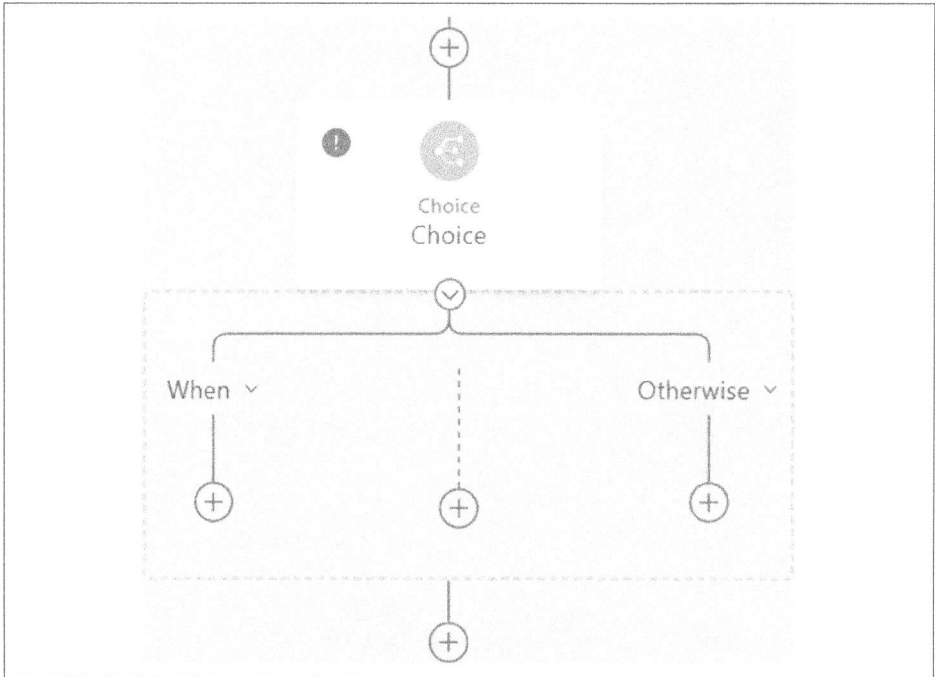

Figure 5-36. ACB Choice router

Notice that the configurations for the Choice router are designed differently. As we configure the routing options, we click on the When clause. A new window opens for us to provide the expression for this particular route, as we see in Figure 5-37.

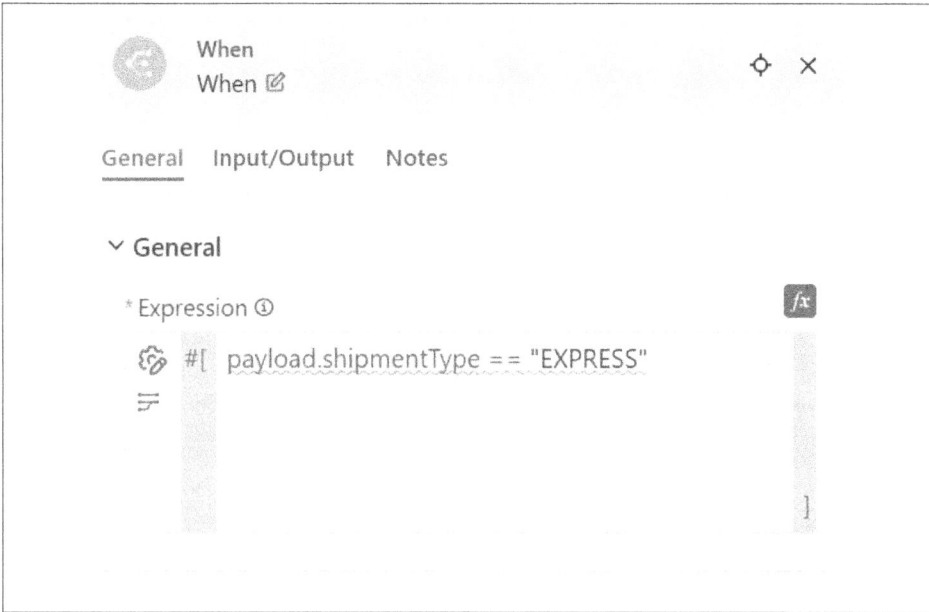

Figure 5-37. When expression configuration

Once multiple routes are defined with processors aligned in each route, the Choice router is configured with the UI that renders as in Figure 5-38.

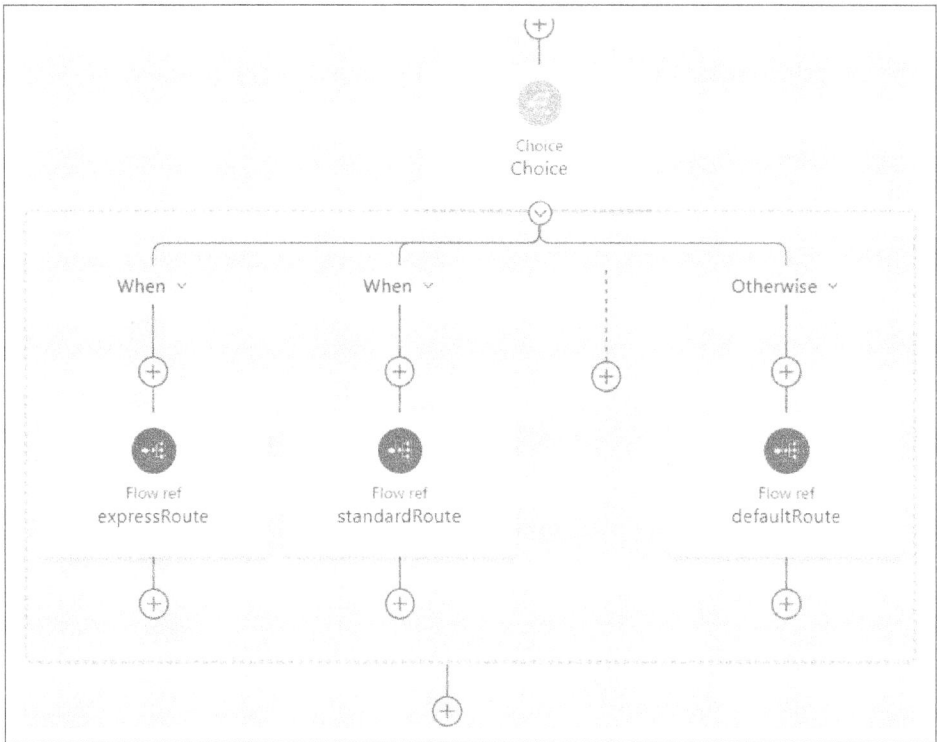

Figure 5-38. Choice router configuration

Routers like Scatter-Gather, Round Robin, and First Successful work just as reliably in ACB as they do in Studio, with the key difference being how they're configured. Instead of dragging routes onto a canvas, ACB uses a more structured, code-first approach—routes are declared inline in XML, and form-based panels guide the setup when needed. This shift offers greater clarity, especially when managing parallel calls, load distribution, or fallback logic. Let's look at the visuals for Scatter-Gather first in Figure 5-39.

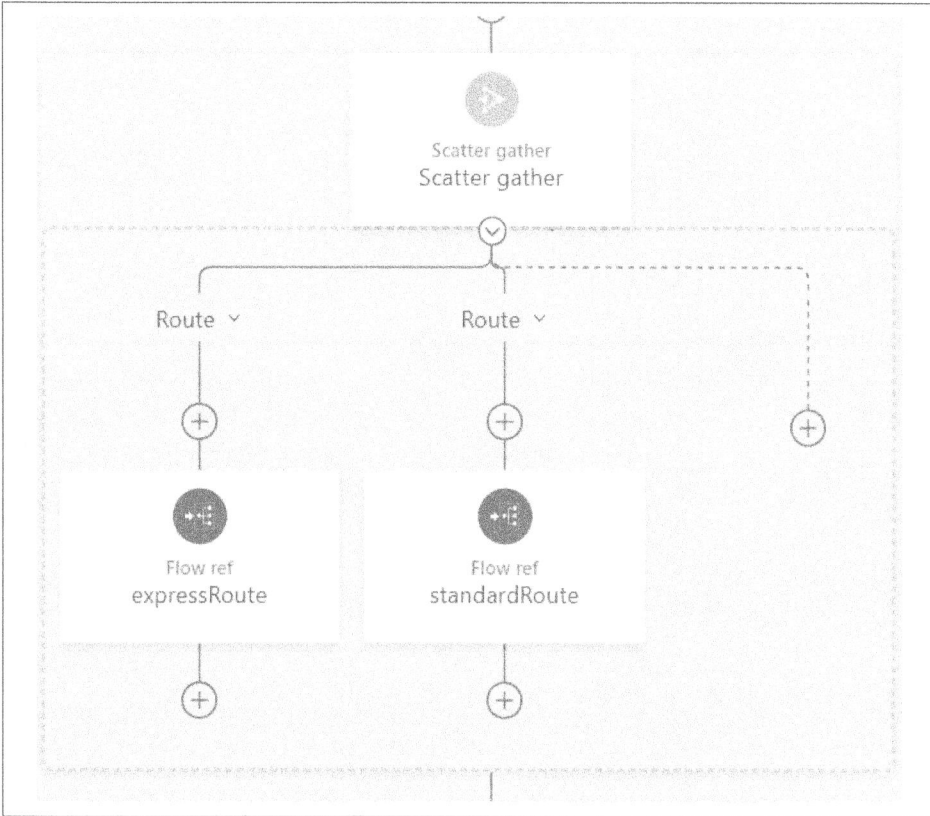

Figure 5-39. Scatter Gather configuration

Next, we will look at Round Robin in Figure 5-40.

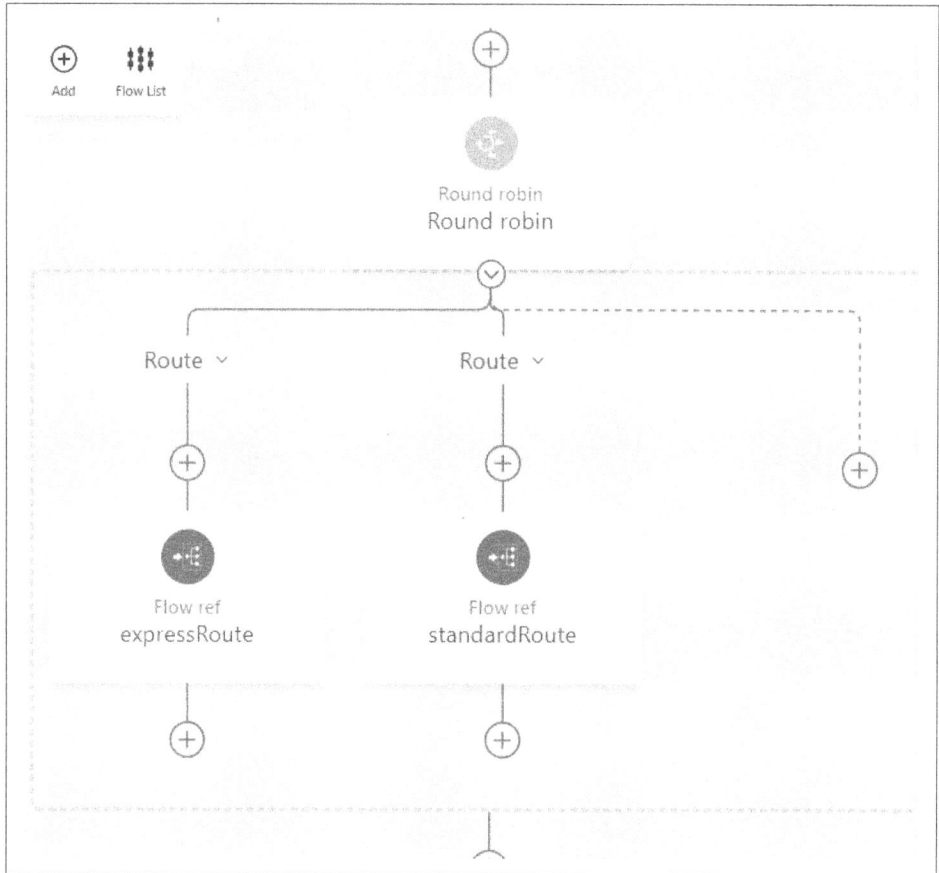

Figure 5-40. Round Robin configuration

And finally, the last router is First Successful shown in Figure 5-41.

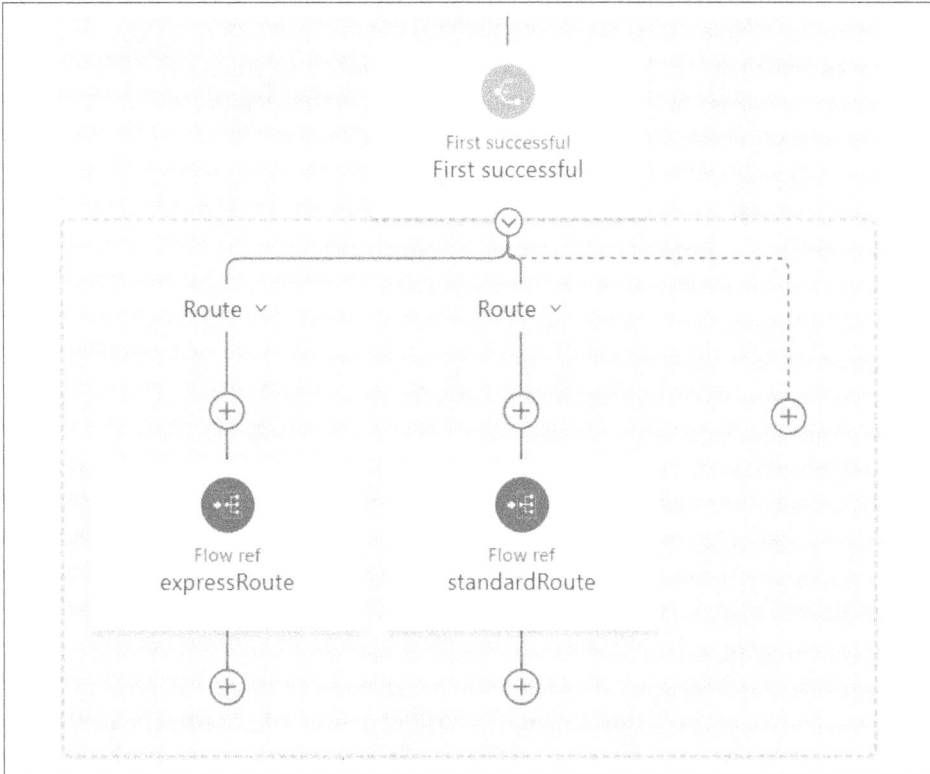

Figure 5-41. First Successful configuration

Summary

This chapter delved into the essential aspects of message orchestration, a vital concept in integration environments. You've learned how to coordinate and manage messages between different systems, services, or components, ensuring they are properly routed, transformed, and delivered based on predefined business logic and rules. This process is crucial for maintaining seamless communication and data flow within complex systems.

Building on the knowledge from Chapter 4, which covered data flow essentials, you now know how to import, transform, store, and process data to extract insights and deliver it to users or systems. You also learned about the importance of logging for error diagnosis and future improvements.

In this chapter, you mastered error handling to ensure reliable message processing, learned to resolve errors confidently, and explored advanced routing techniques like Scatter-Gather, Choice, First Successful, and Round Robin. You also covered transaction management to complete operations consistently and efficiently. Additionally, you learned about using For Each, Parallel For Each, and batch processing to handle large message volumes effectively.

You have now transformed your understanding of message orchestration, making your integration solutions more robust and effective. This knowledge prepares you for more advanced topics in upcoming chapters, enhancing your ability to design, develop, and manage complex integration scenarios efficiently.

By applying these orchestration techniques, you now have the tools to build integration solutions that are robust, scalable, and responsive. As we saw with SRL, real-world integration challenges—like generating real-time delivery quotes or handling multipackage requests—require more than just moving data. They demand intelligent routing, resilient error handling, and efficient message processing. Whether it's looping through packages with For Each, accelerating throughput with Parallel For Each, or managing high-volume recalculations with Batch Jobs, orchestration ensures that systems like SRL's can scale smartly, respond in real time, and keep customers informed every step of the way.

In Chapter 6, we'll embark on an exciting journey into events and storage. We'll explore Anypoint MQ, virtual machine (VM) queues, third-party queues, Object Store, Cache scope, and Redis. These tools will empower you to manage messaging and data storage like a pro, designing resilient, efficient systems ready for any project. By mastering these components, you'll build robust and scalable integration architectures that are fully prepared for the challenges of advanced integration projects. Let's dive into Chapter 6 and continue our adventure.

AsyncAPI

An API-led strategy isn't a one-size-fits-all solution. Different organizations have unique needs, goals, and technical environments, so it's important to tailor the plan to fit those specific circumstances. Each organization must evaluate its unique context to develop an effective API-led strategy.

Suppose event-driven architecture (EDA) is part of your strategy. In that case, allowing different components to react to events in real time can further enhance the responsiveness and scalability of your system. This can be particularly beneficial for applications that require real-time data processing and updates, such as live chat apps, online gaming, or Internet of Things (IoT) systems.

An asynchronous API (async API) is a way for different software programs to talk to each other without having to wait for a response right away. Imagine you're texting a friend. With a regular (synchronous) API, it's as if you send a text and you can't do anything else until your friend replies. But with an async API, you send a text, and while waiting for a reply, you can do other things like play a game or chat with another friend. In this chapter, we will look at async APIs and learn how to design and implement one in ACB.

Event-Driven Architecture

So far in this book, we have focused on REST APIs, where a request is made and a response is awaited. However, there are instances where an immediate response is optional. In such cases, only a confirmation that the request was sent is required, similar to a "fire-and-forget" notification from a sensor indicating a low battery. Along with the notification (event), additional details such as the level of emptiness and the expected duration of device operation can be sent. This additional information is referred to as the event *payload*. EDA uses events to trigger communication between services, commonly found in modern microservices-based applications.

Let's use a broker-centric EDA to understand the core concepts. Figure 6-1 shows the core pieces needed for an event-driven setup to work.

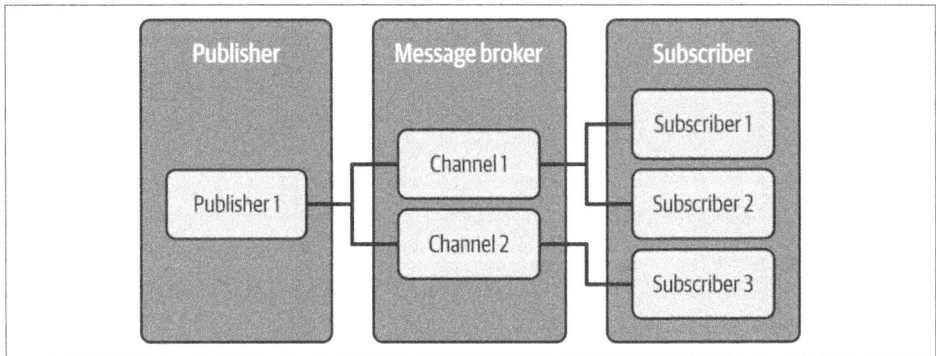

Figure 6-1. Publisher/subscriber mechanism

A *message broker* is a system that receives messages and sends them to interested people or programs. The broker stores messages until they can be delivered, making EDAs reliable even in case of a failure. Examples of message brokers include Anypoint MQ, RabbitMQ, Apache Kafka, and Solace. A *publisher*, also known as a *producer*, is a program that sends messages to the broker, whereas a *subscriber*, also known as a *consumer*, is a program that connects to the broker, specifies the types of messages it wants to receive, and waits to receive those messages.

> Most EDAs are broker-centric, but there are several alternatives. One option is a broker-less architecture, where services communicate directly without a message broker. This reduces complexity but sacrifices reliability and fault tolerance. Point-to-point (P2P) communication allows one-to-one messaging between services, which is suitable for smaller systems but not scalable. Event streaming, such as in Apache Kafka, provides a scalable approach by storing events in a distributed log, although it still relies on a broker-like system. In decentralized architectures, services act as both publishers and subscribers, dynamically discovering each other using tools like Google Remote Procedure Call (gRPC) or service meshes. The actor model, as seen in systems like Akka, enables distributed communication between *actors*, which manage their own state and message passing. Serverless event-driven systems, such as AWS Lambda, handle event processing without needing a dedicated broker, though they offer limited control over infrastructure. Some architectures use a hybrid approach, combining broker-based and direct communication for different types of messages, balancing performance and reliability. Each of these alternatives offers trade-offs in terms of complexity, scalability, and fault tolerance depending on the system's needs.

In this context, a *message* is a form of communication, and in the case of REST APIs, a message refers to a *request*. In Chapter 2, we discussed the OpenAPI Specification (OAS), a well-known standard for defining the various components of REST APIs. It enables developers to precisely outline endpoints, parameters, request bodies, and responses in a format that can be understood by both humans and machines.

Likewise, the AsyncAPI Specification is a framework specifically designed for asynchronous APIs, which are based on events or messages rather than direct requests and responses. The AsyncAPI Specification outlines a set of fields and components that can be utilized in an AsyncAPI document, providing a standardized method for describing how applications communicate using events or messages, whether through message brokers, queues, or direct messaging, as shown in Figure 6-2.

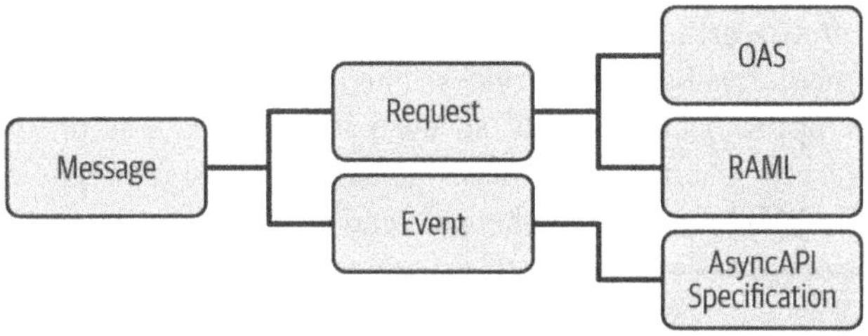

Figure 6-2. Events are messages, but not all messages are events

Now that you are familiar with the OpenAPI spec, let's examine the AsyncAPI from the perspective of the OpenAPI spec.

OpenAPI Versus AsyncAPI

From the perspective of OpenAPI, which is used to describe how traditional request-response systems like REST APIs work, AsyncAPI deals with a different way of communicating called *asynchronous messaging*. Let's break down the differences in simple terms:

Endpoints versus channels

OpenAPI uses endpoints to define where the client can send requests, like specific URLs (for example, */users* or */products*). Each endpoint performs specific actions such as getting, posting, or deleting data.

AsyncAPI uses channels instead of endpoints. A channel represents a topic or event type that messages are sent through. For example, a channel named *user/ signedUp* would be used for messages related to users signing up for a service.

Requests/responses versus events/messages

OpenAPI focuses on requests and responses. A client sends a request (like submitting a form) and the server replies with a response (like showing confirmation).

AsyncAPI talks about events or messages instead of requests and responses. A message is a piece of data sent from one service (the publisher) to another (the subscriber). The subscriber receives and processes the message, but no immediate response is required.

Protocols and brokers

OpenAPI usually works over HTTP/HTTPS, the protocol your browser uses to talk to websites. The client and server communicate directly through URLs.

AsyncAPI often works with message brokers (like Kafka or RabbitMQ), which act as intermediaries between services. The broker stores messages and forwards them to the appropriate services, so even if one service is offline, the message will be delivered when it reconnects. It can also use different communication protocols like MQTT or WebSockets instead of HTTP.

Document structure

An *OpenAPI* document explains the operations (like GET or POST) for each endpoint, the type of data expected in requests and responses, and other details like security and data formats.

An *AsyncAPI* document focuses on defining channels, the structure of the messages, and how they are handled. It also includes details like the type of data being sent, security options, and how different protocols are used.

Interaction style

OpenAPI is based on a client-server model where the client asks for information and waits for the server's reply. This is useful when you need information right away, like loading a web page or submitting an order online.

AsyncAPI works in an event-driven style, where systems communicate by sending messages that might not need an immediate response. For example, a smart home system could send an event when the door is opened, and other devices react without needing a direct request. Figure 6-3 shows the comparison between OpenAPI 3.0 and AsyncAPI 2.6.

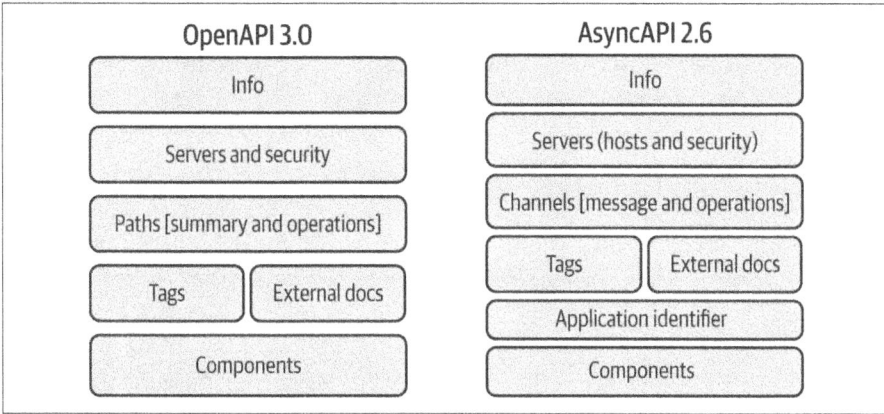

Figure 6-3. OpenAPI versus AsyncAPI

AsyncAPI Object

This element tells you which version of the AsyncAPI Specification is being used. It's like saying which "rule book" the document is following. For example, *asyncapi: 2.6.0* means the document follows version 2.6 of the AsyncAPI rules.

Info

The `info` section gives general information about the API:

`title`
   The name of the API

`version`
   The version number of the API (e.g., 1.0.0); not to be confused with the AsyncAPI I Specification version

`description`
   A short description of what the API does

`contact`
   Information about who to contact if you need help; usually the developer's or support person's email

Servers

The `servers` section lists the servers where the API is available. Servers are the addresses where the messages are sent or received:

url
> The address of the server (for example, *broker.example.com*)

protocol
> The communication method used (for example, MQTT, AMQP, or Kafka)

Channels

The `channels` section is one of the most important parts. It defines the different paths (called channels) through which messages travel. Think of channels as chat rooms where messages are sent and received.

Here are the key components within the `channels` field explained in simpler terms:

address
> A string that shows the address of the channel, like a location where messages can be sent.

messages
> A list of messages that can be sent to this channel by any application at any time.

title
> A clear title for the channel that's easy to understand.

summary
> A brief overview that gives a quick idea of what the channel is about.

description
> A more detailed explanation of the channel, providing extra context about the messages being sent.

servers
> A list of references to the servers where this channel is available. (If there are no servers listed, it means the channel is open on all the servers mentioned earlier.)

parameters
> A collection of parameters included in the channel's address, which can help define specific details.

tags
> A list of tags used to group related channels together logically.

externalDocs
Links to any additional documentation outside of the main API document that explains the channel further.

bindings
A collection where the keys are the names of the communication protocols used, and the values describe the specific details for each protocol related to this channel.

Operations field

The operations field is used to clearly explain the different actions that the application can perform. It provides a structured way to describe whether the application sends or receives messages and what each action is meant to do.

Here are the key components in the operations field:

publish
Defines the operation for sending messages to the channel

subscribe
Defines the operation for receiving messages from the channel

Each operations field has the following attributes:

summary
A brief overview of what the operation does

description
A detailed explanation of the operation, giving more context

operationId
A unique identifier for the operation

tags
A list of tags that help organize and categorize the operations logically

externalDocs
Links to any additional outside documentation that provides more information about the operation

bindings
A collection where the keys are the names of the communication protocols, and the values provide specific details for each protocol related to the operation

traits
> A list of traits that can be applied to the operation, which might modify its behavior or characteristics

messages
> A list of references to the supported message types that this operation can handle

Components

The `components` section is used to store reusable pieces of information. These are like building blocks you can use over and over in different parts of the API document:

schemas
> Defines the structure of the data being sent or received

messages
> Describes the details of messages (like the data format)

securitySchemes
> Lists security methods (like API keys) used to protect the API

Messages

The `messages` section explains the structure of the messages being sent or received. Each message has a payload, which is the actual data being transferred, and sometimes headers, which provide additional information about the message:

name
> The name of the message

payload
> The content or structure of the message data (for example, JSON or XML)

headers
> Additional information about the message (optional)

Bindings

The `bindings` section describes specific settings for each channel or message depending on the protocol being used (such as MQTT, AMQP, or Kafka). Since different communication methods have different rules, bindings allow you to customize these details:

Channel bindings
Special settings for the channel

Message bindings
Special settings for the message

Security

The `security` section explains how the API is protected. It references the security methods listed in the components section (like OAuth or API keys) and specifies which ones are needed to access the API.

Tags

The `tags` section is used to organize and categorize the different parts of the API. It's optional but helps keep things clear and easy to navigate, especially in large documents.

EDA with AsyncAPI

We will use an order-processing scenario to show you how to process orders in real time using Anypoint MQ. Then we will scaffold the API and build out the application logic. We will then run the application and validate the results.

Let's begin by designing an AsyncAPI.

Example of Event-Driven Orders API

In our use case, instead of systems constantly asking, *Has a new order been placed?* or *Has the order been shipped?* the system sends a message (event) when an order is created or updated. For instance:

New Order Event
When a customer places an order, an event is sent to other systems like the warehouse or payment service, notifying them to process the order.

Order Shipped Event
When the order is shipped, the shipping system sends a message to the Orders API, which then updates the customer and other systems (like the inventory manager).

AsyncAPI Design

Let's use the Anypoint Design Center to create an AsyncAPI and then publish it to Anypoint Exchange for consumption. We start by choosing the New AsyncAPI option under Create, as shown in Figure 6-4.

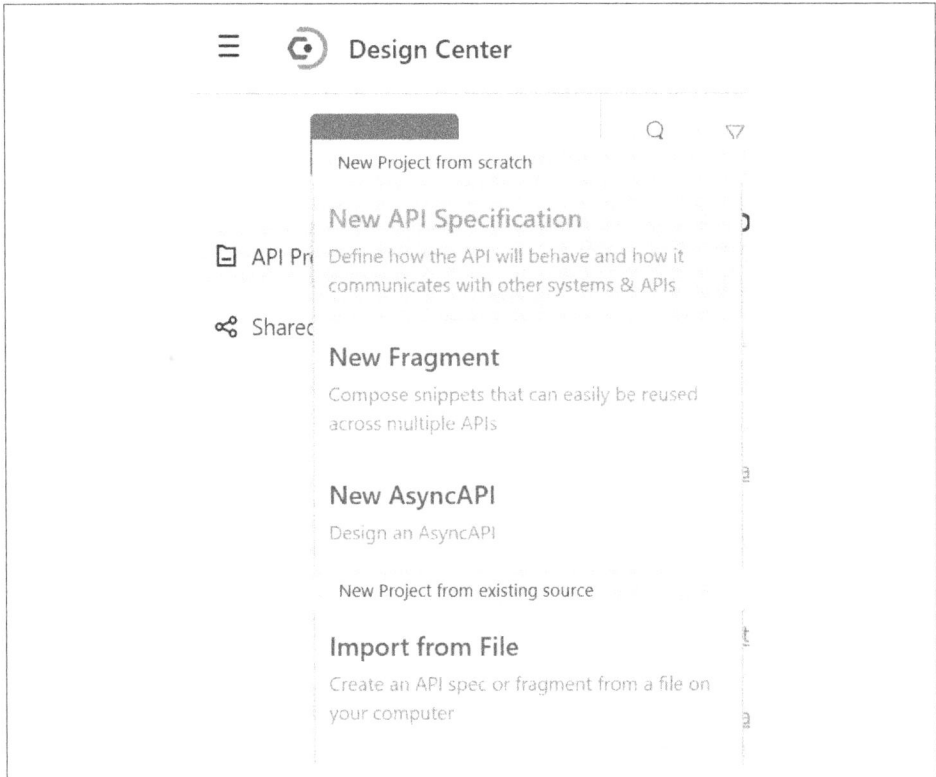

Figure 6-4. Create AsyncAPI

This opens the "New API specification" pop-up, as shown in Figure 6-5.

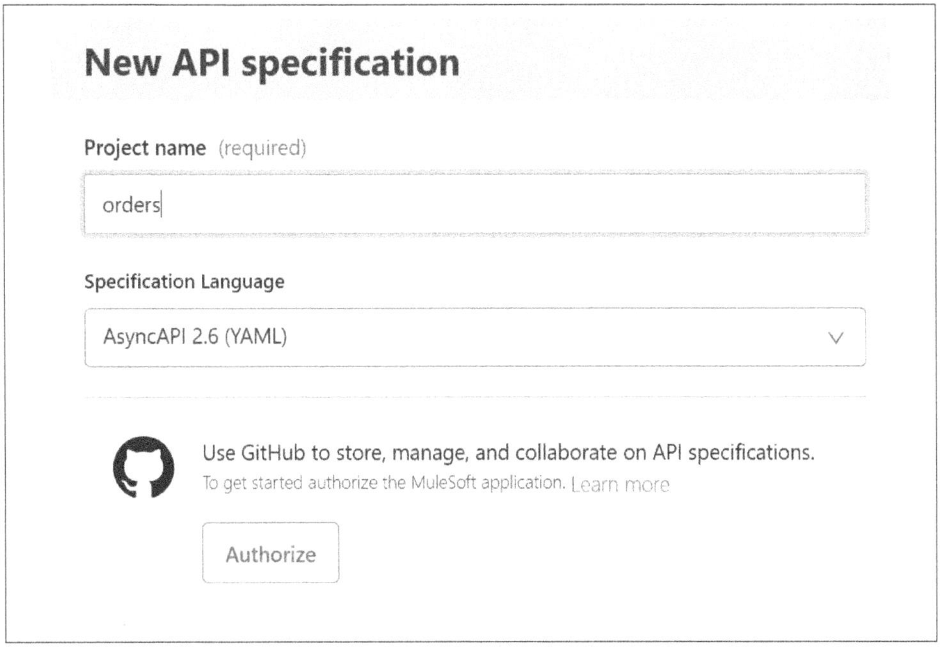

Figure 6-5. New API specification

Next you can see the editor, where you can create the AsyncAPI specification using Design Center. Figure 6-6 shows the editor with a sample AsyncAPI.

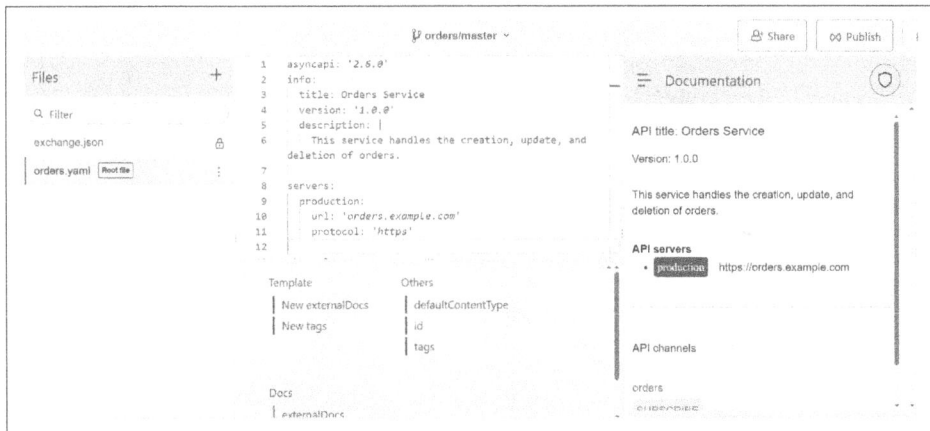

Figure 6-6. AsyncAPI in Design Center

Following is the AsyncAPI specification code outlined. We will be using this as an example for learning purposes:

```yaml
asyncapi: '2.6.0'
info:
  title: Orders Service
  version: '1.0.0'
  description: |
    This service handles the creation, update, and deletion of orders.
servers:
  production:
    url: 'amqp://orders.example.com'
    protocol: 'amqp'
channels:
  orders:
    description: Channel for order events
    subscribe:
      summary: Receive order events
      operationId: receiveOrder
      message:
        contentType: application/json
        payload:
          type: object
          properties:
            orderId:
              type: string
            status:
              type: string
            items:
              type: array
              items:
                type: object
                properties:
                  itemId:
                    type: string
                  quantity:
                    type: integer
  orderShipped:
    description: Channel for order shipped events
    subscribe:
      summary: Receive order shipped events
      operationId: receiveOrderShipped
      message:
        contentType: application/json
        payload:
          type: object
          properties:
            orderId:
              type: string
            shippedDate:
              type: string
              format: date-time
```

```
carrier:
  type: string
trackingNumber:
  type: string
```

Next, hit the "Publish to Exchange" button to publish the AsyncAPI (see Figure 6-7).

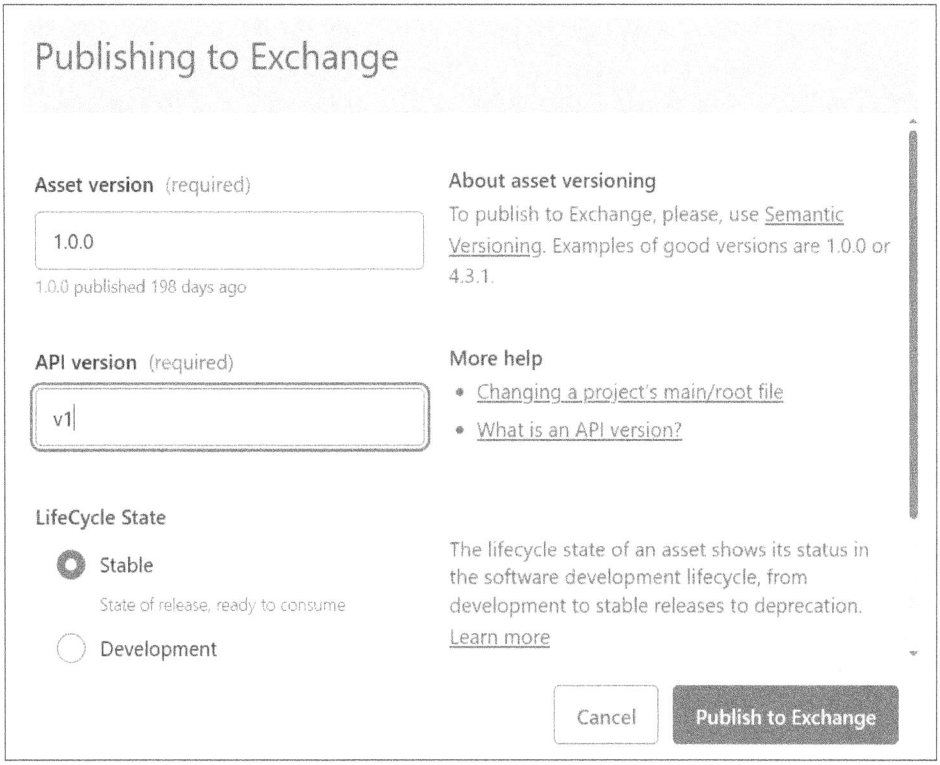

Figure 6-7. Publishing to Exchange

Implementing AsyncAPI

To implement an AsyncAPI, go to Anypoint Code Builder and select "Implement an API" for AsyncAPI. You can choose AsyncAPI by enabling the filters and picking AsyncAPIs from type, as shown in Figure 6-8.

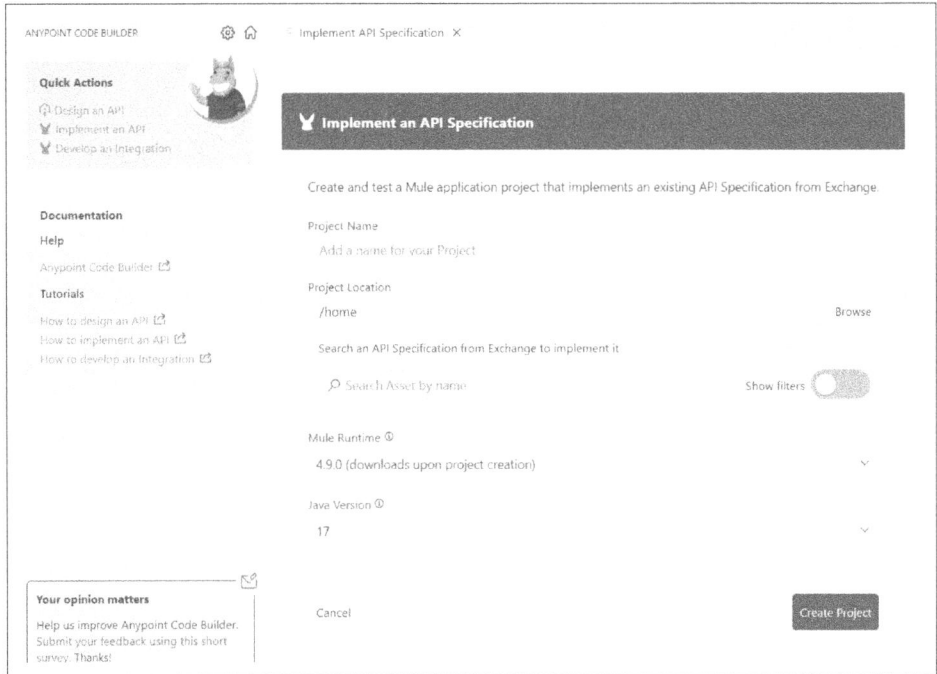

Figure 6-8. Implementing AsyncAPI

Then select the AsyncAPI from the list, as shown in Figure 6-9.

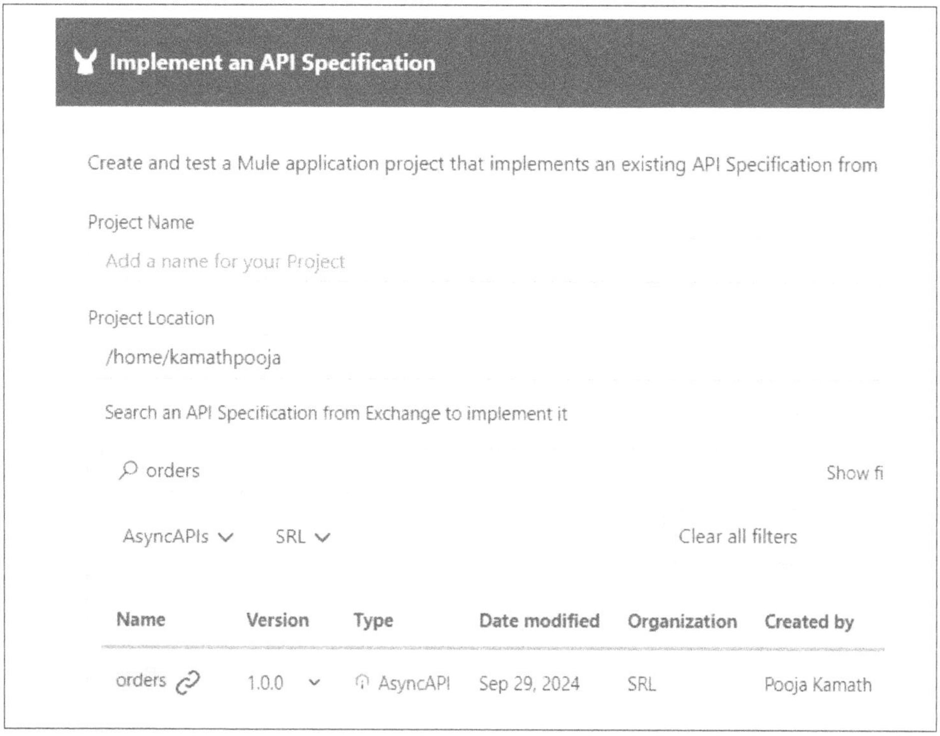

Figure 6-9. AsyncAPI implementation

Scaffolding a Basic Orders API in Mule

At this point, the APIkit scaffolder kicks in and generates a basic structure for your Orders API within a Mule project. For instance, it will automatically generate the code to handle sending *New Order* messages to the warehouse and receiving *Order Shipped* messages from the shipping system. This saves a lot of time, as it automates the creation of the basic communication structure between systems. The structure of the project is shown in Figure 6-10.

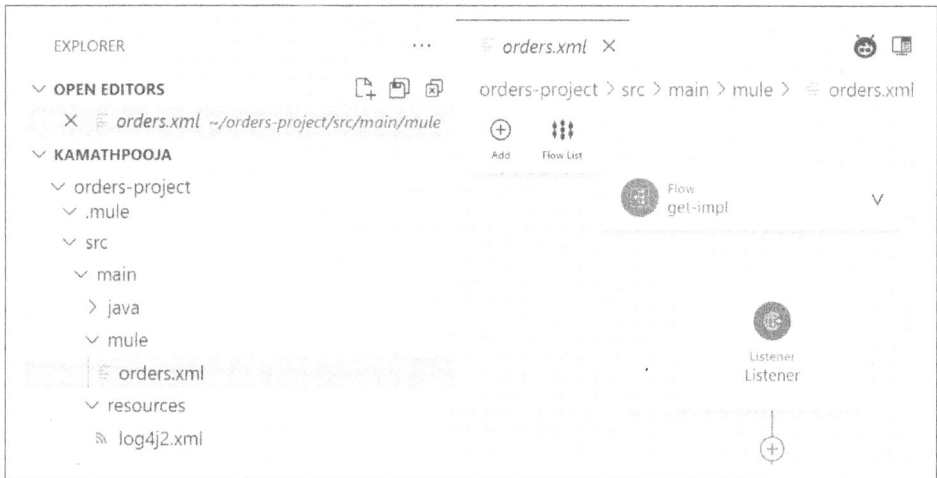

Figure 6-10. AsyncAPI implementation

APIkit for AsyncAPI helps you build event-driven APIs—APIs that send and receive messages when something happens, like an order being placed or shipped. Let's look at how this would work for an Orders API.

Using APIkit for AsyncAPI

With APIkit for AsyncAPI, you define how these messages will be sent or received using asynchronous messaging protocols. For example, your Orders API might use Apache Kafka (a common messaging system) to handle events.

You would create an AsyncAPI specification that describes the following:

- How the Orders API sends a *New Order* message to the warehouse system
- How the Orders API listens for an *Order Shipped* event from the shipping system

APIkit simplifies this process by providing modules you can add and configure. For example, you can set up a `Publish` operation to send a message when a new order is placed, or a `Subscribe` operation that listens for updates like when the order has been shipped.

In *global-configs.xml* you can see the configurations for AsyncAPI APIkit, as shown in Figure 6-11.

Figure 6-11. AsyncAPI APIkit configurations

You can then implement your business logic to complete your project. Once it's complete, you can run the application in run or debug mode to test your project. Run/debug is the same as any other project on ACB.

Later chapters explore deployment. For now, let's look at how to import preexisting AsyncAPI specifications into Design Center.

Importing AsyncAPI Specifications

To import an AsyncAPI specification from Anypoint Exchange or from your computer's local files, follow these steps:

1. *Open the settings.* In the top-right corner of the text editor, you'll see a gear icon. Click on this icon to access the Settings menu.

2. *Choose your import option.* You have two main options to import an AsyncAPI specification:

   a. *Import from Exchange.* When you select this option, you will see two lists:

      i. *API Specifications from Your Organization:* This list includes all the API specifications available in Anypoint Exchange from the business organization your user ID is connected to.

      ii. *API Specifications Published by MuleSoft:* You can also access API specifications published by MuleSoft and available in Anypoint Exchange.

b. *Import from Local Filesystem.* This option allows you to import an AsyncAPI specification directly from your computer. Simply choose the file from your local storage and upload it to the API Designer.

3. *Work with your AsyncAPI specification.* Once your AsyncAPI specification is imported, you can do any of the following:

   a. *Edit and develop.* Make changes or develop your AsyncAPI specification directly in API Designer.

   b. *View documentation.* See the documentation included with the AsyncAPI specification to better understand the API and how it works.

   c. *Publish back to Anypoint Exchange.* Once you've made edits or developed the AsyncAPI specification, you can publish it back to Anypoint Exchange for other users in your organization to access and use.

By following these steps, you can easily manage, edit, and share your AsyncAPI specifications within your organization or from other sources. This makes collaborating on API development simpler and more efficient.

Building from Exchange and Updating Your API

After the initial API setup, you can pull in additional components or other APIs from Anypoint Exchange. For example, you could import a payment service API that handles payment confirmations so that your Orders API can integrate with the payment system whenever a new order is placed. MuleSoft only supports implementing one AsyncAPI into one project, but you can add many REST APIs.

Suppose you make changes to the AsyncAPI specification, such as adding a new status for *Order Delivered*. In that case, you can re-scaffold the Orders API in ACB or Anypoint Studio. This will update the API to handle the new event without you having to manually write new code.

Example for Re-Scaffolding

Let's say your Orders API initially handled only two events: *New Order* and *Order Shipped*. Later, you decide to add a new event, *Order Delivered*, to notify customers when their package has arrived. You update your AsyncAPI specification with this new event, and then re-scaffold the Orders API in ACB. This process automatically updates the API to manage the new *Order Delivered* event, without you having to start from scratch.

In this way, APIkit for AsyncAPI helps you quickly create, update, and manage an event-driven Orders API, making it easier to keep systems like inventory, shipping, and customer notifications in sync through real-time messaging. You can focus on improving the logic and performance of the API while APIkit handles the basic structure and communication.

Validating AsyncAPI Documents

When you validate an AsyncAPI document, you're making sure that it follows the proper rules. This can mean two different things:

Validating against the specification
   Making sure the document follows AsyncAPI's official rules

Validating against best practices or company rules
   Checking if the document meets internal guidelines; also called linting

Validating Against the Specification

This type of validation ensures that your AsyncAPI document is written correctly according to the official AsyncAPI specification. This section discusses a few tools you can use for this.

AsyncAPI on Anypoint Designer

API Designer is a visual tool that makes validation easy. It checks the document for any errors using the AsyncAPI JavaScript parser. When there's a problem, the tool highlights the error with a red underline, and the Diagnostics section provides detailed feedback on what went wrong.

For example, if your document is missing important content or has syntax errors, you might get an error message like this: *Empty or invalid document, please fix errors/ define AsyncAPI document.*

Validating AsyncAPI with ACB

ACB has tools for validating ACB. ACB's governance rules help organizations create specific rules and best practices for their AsyncAPI documents. This ensures that teams and projects maintain consistency and quality. You can write custom rules or use Spectral, an open source tool for defining and enforcing rule sets that ACB integrates with. Governance rule sets can be managed centrally, making it easy to maintain consistency and code quality.

AsyncAPI CLI

You can also use the AsyncAPI CLI to validate your documents locally or as part of an automated CI/CD pipeline. For example, to validate a document, use the following command:

```bash
asyncapi validate asyncapi.yaml
```

This checks your file to ensure it meets the AsyncAPI standards.

Parsers

AsyncAPI provides official JavaScript and Go parsers that can be used to validate documents programmatically. These parsers use JSON Schema to ensure that your document is properly formatted according to the AsyncAPI specification.

> While JSON Schema is helpful, it may not catch every type of error. That's why the official parsers have extra features to fully validate documents, especially if you're building your own parser.

Validating Against Best Practices or Company Rules (Linting)

Although validating against the specification is important, you may also want to ensure that your document follows company-specific guidelines. This is known as *linting.* For example, you might want all documents to include optional properties, like a summary, even though AsyncAPI doesn't require it.

Here's an example: The summary field is optional in AsyncAPI, but your company may decide to make it mandatory for consistency. To enforce this rule across your organization, you can use a tool like Spectral.

Using Spectral for linting

Spectral is an open source tool that allows you to create custom rules for validating your AsyncAPI documents. Here's how to get started:

1. *Install Spectral on your computer.* Create a file called *.spectral.yaml* where you will define your own rules. Here's an example of a rule you might write:

   ```
   {
     "rules": {
       // Add your own rules here
     }
   }
   ```

2. *Create a custom rule.* Let's say you want to ensure that all document titles start with an uppercase letter. You can create a rule like this:

```json
{
  "rules": {
    "valid-document-version": {
      "message": "Application title must start with upper case",
      "severity": "error",
      "given": "$.info",
      "then": [
        {
          "field": "title",
          "function": "pattern",
          "functionOptions": {
            "match": "^[A-Z]"
          }
        }
      ]
    }
  }
}
```

3. *Run Spectral lint.* Once you've set up your custom rules, you can validate your AsyncAPI document using the Spectral CLI with this command:

```
spectral lint asyncapi.yaml
```

This will check to see whether your document follows both the AsyncAPI specification and the custom rules your organization has set.

Why validation is important

Whether you're validating against the official specification or your company's rules, validation is crucial for maintaining consistent and error-free AsyncAPI documents. It helps ensure that your application's communication with other services is reliable and meets industry standards.

By using tools like AsyncAPI Studio (*https://studio.asyncapi.com*), CLI, and Spectral, you can catch issues early and ensure your event-driven systems run smoothly.

Summary

This chapter covered the fundamentals of event-driven architecture (EDA), where systems communicate by sending and receiving events in real time, allowing for more efficient and responsive communication compared to traditional request-response architectures. It introduced AsyncAPI, a specification designed to document and implement APIs that work with event-driven systems, similar to how OpenAPI serves request-response APIs.

The chapter compared AsyncAPI and OpenAPI, highlighting key differences in their design and communication models:

- OpenAPI is for traditional, synchronous APIs where requests and responses are handled directly by the server.
- AsyncAPI, in contrast, manages asynchronous communication, where events (messages) are sent when something occurs, and the receiving systems act upon these messages independently.

The chapter walked through how to design event-driven APIs using AsyncAPI specifications. It covered the key components of AsyncAPI—such as channels, messages, and operations—that define how different systems interact through events.

The chapter also introduced APIkit for AsyncAPI, a tool that automates the creation of event-driven APIs. APIkit helps generate the skeleton code for an API based on an AsyncAPI specification, allowing developers to focus on building business logic rather than managing basic communication setup. The tool simplifies the integration of asynchronous messaging protocols like Kafka and MQTT.

Finally, the chapter discussed using Anypoint Code Builder to scaffold and implement an AsyncAPI specification. Developers can use this tool to quickly set up and modify APIs, whether they are handling new events or integrating additional services. The chapter concluded by emphasizing how these tools streamline the development process for building efficient, event-driven systems in real-world applications.

Chapter 7 focuses on handling events at scale. These tools are crucial for maintaining smooth operations, ensuring reliable message delivery, and efficiently managing data persistence and caching, all contributing to robust, high-performance integrations.

CHAPTER 7
Events and Storage

Events and storage are a critical part of building smart, scalable integration solutions. Think of them as the backbone of modern systems. This chapter breaks down how to handle real-time message flows and data storage like a pro. You'll dive into tools like Anypoint MQ, virtual machine (VM) queues, third-party queues, Object Store, Cache scope, and Redis, all designed to help you build systems that are both resilient and responsive. In Chapter 6, we learned the dynamics of event-driven architecture and the fundamentals of asynchronous messaging; now we will dive deeper into the mechanics of handling these events at scale.

These aren't just tools. They're your secret weapons for keeping everything running smoothly, whether you're managing message queues or optimizing storage for high volumes of data. From ensuring reliable message delivery with queuing systems to efficiently handling data persistence and caching, you'll see how each component fits into the bigger picture of building rock-solid, high-performance integrations.

Take Super Routes Logistics (SRL), for example. Their system must manage thousands of quote requests, delivery confirmations, and driver updates every day. To stay responsive and scalable, they rely on tools like Anypoint MQ for message queuing, Object Store for tracking delivery sessions, and Redis for caching dynamic traffic data—all while keeping operations smooth and customer expectations met.

One key question when discussing queues is: how do you know which queuing product to use? This is where understanding your specific use case becomes most important. For instance, Anypoint MQ is ideal when you need reliable, cloud-based messaging for scalable, distributed systems. It ensures persistent, asynchronous communication, making it perfect for scenarios where message delivery order and reliability are essential. On the other hand, VM queues might be more suitable for internal, lightweight messaging within Mule applications, where performance and speed are prioritized over persistence. Third-party queues like RabbitMQ and Kafka come into play when you need to integrate with external systems, bringing added flexibility.

By the end of this chapter, you'll not only know how to orchestrate event-driven architectures that move messages seamlessly, but you'll also know when to use which queuing product based on your system's needs. Whether you're streamlining data access with Object Store or boosting performance with Redis, you'll have the confidence to tackle even the most complex integration challenges.

Set up persistent queues in Anypoint MQ to make sure no message goes missing in action during an outage, because who wants to lose an important shipping order in the chaos? And don't forget dead letter queues! They're like your system's lost and found, catching failed messages so you can fix them up and send them on their way without causing a traffic jam. Keep your message flow smooth and drama-free!

Anypoint MQ

Let's dive into the details of Anypoint MQ, your first option for managing message queues.

Anypoint MQ is MuleSoft's fully managed cloud messaging service, designed to handle asynchronous communication across distributed systems. It's perfect for scenarios where reliability, scalability, and message persistence are key. By queuing messages, Anypoint MQ ensures that no data is lost during transmission, even if some systems experience downtime or performance issues.

At SRL, Anypoint MQ is used to queue shipping requests from their customer portal. Each order message is stored until it's processed by downstream systems like the route planner and cost-analysis engine. This ensures that even during traffic surges or system slowdowns, no order is lost—guaranteeing a smooth and transparent experience for their SMB customers.

Here's how Anypoint MQ works in practice:

Persistent queuing
Messages are stored in a queue until they are successfully processed, guaranteeing reliable delivery. This makes it ideal for tasks like order processing or payment transactions where losing a message is simply not an option.

Asynchronous communication
Anypoint MQ allows different systems to communicate at their own pace. For instance, if one system is processing orders faster than another can handle them, messages are queued until the slower system is ready. This prevents system overloads and keeps everything moving smoothly.

Advanced features

Anypoint MQ supports first in, first out (FIFO) delivery, ensuring that messages are processed in the exact order they were received. Additionally, you can set up *dead letter* queues that catch failed messages for later review and troubleshooting, which is great for maintaining system reliability and fixing issues without disrupting ongoing processes.

Scalability

Built for the cloud, Anypoint MQ can handle large volumes of messages across multiple environments, whether you're dealing with thousands or millions of transactions daily. It's designed to scale as your workload increases, making it a great choice for fast-growing businesses or systems with unpredictable traffic spikes.

Multitenant and secure

Anypoint MQ is part of the MuleSoft Anypoint Platform, meaning you get multitenancy, built-in security features, and seamless integration with the rest of your Mule applications. You can define permissions, manage access controls, and monitor queue activity in real time through the Anypoint MQ dashboard.

Integration with Mule flows

Setting up Anypoint MQ is simple. Once you've added it to your Anypoint Platform account, you can easily integrate it into your Mule flows by using the Anypoint MQ connector. Drag and drop the connector into your flow, connect it to your queue, and define your message-processing rules. You can quickly set up asynchronous message processing with minimal configuration.

Anypoint MQ is especially useful for distributed systems or complex integrations where you need to manage communication between multiple applications in different locations or on different schedules. It acts as the main source of your messaging architecture, ensuring your systems stay connected and available under any condition.

Anypoint MQ is an additional *entitlement* on your Anypoint Platform account, meaning it's not included by default with trial accounts. However, if your company's platform account doesn't have Anypoint MQ enabled, you can easily request to try it out. This way, you can evaluate whether it's the right solution for your messaging and integration needs before fully committing. It's a great opportunity to see how Anypoint MQ can enhance your system's performance and reliability.

Let's get started! Setting up Anypoint MQ within the MuleSoft Anypoint Platform is a straightforward process. This section shows how to do it.

To access Anypoint MQ, log into your Anypoint Platform account. From the Anypoint Platform Home, click on MQ from the navigation menu. This will bring you to the Anypoint MQ dashboard, where you can manage your queues and messages.

Figure 7-1 shows the Anypoint Platform Management Center options. When a platform account is provisioned with Anypoint MQ, you will see MQ listed as an option. Click the MQ hyperlink.

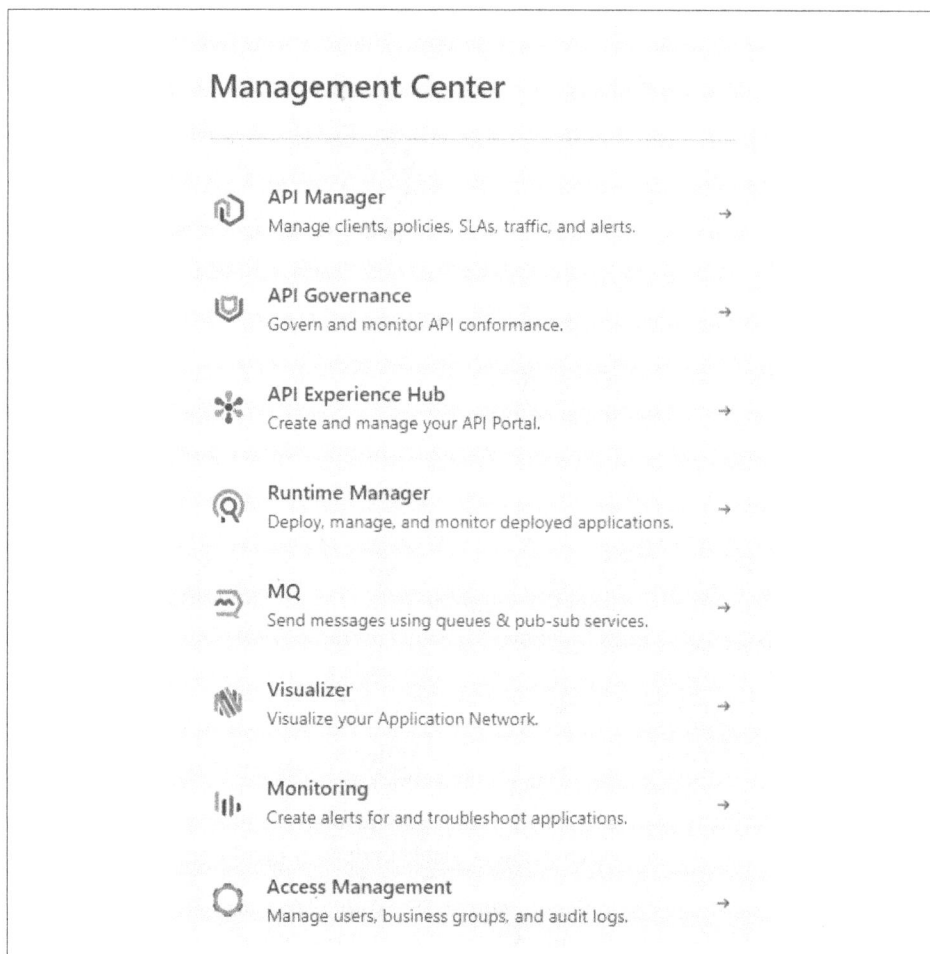

Management Center

API Manager
Manage clients, policies, SLAs, traffic, and alerts. →

API Governance
Govern and monitor API conformance. →

API Experience Hub
Create and manage your API Portal. →

Runtime Manager
Deploy, manage, and monitor deployed applications. →

MQ
Send messages using queues & pub-sub services. →

Visualizer
Visualize your Application Network. →

Monitoring
Create alerts for and troubleshoot applications. →

Access Management
Manage users, business groups, and audit logs. →

Figure 7-1. Anypoint Platform Management Center

Now create a new queue. Once in the Anypoint MQ dashboard, click Create Queue.

Figure 7-2 shows the Anypoint MQ dashboard; click the "+" icon to create a new queue.

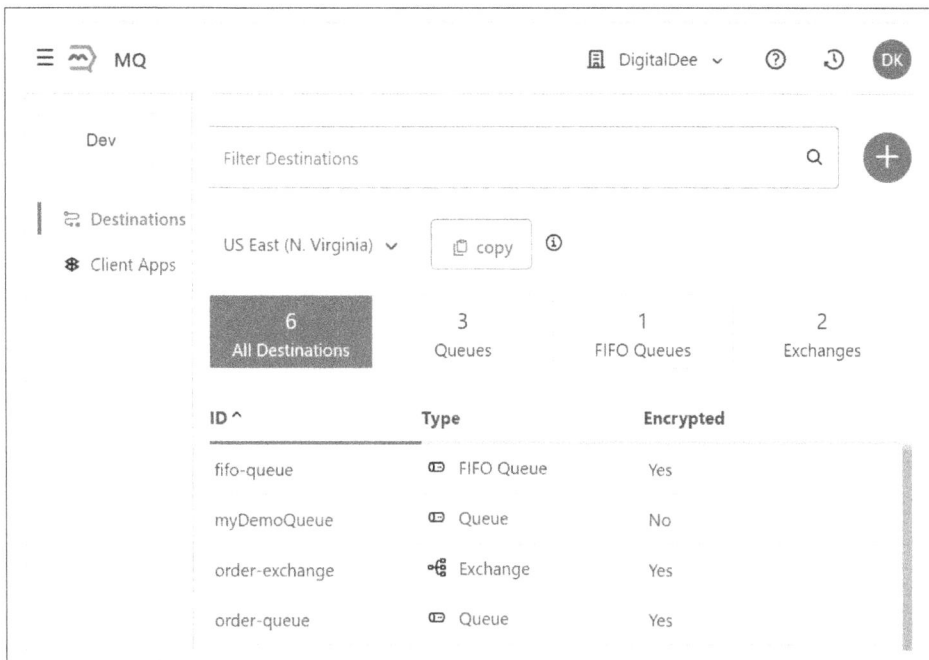

Figure 7-2. Anypoint MQ: creating a queue

Figure 7-3 shows the Create options. You can create a Queue, Exchange, or FIFO Queue.

Figure 7-3. Queue types to choose from

Give your queue a name, and set specific configurations such as message retention (how long a message should remain in the queue), maximum message size, and dead letter queue settings (for failed messages).

Figure 7-4 shows the Create Queue options to name and configure the queue.

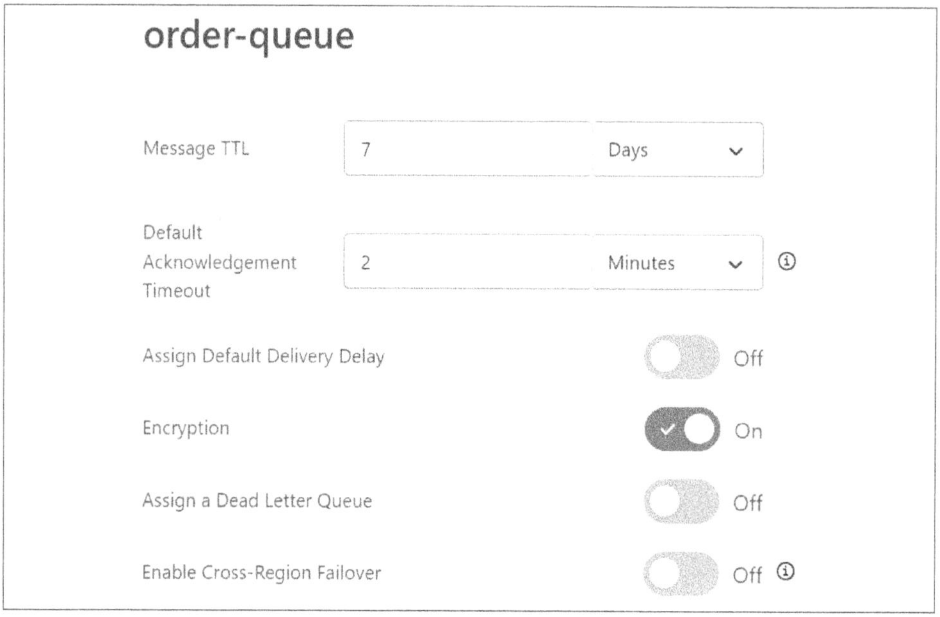

order-queue

Message TTL	7	Days ⌄
Default Acknowledgement Timeout	2	Minutes ⌄ ⓘ
Assign Default Delivery Delay		Off
Encryption		On
Assign a Dead Letter Queue		Off
Enable Cross-Region Failover		Off ⓘ

Figure 7-4. Anypoint MQ Create Queue options

You can create multiple queues for different purposes like order processing, notifications, or inventory updates. Click Create Queue to finalize your queue.

Figure 7-5 shows the new queue that you created.

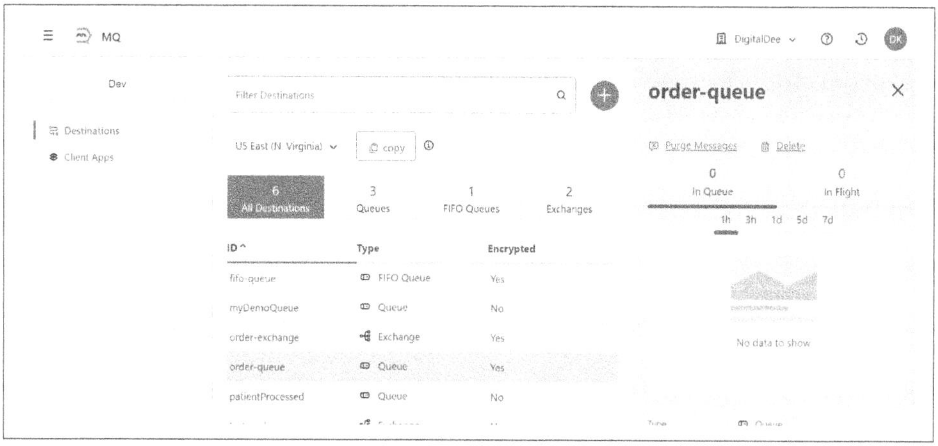

Figure 7-5. Anypoint MQ new order queue

Let's move on and create an Exchange next. By creating an Exchange, you're setting up a place where teams can collaborate effectively by accessing shared components, reducing development time, and ensuring consistency across projects. Once your assets are in the Exchange, they can be easily accessed, modified, or reused across different applications, saving you much time for future integrations. Let's dive in and set it up.

Figure 7-6 shows the Create Exchange options.

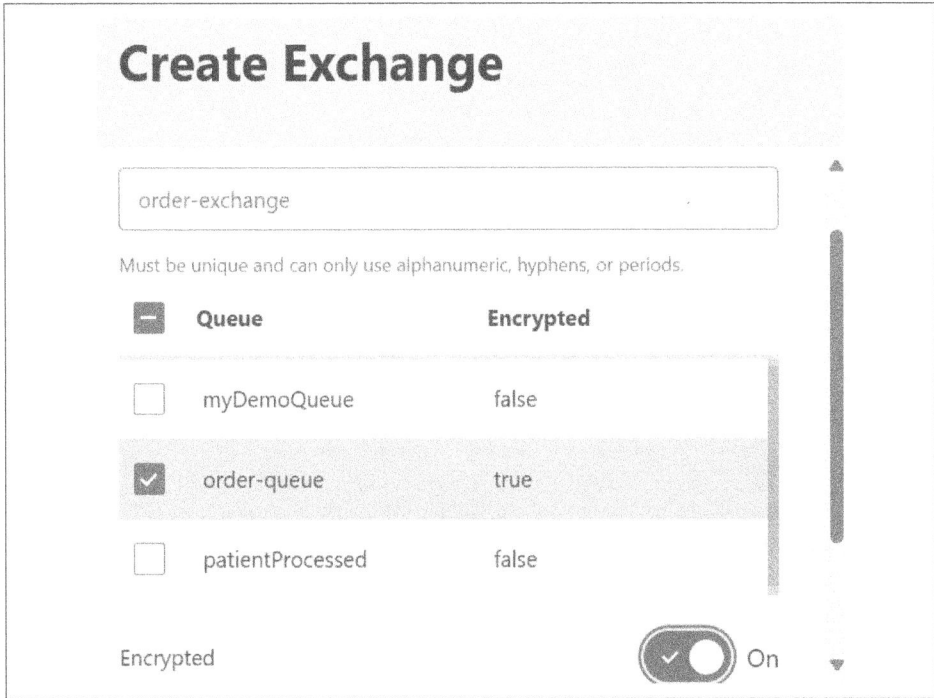

Figure 7-6. Anypoint MQ Create Exchange options

Figure 7-7 shows the new exchange that you created.

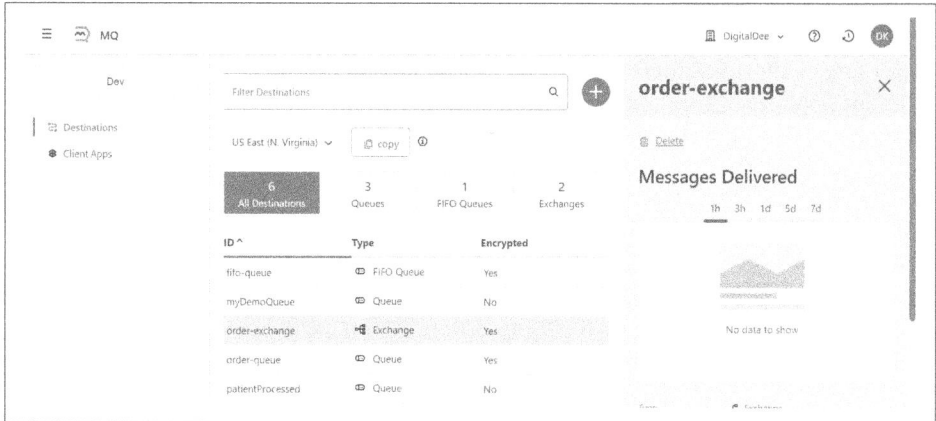

Figure 7-7. Anypoint MQ new order exchange

Next, let's create a FIFO queue. A FIFO queue ensures that messages are processed in the exact order in which they were received, which is essential for scenarios where the sequence of message processing matters, such as in order-processing systems or financial transactions. By using a FIFO queue, you can guarantee that your messages are handled in a reliable, sequential manner, preventing issues that could arise from out-of-order processing.

SRL uses FIFO queues to maintain the order of quote requests as they come in. Since quotes can vary based on real-time conditions like driver availability or traffic, preserving the sequence is critical to ensure fairness and data integrity when sending price estimates to customers.

Setting up a FIFO queue allows you to maintain data consistency and integrity, especially in workflows where message order impacts the outcome. Let's set one up to ensure our message flow stays organized and orderly.

Figure 7-8 shows the FIFO queue options to name and configure the queue.

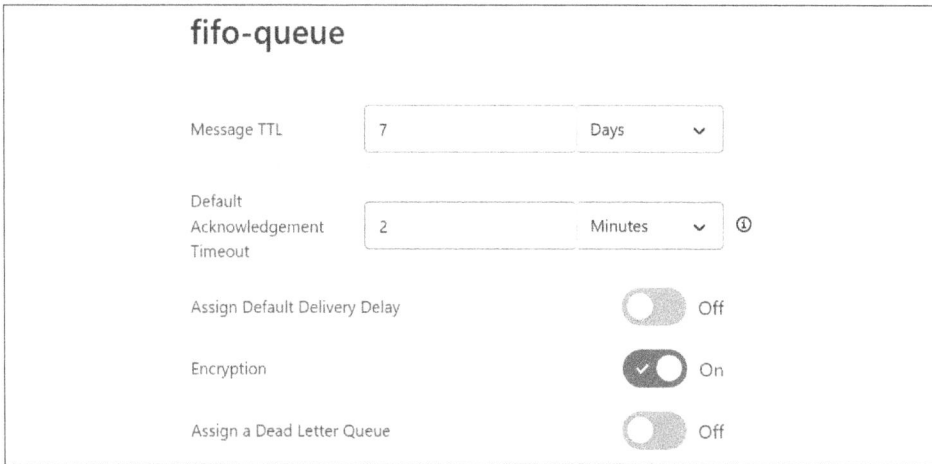

Figure 7-8. FIFO queue options

Figure 7-9 shows the new FIFO queue that you created.

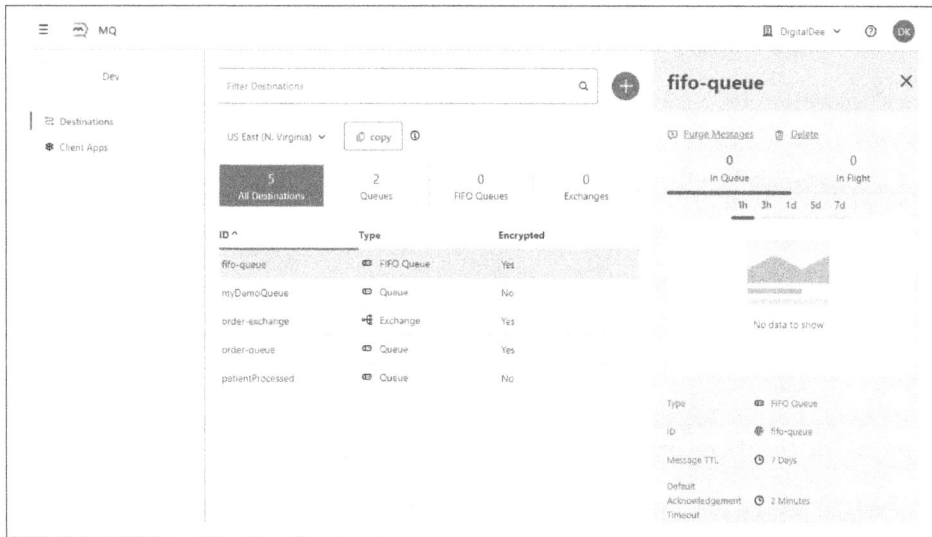

Figure 7-9. Anypoint MQ new FIFO queue

Now we'll set up queue permissions and define who has access to the queue. You can specify roles and permissions for each queue, such as which users can send, receive, or purge messages. This ensures security and proper governance over your messaging system.

To begin integrating the queue into your Mule flows, open Anypoint Studio and drag the Anypoint MQ connector from the Mule Palette into your flow. Configure the connector by selecting the queue name you just created in the Anypoint MQ dashboard. Define the operations you want to perform on the queue (for example, send messages, consume messages). Connect the rest of your flow to the MQ connector to define how the messages are processed and handled.

Figure 7-10 shows the Anypoint MQ module from Exchange.

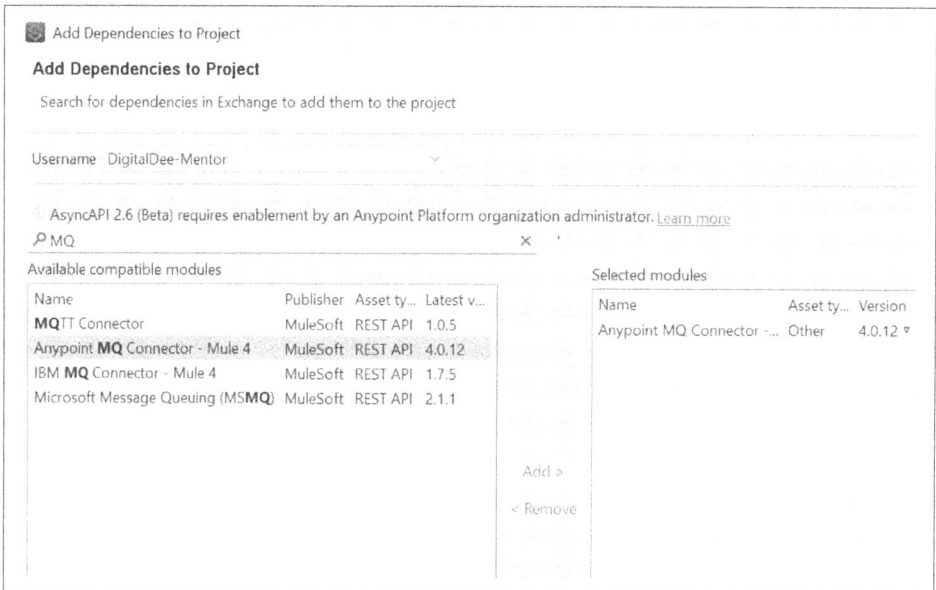

Figure 7-10. Add Anypoint MQ module from Exchange

The Anypoint MQ Publish operation is a core feature that allows you to send (publish) messages to a queue in Anypoint MQ. This is essential for enabling asynchronous communication between different systems, applications, or services. When you publish a message, it is placed in the specified queue, where it waits to be consumed by a consumer or processed by another system.

Figure 7-11 shows the Publish operation.

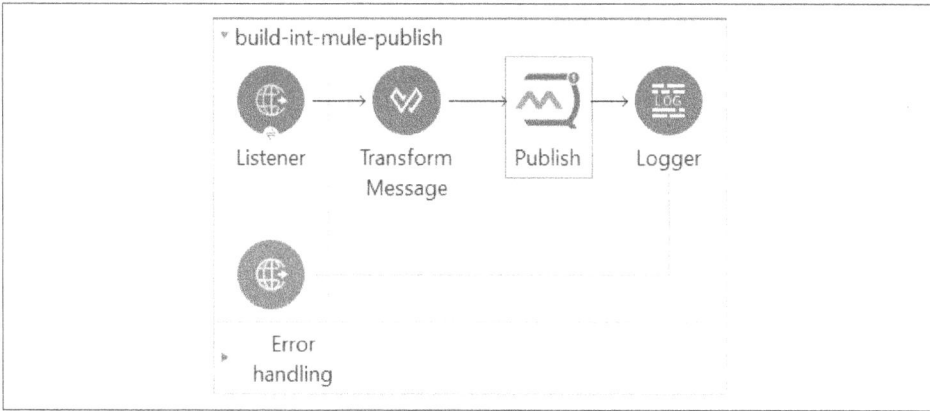

Figure 7-11. Anypoint MQ `Publish` operation

Anypoint MQ Subscriber is a key feature of Anypoint MQ that allows you to receive messages from a queue or topic in a publish-subscribe model. Unlike the `Consume` operation, which retrieves messages for a single consumer from a queue, the Subscriber pattern enables multiple consumers to receive copies of messages, making it ideal for broadcast or fan-out scenarios where the same message needs to be delivered to multiple systems or services.

Figure 7-12 shows the Subscriber source.

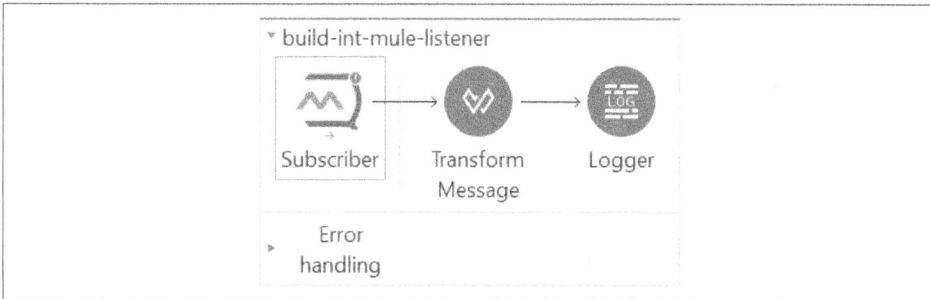

Figure 7-12. Anypoint MQ Subscriber source

The Anypoint MQ `Consume` operation is the counterpart to the `Publish` operation, allowing applications to retrieve (consume) messages from an Anypoint MQ queue. It enables your system to process messages that have been queued, ensuring that tasks such as order processing, notifications, or other operations can be handled efficiently and asynchronously.

Figure 7-13 shows the Consume operation.

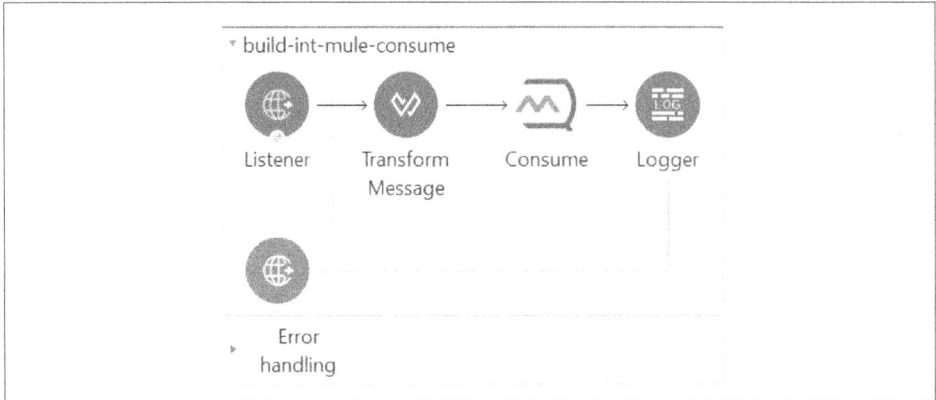

Figure 7-13. Anypoint MQ Consume operation

Let's talk about managing your queues. Back in the Anypoint MQ dashboard, you can monitor the status of your queues. You'll have visibility into message counts, queue length, and message age. You can also review logs, track message delivery, and set up alerts for specific events, such as when a queue exceeds a certain size (see Figure 7-14).

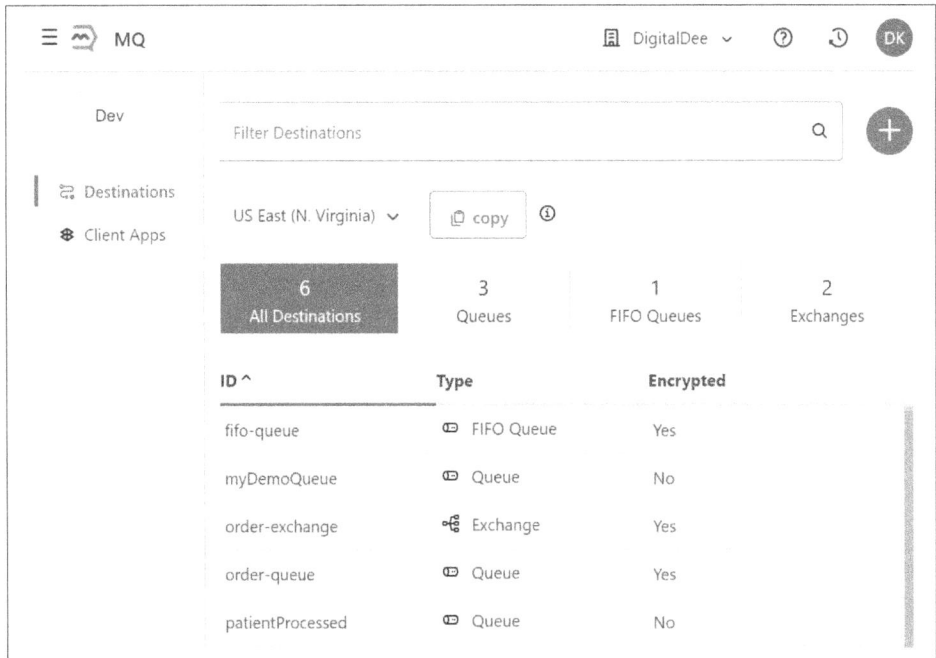

Figure 7-14. Anypoint MQ dashboard

After configuring the queue and connecting it to your flows, test the system by sending a few messages to the queue. Ensure the messages are properly queued, consumed, and processed as expected. If any issues arise, check the dead letter queue for failed messages, and adjust your configuration as needed.

For SRL, if a message fails due to an unavailable driver service or missing payload data, it's automatically routed to a dead letter queue. Their team can inspect these messages, correct the issue, and reprocess them—preventing lost orders while maintaining trust and reliability.

By following along in this section, Anypoint MQ will be fully integrated into your environment, enabling asynchronous, reliable message processing for your integration use cases. It's an easy setup that gives you full control over your messaging system, with the flexibility to scale and adapt to your needs.

VM Queues

The next type of queuing option is VM queues, a commonly used option within MuleSoft for handling intra-application communication. Unlike Anypoint MQ, which is designed for cross-application or distributed system communication, VM queues are specifically intended for communication within the same Mule application. They provide an efficient, lightweight way to pass messages between flows and components within a single Mule runtime instance.

VM queues are confined to a single Mule runtime instance, meaning they cannot be used to communicate across different Mule applications or across distributed Mule runtime instances. They are specifically meant for internal communication within the same application.

By default, VM queues are stored in memory, which makes them extremely fast for passing messages between flows in the same Mule app. However, this also means that the messages are nonpersistent; if the Mule application restarts or the server crashes, the messages in the VM queue will be lost.

You can configure persistent VM queues to store messages on disk. In this case, messages are written to a file system, providing a more durable solution. If the Mule runtime is restarted, messages can be recovered from disk. However, using persistent queues may result in slower performance due to disk I/O operations.

VM queues do not have the same management features as Anypoint MQ—there is no Exchange or dashboard for VM queues. They are configured and managed directly in the Mule flow through Anypoint Studio or Anypoint Code Builder (ACB), with no centralized management or visualization like you would find with Anypoint MQ.

To use VM queues in your Mule application, you'll need to add the VM module in Anypoint Studio or ACB.

Figure 7-15 shows the VM queue module.

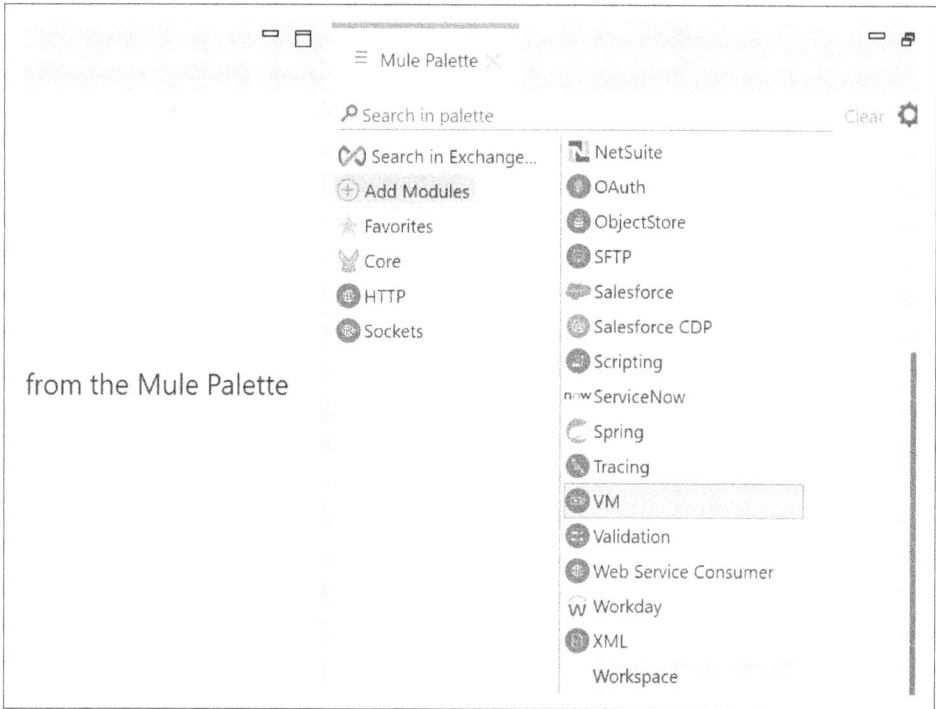

Figure 7-15. Add Anypoint VM module

The VM Publish operation allows you to send (publish) messages to a VM queue within the same Mule application. This is essential for enabling asynchronous communication between different flows or components within the same Mule runtime. When you publish a message, it is placed in the specified VM queue, where it waits to be consumed by another flow or component within the same application.

Figure 7-16 shows the VM Publish operation.

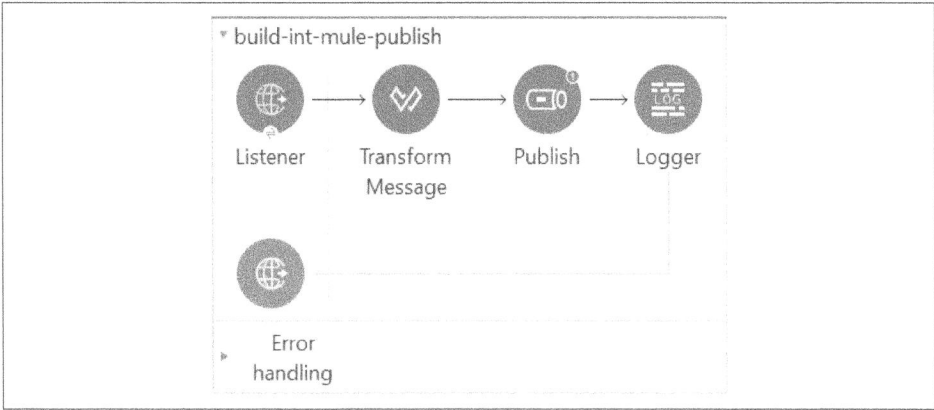

Figure 7-16. VM Publish *operation*

The VM Publish-Consume operation is a unique feature that allows you to publish a message to a VM queue and wait synchronously until the designated flow consumes the message. Unlike the asynchronous behavior of standard Publish and Consume operations, the Publish-Consume operation does not return control to the publishing flow until the message has been processed and consumed by the target flow or component.

Figure 7-17 shows the VM Publish-Consume operation.

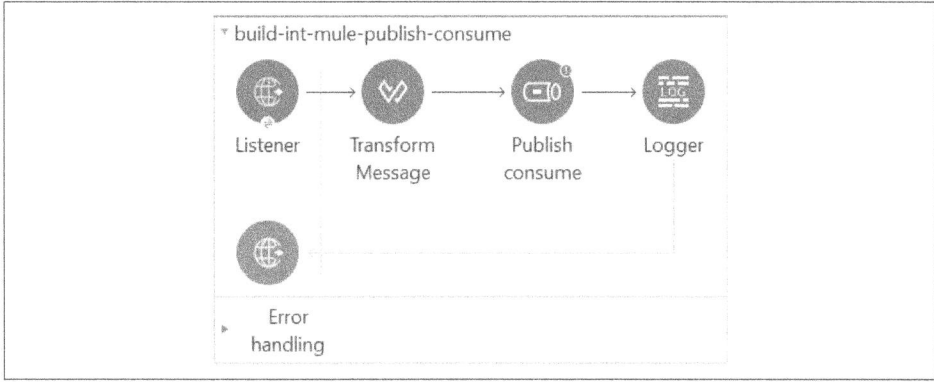

Figure 7-17. VM Publish-Consume *operation*

The VM Listener is a key feature of VM queues in MuleSoft that allows you to receive messages from a VM queue. The VM Listener operates in a point-to-point messaging model, where only one consumer (flow) retrieves each message from the queue. It is designed for use within a single Mule application and enables asynchronous communication between flows or components. Each message is consumed by one flow, ensuring that message processing is done in a controlled and sequential manner (see Figure 7-18).

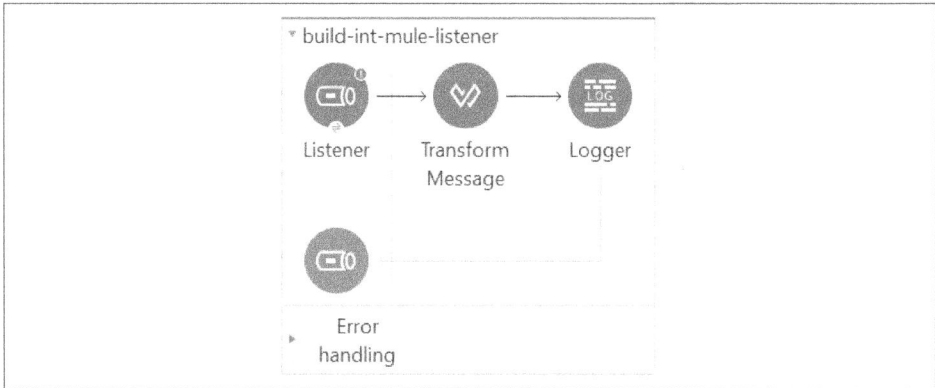

Figure 7-18. VM Listener operation

The VM Consume operation is the counterpart to the VM Publish operation, allowing flows within the same Mule application to retrieve (consume) messages from a VM queue. It enables asynchronous communication within the application, allowing messages to be processed by different flows or components (see Figure 7-19).

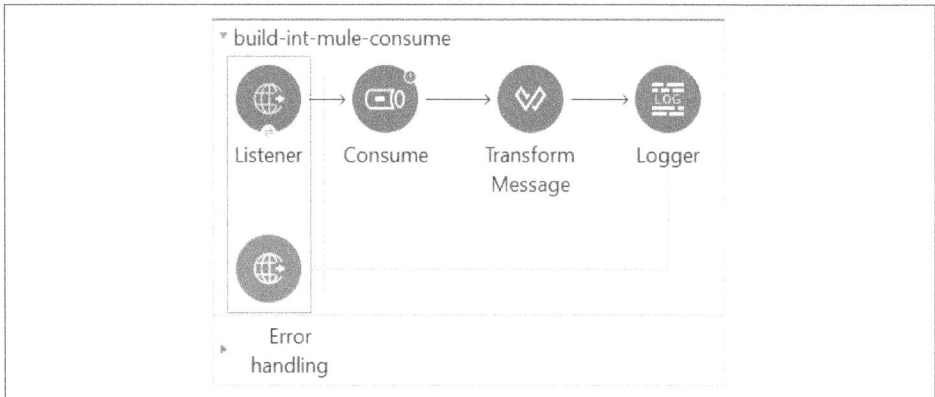

Figure 7-19. VM Consume operation

Third-Party Queues

Another option is third-party queues like RabbitMQ and Kafka. RabbitMQ shines when you need flexible message routing and asynchronous tasks, helping your services talk to each other without getting in each other's way. Kafka is all about speed and scale, built for high-volume data streaming and event-driven architectures that need real-time responsiveness. Both are easy to plug into your MuleSoft flows, giving you reliable, scalable messaging to keep everything humming along seamlessly.

RabbitMQ, Kafka, and Anypoint MQ are all built for distributed messaging between applications, offering persistent storage for reliable message delivery, even during failures. They are scalable, handle large volumes of messages, and provide centralized management tools for monitoring and managing message flows, unlike VM queues, which are limited to intra-application communication.

SRL integrates with third-party analytics and tracking platforms using Kafka. Shipment telemetry data—like package scans or delivery timestamps—are streamed in real time to external systems for analysis, enabling smarter routing decisions and predictive delivery estimates.

Object Store

Let's shift gears and talk about how the Object Store is the perfect complement to message queues when it comes to data management in your MuleSoft applications. While message queues handle the reliable delivery of messages between different parts of your system, Object Store focuses on the storage and retrieval of data that needs to be available for a longer period of time. Whether you're caching API responses, managing user session states, or tracking the status of long-running processes, Object Store gives you the flexibility to store and access data across different flows and applications. It's the tool you'll turn to when you need to persist data temporarily or long term, ensuring that your application has everything it needs to keep running smoothly.

You can configure Object Store to save your data in two ways:

- In-memory for quick access
- Persistent storage if you want the data to be available after a restart

So, whether you're just caching (Cache scope is discussed in "Cache Scope" on page 191) something for a few seconds or need to hold onto user sessions, Object Store is a solid tool to use for your solution.

SRL uses Object Store to track session states during multistep quote flows. For example, when a customer starts a quote, their partial data is temporarily stored across flows so that they can resume without starting over. It's also used to keep a lightweight, persistent record of recent quote statuses, which can be retrieved instantly without querying downstream systems.

At Super Route Logistics, Object Store isn't just a behind-the-scenes tool—it's the magic that keeps quote flows smooth, smart, and stress-free. Here's how it works:

- When a customer starts a quote, their early inputs—like pickup location, delivery preferences, and cargo details—are stashed in Object Store under a unique session key.

- As they move through the steps, that data is retrieved and updated across multiple flows—no re-entry required.

- If they step away (life happens!), the system checks if their session still exists and lets them pick up right where they left off.

- A built-in TTL ensures that if a session goes stale, it quietly disappears without cluttering the system.

- Once the quote is submitted or the timer runs out, the session data is cleared—keeping things clean, fast, and ready for the next customer.

By using Object Store this way, SRL delivers a seamless experience while staying lightweight under the hood. Now that's what we call smart logistics.

The benefits of the Object Store extend even further, as it's not limited to use within a single flow. You can share data across different parts of your application or even across multiple applications. Need to keep a running count, store some session info, or hold onto a cache of frequently used data? No problem. You can also set a time-to-live amount (TTL) to automatically clear out data when it's no longer needed—so you never end up with stale info cluttering things up.

And if you're deploying your application to CloudHub, Object Store has built-in redundancy, ensuring that your data is safe and available even if you're spread out across nodes or regions. Now, let's dive into the operations you'll be using:

Store

Want to save something important for later? Use the `Store` operation to drop a key-value pair into Object Store. It's like filing a document under a label. Next time you need it, you'll know exactly where to look. And if the key already exists? No problem, Object Store just updates it for you.

Retrieve

When you need to pull data back, the `Retrieve` operation has your back. Just hand it the key, and you'll get back the value you stored. If the key's not there, it'll either give you nothing or a default value you've set. It's like reaching back into that labeled drawer and grabbing what you need.

Remove

Done with something and want to clear it out? The Remove operation deletes that key-value pair, cleaning up what you no longer need. It's perfect for clearing expired sessions or old cache data you don't want to hang around.

Contains

Before you go looking for something, you might want to check if it's actually there. The Contains operation is like a quick peek into Object Store to see if your key exists, returning a simple yes or no.

All Keys

Need to see what's hanging out in Object Store? The All Keys operation gives you a list of everything stored there, kind of like getting an inventory of your entire filing system. It's a great way to monitor or clean up stored data.

Clear

Want to wipe everything out and start fresh? The Clear operation is the quick reset button that removes all key-value pairs in Object Store. It's a great tool for doing a full cleanup when necessary.

TTL (time-to-live)

If you don't want data sticking around forever, use the TTL feature to automatically expire key-value pairs after a set amount of time. Object Store takes care of removing the data for you once its usefulness is outlived—no manual cleanup is needed.

With these operations, you've got everything you need to manage data like a pro. Whether it's storing, retrieving, removing, or keeping tabs on all the keys, Object Store gives you the flexibility to handle your data effortlessly across different flows and apps.

Cache Scope

Now that you're familiar with the Object Store, it's time to see how it works alongside the Cache scope to optimize data management in your MuleSoft applications. Object Store is your go-to for persisting data across flows and applications, while the Cache scope helps reduce redundant operations by storing frequently used data for quick access. Together, they form a powerful duo: Object Store provides the underlying storage, and the Cache scope acts as the layer that checks whether the data is already available before making API calls or database queries. This combination not only improves performance but also ensures that your application runs more efficiently by minimizing unnecessary data retrieval.

The Cache scope in MuleSoft works by storing the results of operations, like API calls or database queries. When a request comes in, MuleSoft checks if the result is already cached; if so, it retrieves it directly from the cache. If not, the operation is executed, and the result is cached for future use. The cache is backed by Object Store, where the data can be stored either in-memory or persistently, depending on your configuration. You can also set a TTL to control how long the data stays cached before being refreshed. By using the Cache scope, you significantly improve performance by minimizing redundant operations and reducing the load on external systems.

SRL wraps high-latency API calls—like those to Google Maps—in a Cache scope, storing the results temporarily in Object Store. This allows them to avoid repetitive traffic lookups for the same region during peak quoting times, improving response speed and reducing API costs.

Here's how to set up the Cache scope in MuleSoft:

1. *Add the Cache scope.* In Anypoint Studio or ACB, add the Cache scope and drop it into your flow around the operation or set of operations you want to cache (such as API calls, database queries, or any other heavy processing task).

2. *Configure the Cache scope.* In the Properties panel of the Cache scope, you can adjust key settings including the following:

    a. *Expiration (TTL).* Set the TTL to define how long the cached data should persist before expiring and needing to be refreshed.

    b. *Caching strategy.* Specify how the cache should behave. By default, the scope uses Object Store as the backend, but you can also customize how cache entries are identified and stored.

3. *Define caching keys.* The Cache scope automatically generates a cache key based on the input. If you need more control, you can define a custom key, which is especially useful when caching based on specific parameters (like query strings or path variables).

4. *Test the cache.* Deploy your flow and execute it. On the first run, the data is processed and stored in the cache. On subsequent runs, the Cache scope retrieves the result from the cache, and there is no need to run the complete process again.

Redis

Redis takes things a step further. The Cache scope works great for managing short-term data within MuleSoft flows, but Redis is a more scalable and high-performance solution for caching and data storage across distributed systems. Redis is an in-memory data store known for its speed, and its superpower is being able to cache large amounts of data or share cached information across multiple applications. By integrating Redis with MuleSoft, you unlock the ability to handle more complex caching scenarios, making it perfect for enterprise-level applications where speed and scalability are critical.

Redis is an open source, in-memory data store that provides ultrafast data access, making it ideal for high-performance applications. Unlike the Cache scope, which is limited to your local Mule application, Redis allows you to store and share data across multiple systems, making it perfect for distributed environments. Whether you're storing session data, caching API responses, or managing real-time analytics, Redis delivers the speed and scalability modern applications demand.

Redis is a highly versatile key-value store that supports various data structures such as strings, lists, sets, hashes, and sorted sets. This flexibility allows Redis to handle a wide range of use cases, from simple caching and session management to more complex operations like real-time analytics, messaging, and leaderboards. Its in-memory storage makes it extremely fast, while features like persistence, automatic expiration, and high availability through clustering ensure both speed and reliability in large-scale applications.

To use Redis with MuleSoft, start by adding the Redis Connector in Anypoint Studio or ACB and configuring your connection with the host, port, and any authentication you need. Once you have configured the connector, you can easily use Redis in your flows for things like setting and getting key-value pairs, managing expiration (TTL), or handling list data. Whether you're caching API responses or managing sessions, you can use Redis CLI to check your data.

For SRL's multiregion platform, Redis serves as the central caching layer for storing recent quote results, driver shift statuses, and regional delivery trends. This enables fast data access across distributed applications, especially during high-demand hours when performance is critical.

Anypoint Code Builder

Everything you've learned about working with queues—whether it's Anypoint MQ, VM queues, or third-party options—applies equally in ACB. The runtime behavior doesn't change. What's different is how you configure those components. ACB introduces a streamlined interface where you define queues, connectors, and properties using lightweight forms and inline YAML or XML views. While Studio relies heavily on drag-and-drop from the palette, ACB emphasizes clarity through declarative structure and contextual wizards.

Before we can start publishing or consuming messages in our Mule flow, we need to bring the Anypoint MQ Connector into the project. This connector enables us to integrate with the Anypoint MQ service—without it, we won't be able to access the Publish, Consume, or Subscribe operations required to interact with queues.

Let's begin by adding the Anypoint MQ Connector using the UI inside ACB. In this example, we'll use the Add Component feature. As shown in Figure 7-20, we search for "mq" and select "Anypoint MQ Connector - Mule 4" from the list. Once selected, the connector is added to our project's dependencies and becomes available for use within our flow configuration.

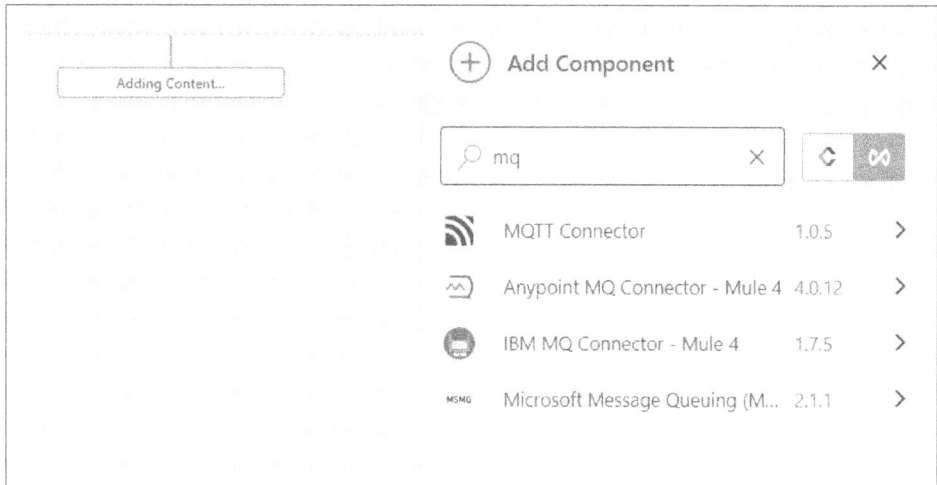

Figure 7-20. Add Component MQ

Once the connector is added, ACB loads and displays the available operations for Anypoint MQ—including Publish, Consume, Subscribe, Ack, and Nack. These operations follow the same logic and behavior you're familiar with in Anypoint Studio, but in ACB, the configuration experience is more transparent, modular, and declarative. This makes it easier to understand how data flows through the application and how each component contributes to the overall messaging behavior.

After adding the connector, the next step is to create a connection to the Anypoint MQ service. This connection defines the client ID, client secret, and the MQ region that your application will use to authenticate and interact with queues. As shown in Figure 7-21, the connection panel in ACB provides a clear and guided interface for entering these values. Once saved, this connection becomes reusable across all MQ operations within your flow.

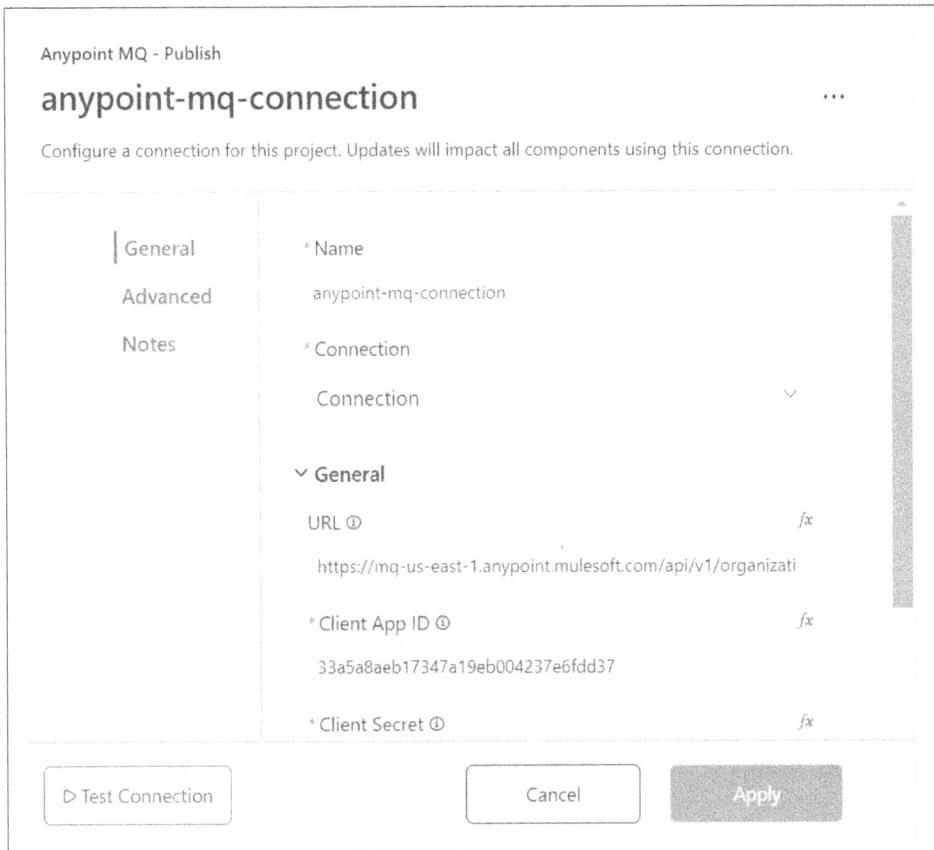

Figure 7-21. Create MQ Connection

Now that the connection is created and successfully tested, we're ready to use the Publish operation in our flow. In the ACB interface, we select Publish from the list of available operations, which automatically inserts it into the Mule flow.

This operation is used to send messages to an Anypoint MQ queue, and just like in Studio, we'll need to configure key details to make it work properly. The most important field here is the Destination, which defines the name of the queue where the message should be delivered. As shown in Figure 7-22, the configuration panel in ACB makes it easy to enter the queue name and any additional properties such as delivery delay or message TTL. With just a few clicks, the Publish operation is fully wired into your flow—ready to send data asynchronously and reliably.

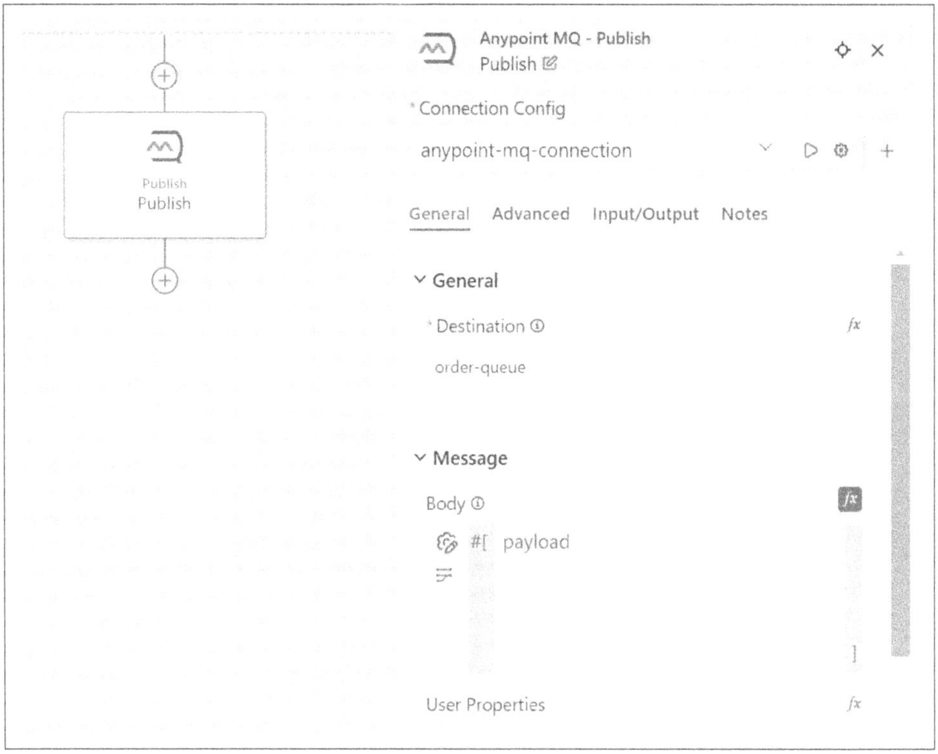

Figure 7-22. Configure Publish operation

To complete the asynchronous flow, we can now set up a second flow using the Consume operation to retrieve messages from the queue. This operation allows your application to process messages that have been published to the queue, enabling end-to-end message handling within your integration.

As shown in Figure 7-23, configuring the Consume operation in ACB is straightforward.

You'll specify the queue name (Destination) and can fine-tune behavior by adjusting additional settings such as acknowledgment mode, timeouts, and polling intervals. These options help ensure that your application retrieves messages reliably and with the right cadence for your use case.

With both Publish and Consume in place, your message flow is fully functional—ready to deliver robust, decoupled communication between services in a modern, event-driven architecture.

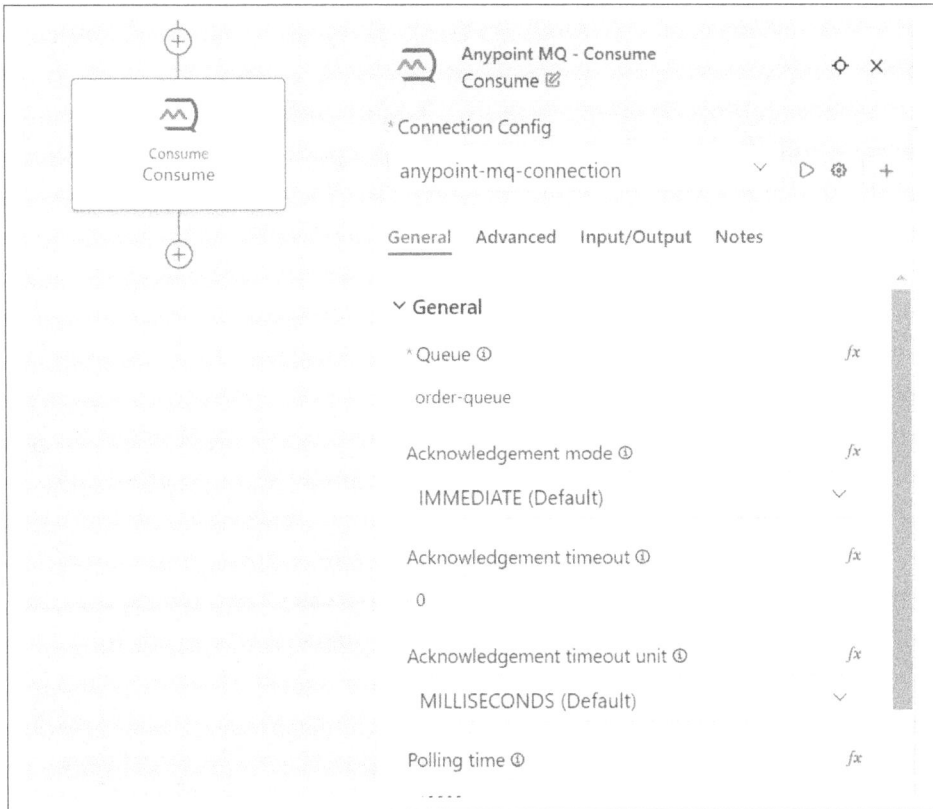

Figure 7-23. Configure Consume operation

Let's go one step further and create a new flow that reacts to messages in real time using the Subscribe operation. In ACB, this is your event-driven trigger—when a message lands in the queue, the flow fires automatically.

Create a new flow, hit the "+", and search for "mq:subscriber". Drop it in, then configure the queue name (Destination) and any extras like reconnection strategy or consumer settings. Just like that, you've got a flow that listens and responds the moment data shows up—no polling required.

This setup is great for real-time updates, alerts, or syncing events across systems. And ACB makes it clean and easy, with all the power of pub/sub messaging at your fingertips as you can see in Figure 7-24.

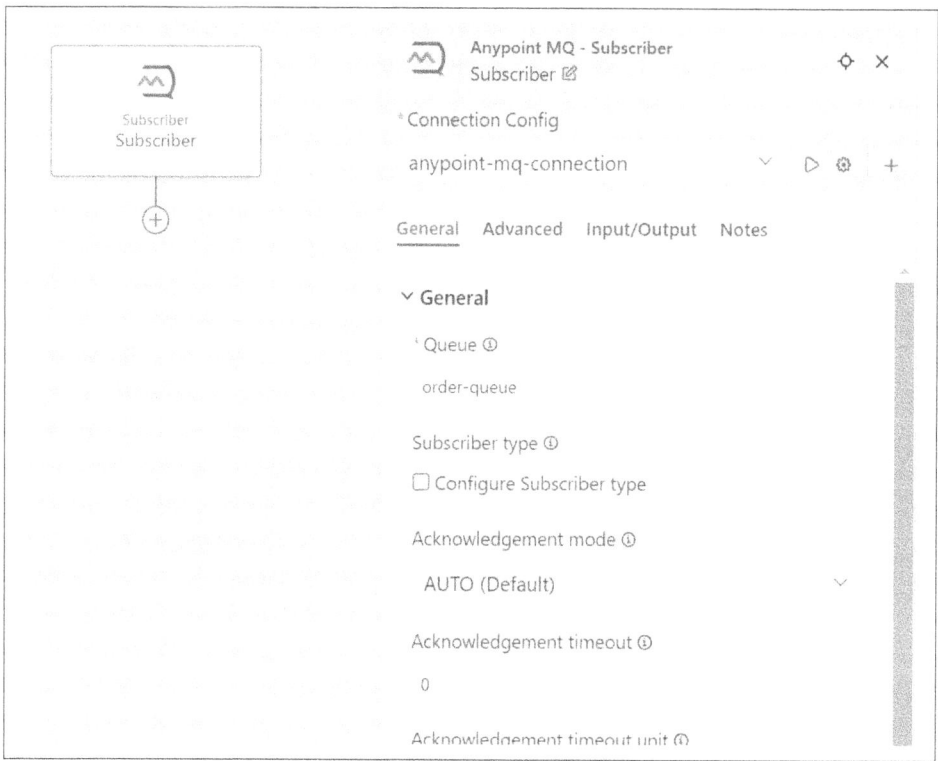

Figure 7-24. Configure Subscribe operation

And just like that, your flows are live in ACB. The message logic is still the same. But the way you build it? That's where ACB levels up the experience. No dragging components or digging through menus—just clean panels, inline editing, and a modern development experience that gives you full visibility into what's happening behind the scenes.

This isn't just "studio in a different outfit"—this is building smarter. You've added the MQ connector, created a reusable connection, and set up flows that publish, consume, and subscribe with ease—all from a sleek, code-first environment that keeps your work fast, clean, and scalable.

Summary

This chapter tackled the backbone of modern integrations: events and storage. You've unlocked the secrets of Anypoint MQ, VM queues, and third-party queues like RabbitMQ and Kafka, and now you know exactly when to use each one. Whether you need cloud-based messaging for large, distributed systems or fast, internal communication with VM queues, you're ready to make those calls with confidence. And let's not forget the magic of Object Store for keeping your data right where you need it, the Cache scope for supercharging your performance, and the powerhouse that is Redis for handling high-speed, distributed caching with ease.

We saw how these tools power real-world solutions like SRL, where reliable queuing and smart storage ensure smooth, scalable operations. SRL uses Anypoint MQ to manage shipping requests, Object Store to maintain session state, and Redis to deliver high-speed access to traffic and pricing data. Their success shows how the right integration patterns can transform complex systems into efficient, responsive platforms.

By mastering these tools, you've learned how to design systems that are not only resilient but also highly responsive. You now know how to ensure reliable message delivery, scale up your message flows, and manage data like a pro. Whether you're orchestrating event-driven architectures, streamlining data access, or optimizing storage, you've got the skills to build solid, high-performance integrations that can tackle even the most complex challenges.

Chapter 8 transitions into the world of DataWeave, where things get even more exciting. While the queuing systems and storage solutions we've covered handle moving and storing your data, DataWeave is your go-to for transforming it. It's the ultimate tool for shaping, enriching, and translating data from one format to another, ensuring that it's ready for any system or application it touches. Whether you're transforming JSON to XML, flattening nested structures, or cleaning up datasets, DataWeave makes it smooth, efficient, and powerful.

So buckle up—we're about to dive into how you can wield DataWeave to transform your data with the same confidence and precision you've applied to managing events and storage. Let's keep the momentum going and make your integrations not just smart and scalable, but fully data-driven!

CHAPTER 8

DataWeave: The Language of Integration

In Chapter 7, we examined the essential tools that keep modern integrations running smoothly. From message queues like Anypoint Message Queue (MQ), VM queues, RabbitMQ, and Kafka to data storage options like Object Store and Redis, you mastered strategies for reliable, scalable system design. With these skills, you can manage data flow and storage confidently and precisely.

At Super Routes Logistics (SRL), the team regularly transforms shipping, customer, and carrier data between systems. In this chapter, you'll see how SRL uses Data-Weave to streamline everything from order formatting to complex joins—turning raw logistics data into actionable insights. Moving and storing data is only part of the story—DataWeave brings your data to life. Whether you're reshaping JSON into XML, simplifying nested structures, or merging datasets, DataWeave is your ultimate ally. Think of it as your integration magic wand, effortlessly turning messy data (as someone might call it, gnarly XML) into polished, actionable formats.

DataWeave is more than just a tool—it's your ultimate companion for data transformation. With its intuitive syntax and powerful features, it empowers you to handle data with both efficiency and precision. We'll begin by exploring what makes Data-Weave unique, then move into practical ways to use it effectively. In this chapter, you'll uncover its syntax, core principles, and best practices. Get ready to take your integration skills to the next level!

Before we start, meet the DataWeave playground, a hands-on environment where you can experiment with transformations, debug scripts, and test your ideas in real time. Think of it as your lab to refine and perfect your data magic. Let's explore how DataWeave can elevate your integrations to a new level with the DataWeave playground shown in Figure 8-1.

Figure 8-1. DataWeave playground

Features include:

Script editor
Write and edit DataWeave transformations.

Debugging tools
Test and debug scripts with immediate feedback.

Data Viewer
Visualize input and output data side by side.

Tutorials
Interactive challenges guide you through mastering DataWeave with practical, hands-on examples.

> Learning DataWeave? Take advantage of the interactive tutorials (*https://oreil.ly/MtAJi*) available in the DataWeave playground. These challenges guide you step by step through common transformation scenarios, helping you practice and master DataWeave with real-world examples.

As you explore the DataWeave playground, you've taken the first steps into the exciting realm of data transformation. With its intuitive tools and interactive challenges, you now have a solid foundation to start mastering DataWeave. But this is just the beginning of your journey. Ahead lies the heart of DataWeave, where its essential principles and powerful techniques await.

DataWeave: The Essentials

DataWeave opens the door to a world where data transformation feels less like a task and more like an adventure. Picture venturing into an enterprise of tangled JSON, cryptic XML, and sprawling CSV files—only to emerge with perfectly structured, seamless outputs. Designed to tame the chaos of disparate data formats, DataWeave equips you with the tools to map, convert, and enrich data with precision and creativity.

Functional Programming Principles

At its core, DataWeave applies functional programming principles: it emphasizes *immutability* (keeping data unchangeable), *declarative logic* (describing the desired outcome), and *pure functions* (self-contained pieces of logic that take input, perform a specific task, and return output).

Here's a little bit more about functional programming:

Data is immutable
> Once created, it remains unchanged. Transformations produce entirely new data structures, eliminating side effects and making scripts more predictable and easier to debug.

Declarative logic further simplifies tasks
> You focus on the outcome rather than the steps to achieve it. For example, instead of looping through a dataset manually, you can simply state, *Show me all items priced below $20.*

Pure functions are reliable and reusable
> Independent and consistent, they enhance reliability and make your scripts easier to maintain.

You focus on defining what your data should look like, and DataWeave handles the *how* seamlessly. The result is cleaner, more efficient, and highly reliable scripts with no unnecessary complexity.

The Evolution of DataWeave

DataWeave, created by MuleSoft, first appeared in Mule 3.7 in 2015, replacing the old DataMapper. DataMapper was a graphical tool that many found cumbersome and limiting when it came to complex transformations. DataWeave emerged as a powerful, text-based scripting solution, offering a much-needed upgrade to integration professionals. With its intuitive syntax and robust capabilities, DataWeave quickly proved its versatility, handling everything from straightforward field mappings to intricate multistep transformations.

Over time, it has become an essential tool for data integration, enabling developers to tackle challenges with flexibility and precision.

Key features include the following:

Text-based scripting
Simplifies writing and debugging transformations.

Wide format support
JSON, XML, CSV, Excel, and even Avro types.

Extensibility
Reusable scripts and libraries for efficiency.

Advanced annotations
Metadata support was introduced in DataWeave 2.8.0.

The latest version, DataWeave 2.8.0, was released in October 2024 as part of Mule 4.8.0, bringing even more capabilities to this powerhouse tool.

DataWeave in Salesforce: A Revolutionary Tool

Beyond its use in MuleSoft integrations, DataWeave has transformed how Salesforce Flows handles data. Thanks to the DataWeave in Apex feature, you can now weave complex data transformations directly into Apex code within Salesforce. Imagine transforming CSV files into polished Salesforce objects or merging datasets without writing endless lines of custom Apex. It's like having an on-demand data wizard inside your flow builder, ready to tackle even the trickiest transformations.

Even better, DataWeave seamlessly integrates within Salesforce's execution limits, like heap size and CPU time, ensuring smooth and efficient performance. Whether you're reformatting data for analytics or syncing external data sources, DataWeave takes the heavy lifting out of data manipulation, leaving you with a more streamlined and dynamic workflow.

DataWeave Basics

Let's get started with the basics and explore the core components of DataWeave, including its syntax, data formats, and practical applications. From writing your first script to navigating tools like the DataWeave playground, this section is designed to equip you with the essential knowledge and confidence to begin transforming data effectively.

DataWeave structure

DataWeave scripts are structured into three sections (see Figure 8-2):

Header
> Declares output `mimeType` and any relevant functions or variables that will be utilized within the executed script

Delimiter
> Separates the header from the body

Body
> Executable script that will be put into format as declared by header

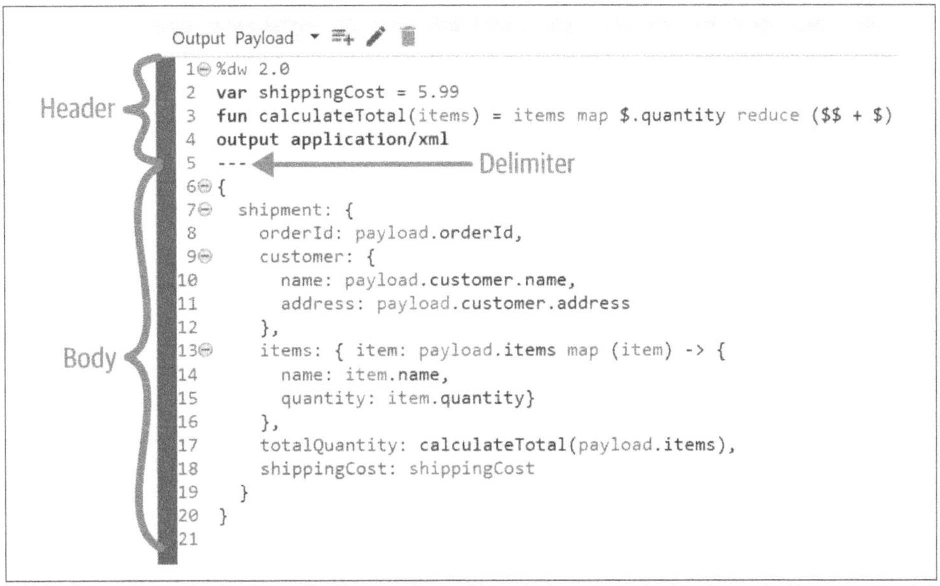

```
    Output Payload  ▼ ≡+ ✎ 🗑
    1⊖ %dw 2.0
    2   var shippingCost = 5.99
    3   fun calculateTotal(items) = items map $.quantity reduce ($$ + $)
    4   output application/xml
    5   ---          ◄─────────────── Delimiter
    6⊖ {
    7⊖   shipment: {
    8        orderId: payload.orderId,
    9⊖       customer: {
    10         name: payload.customer.name,
    11         address: payload.customer.address
    12       },
    13⊖      items: { item: payload.items map (item) -> {
    14         name: item.name,
    15         quantity: item.quantity}
    16       },
    17       totalQuantity: calculateTotal(payload.items),
    18       shippingCost: shippingCost
    19     }
    20  }
    21
```

Figure 8-2. DataWeave structure

Understanding input and output formats

Notice line 4 of the code in Figure 8-2. It begins with output, which will identify the output data format to use. DataWeave supports a wide range of formats; refer to MuleSoft's official documentation (*https://oreil.ly/iNwgu*) for the entire listing. In this book, we will just mention a few:

JSON
> Commonly used for APIs and lightweight data exchange.

XML
> Used in enterprise integrations and legacy systems.

CSV
> Ideal for flat-file data.

Excel
> Useful for structured data reports.

DWL (DataWeave Language)
> A specialized format for saving reusable DataWeave scripts, DWL files are used to modularize and manage complex transformations, allowing developers to maintain consistency and reuse logic across projects. They are also an excellent format for testing and refining scripts in development environments before deploying them to production.

You will learn how to configure the input and output formats in the script's header and adapt transformations for each format seamlessly. Imagine receiving input data in JSON format from a web API and needing to transform it into XML for compatibility with a legacy system. Or perhaps you need to make a simple change, like reformatting a date, or handle something more complex, like restructuring an entire dataset. DataWeave handles these transformations precisely and efficiently, ensuring every step aligns seamlessly. This flexibility empowers you to meet the diverse demands of integration workflows, making data exchange across platforms feel effortless. By dynamically converting between formats, such as JSON to XML for enterprise communication, DataWeave ensures smooth and adaptable data handling across various systems.

DataWeave types

The DataWeave body is the powerhouse of your transformations, built with one or more expressions that come together to produce the final output. DataWeave expressions generate specific types, ranging from simple primitives like `Strings`, `Numbers`, `Booleans`, `Dates`, `Times`, and `DateTimes` to more dynamic structures like `Arrays` and `Objects`. These building blocks make DataWeave a versatile and efficient tool for any integration scenario:

- Primitive types:
  - `String`: "Hello, World!"
  - `Number`: 42
  - `Boolean`: True (or false)
  - `Date`: |2024-12-24|
  - `Time`: |14:30:00|
  - `DateTime`: |2024-12-24T14:30:00|

- `Arrays`: Lists represented as [value1, value2, value3] for handling ordered data collections
- `Objects`: Structured key-value pairs like { key1: value1, key2: value2 }

What makes DataWeave so powerful is its ability to dynamically create array values, object keys, and object values from other expressions, giving you the flexibility to handle transformations easily.

Where DataWeave is used

DataWeave scripts can be utilized in various scenarios across MuleSoft applications to meet diverse transformation needs. Here are some common use cases:

Transform Message
Often used in the Transform Message component (see Figure 8-3) within a Mule flow to reshape and convert data formats as they move between systems.

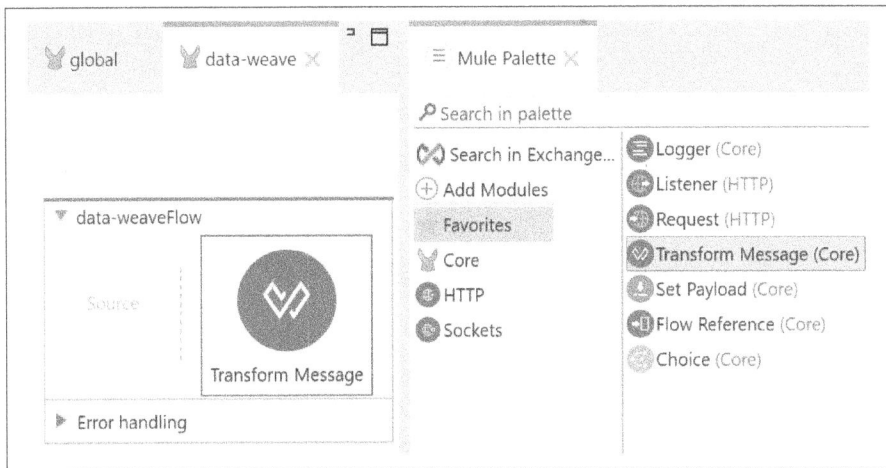

Figure 8-3. Transform Message processor

Processors with `fx` *option*
DataWeave expressions can be leveraged in processors that support the `fx` (function) option, such as Set Variable shown in Figure 8-4, to define custom logic dynamically.

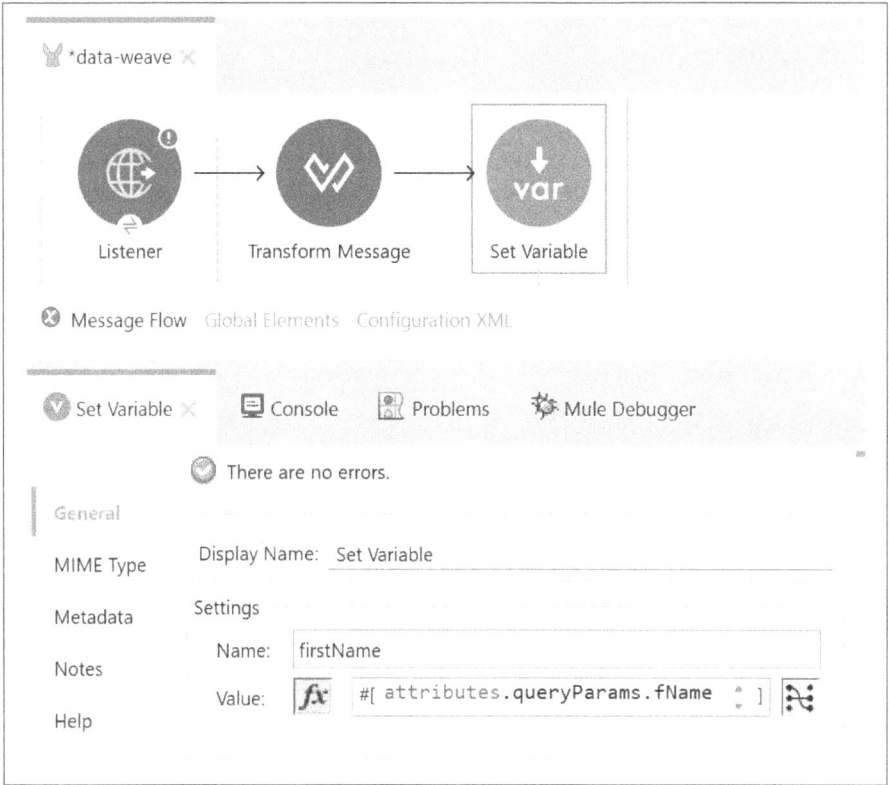

Figure 8-4. Processors with the function option

DataWeave as an expression

This is achieved by wrapping the code in #[*dataWeave code block*] syntax, as shown in Figure 8-5.

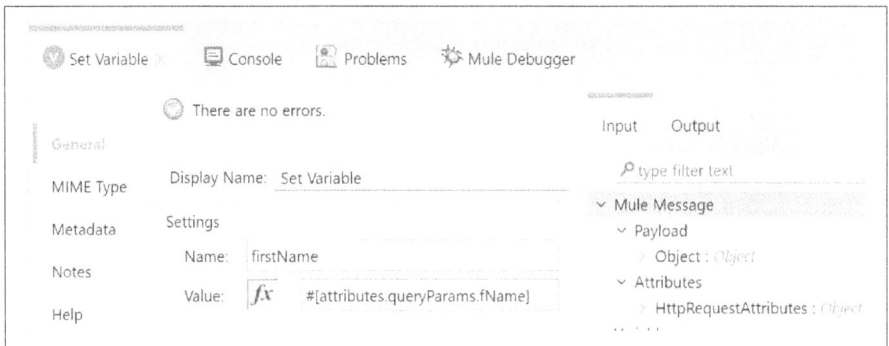

Figure 8-5. Expression syntax

DWK libraries and modules

DataWeave scripts can be stored in DWL files or custom modules for reusable, modularized transformations. These allow for consistent logic and efficient management of complex transformations across multiple projects, which we will use later in this chapter.

Writing your first transformation

When learning a new programming language, a common starting point is a "Hello World" example. In DataWeave, this first step introduces the basics of data transformation. Even a simple script can demonstrate key concepts and set the foundation for more complex integrations. This guide will walk you through writing your first transformation and understanding the core structure of a DataWeave script.

We start with a simple JSON input—a straightforward key-value pair where the key is "name" and the value is "World":

```
{
  "name": "World"
}
```

This is how it works:

- Using DataWeave, we access the payload, which holds the input data, and extract the "name" value.

- We combine this value with the static text "Hello, " and add an exclamation mark, using the ++ operator to construct a complete greeting.

- The result is wrapped in a new JSON object under a key called message.

Here's the DataWeave code:

```
%dw 2.0
output application/json
---
{
  message: "Hello, " ++ payload.name ++ "!" as String
}
```

The output shown in Figure 8-6 shows the final result. It is a structured JSON object delivering a greeting: "Hello, World!"

```
OUTPUT          JSON

1   {
2       "message": "Hello, World!!"
3   }
```

Figure 8-6. JSON output from DataWeave script

SRL uses DataWeave daily to transform complex datasets between systems—whether it's converting incoming orders, enriching them with customer preferences, or reformatting them for external carrier APIs. By applying the techniques we've explored so far, SRL ensures that its operations remain efficient, scalable, and tailored to partner requirements.

Now it's time to take the next step into real-world applications. Let's bring this to life with our SRL shipping use case. Imagine you're managing shipments for a global ecommerce business. You receive order data in JSON and need to convert it into an XML format to send to a shipping partner. This is where the true power of DataWeave shines—allowing you to seamlessly transform data structures while meeting the unique requirements of business processes.

Your input data is as follows:

```
{
  "orderId": "78910",
  "customer": {
    "name": "Jane Smith",
    "address": "456 Oak Avenue, Metropolis, NY, 10101"
  },
  "items": [
    {
      "name": "Smartphone",
      "quantity": 2
    },
    {
      "name": "Charging Cable",
      "quantity": 5
    },
    {
      "name": "Phone Case",
      "quantity": 1
    }
  ]
}
```

The DataWeave code:

```
%dw 2.0
var shippingCost = 5.99
fun calculateTotal(items) = items map $.quantity reduce ($$ + $)
output application/xml
---
{
  shipment: {
    orderId: payload.orderId,
    customer: {
      name: payload.customer.name,
      address: payload.customer.address
    },
    items: { item: payload.items map (item) -> {
      name: item.name,
      quantity: item.quantity}
    },
    totalQuantity: calculateTotal(payload.items),
    shippingCost: shippingCost
  }
}
```

Here's how it works:

- Declare a variable (`shippingCost`) to represent a constant value that can be used consistently throughout the script. This helps simplify future updates to the shipping cost since it only needs to be changed in one place.

- Create a function (`calculateTotal`) to dynamically compute the total quantity of items by using the `map` function to extract quantities from each item and the `reduce` function to sum them up. This approach is both concise and efficient for handling lists of varying sizes.

- Use the `map` function to iterate through the `items` array, transforming each object in the array into a new format. Specifically, we are creating a simplified representation of each item, extracting its `name` and `quantity` fields.

- Build the XML structure dynamically by combining the output of the function, variable, and mapping logic into a simplified format. This ensures that the final output aligns with the requirements of the shipping partner's system.

- Integrate all these components into the transformation, making the script both flexible and reusable for similar scenarios in the future.

Here's the output:

```
<?xml version='1.0' encoding='UTF-8'?>
<shipment>
  <orderId>78910</orderId>
  <customer>
```

```
    <name>Jane Smith</name>
    <address>456 Oak Avenue, Metropolis, NY, 10101</address>
  </customer>
  <items>
    <item>
      <name>Smartphone</name>
      <quantity>2</quantity>
    </item>
    <item>
      <name>Charging Cable</name>
      <quantity>5</quantity>
    </item>
    <item>
      <name>Phone Case</name>
      <quantity>1</quantity>
    </item>
  </items>
  <totalQuantity>8</totalQuantity>
  <shippingCost>5.99</shippingCost>
</shipment>
```

This script transforms your JSON order data into a well-structured XML, perfectly tailored for the logistics workflow. It is now converted into an XML format to send to your shipping partner.

Simple Transformations: Dates

Working with dates in DataWeave is straightforward, thanks to its robust support for date and time manipulations. Whether you're parsing, formatting, or extracting parts of a date, DataWeave empowers you to get it done efficiently.

Parsing dates

Turning a date string into a date object is often step one when working with shipping schedules or delivery timelines. DataWeave supports many ISO 8601 date formats, which ensures compatibility across systems. For a comprehensive guide to ISO 8601 formats, you can refer to the Wikipedia article "ISO 8601" (*https://oreil.ly/jEOmE*).

Here's the DataWeave code:

```
%dw 2.0
output application/json
---
{
  deliveryDate: "2023-12-31" as Date
}
Output:
{
  "deliveryDate": "2023-12-31T00:00:00Z"
}
```

Formatting dates

Need to format shipping dates for an external system or customer-friendly output? No problem; here is how to do that.

Here's the DataWeave code:

```
%dw 2.0
output application/json
---
{
  formattedDeliveryDate: ("2023-12-31" as Date) as String {format: "mm/dd/yyyy"}
}
```

Here's the output:

```
{
  "formattedDeliveryDate": "12/31/2023"
}
```

Extracting date components

Drill down into delivery dates to extract exactly what you need for your logistics system. Here's the DataWeave code:

```
%dw 2.0
output application/json
---
{
  year: ("2023-12-31" as Date).year,
  month: ("2023-12-31" as Date).month,
  day: ("2023-12-31" as Date).day
}
```

And here's the output:

```
{
  "year": 2023,
  "month": 12,
  "day": 31
}
```

These simple yet effective transformations handle many date-related tasks with ease and precision, perfect for keeping your shipping operations on track.

Complex Transformations: filter, map, reduce

At SRL, managing thousands of shipments daily means dealing with sprawling datasets that require more than simple transformations. Whether it's isolating express deliveries for priority handling, generating shipment labels tailored to each region, or calculating total freight weight for invoicing, the team relies heavily on DataWeave's advanced capabilities to streamline the process.

Sometimes you need to tap into DataWeave's advanced capabilities to tackle complex shipping data scenarios. Let's explore some of its functions, such as filter, map, and reduce, which allow you to efficiently refine, reshape, and aggregate your data. These tools are essential for creating meaningful and actionable outputs from even the most intricate datasets.

filter function

The filter function in DataWeave is a powerful tool for refining your data by removing elements that don't meet specified conditions. Think of it as a way to sift through your data and keep only what's relevant to your use case. It works seamlessly with both arrays and objects, making it highly versatile for various transformation scenarios. Let's say SRL needs to filter shipments based on specific criteria, such as those scheduled for express delivery. Here is an example:

- With arrays, you might use filter to retain only the orders that are marked "Express."

- With objects, you can apply filter to keep only the key-value pairs where the value meets a certain condition.

Here's the DataWeave code:

```
%dw 2.0
output application/json
---
{
  expressShipments: [
    {id: 1, deliveryType: "Standard"},
    {id: 2, deliveryType: "Express"},
    {id: 3, deliveryType: "Express"}
  ] filter ((shipment) -> shipment.deliveryType == "Express")
}
```

And here's the output:

```
{
  "expressShipments": [
    {"id": 2, "deliveryType": "Express"},
    {"id": 3, "deliveryType": "Express"}
  ]
}
```

map function

The map function in DataWeave is your go-to tool for transforming data structures by applying a defined logic to each element in an array or object. It's like crafting a personalized transformation for every item, whether it's reshaping, reformatting, or enriching your data.

With map, you can iterate through arrays or objects, apply changes to each element, and return a new array or object with the modified data. It's incredibly useful for scenarios where data needs to be structured differently for downstream systems. Here's how it works:

- For arrays, it transforms each element based on the logic you define.

- For objects, it applies changes to values and keys (if needed), creating a new object. Think of it as DataWeave's version of a shipping label generator.

Here's the DataWeave code:

```
%dw 2.0
output application/json
---
{
  shipmentLabels: [
    {id: 1, destination: "New York"},
    {id: 2, destination: "Los Angeles"}
  ] map ((shipment) -> {label: "SHIP TO: " ++ shipment.destination})
}
And here's the output:
{
  "shipmentLabels": [
    {"label": "SHIP TO: New York"},
    {"label": "SHIP TO: Los Angeles"}
  ]
}
```

reduce function

The reduce function in DataWeave is a powerful tool for combining elements of an array into a single value or summary. It's especially useful for aggregating data, such as calculating totals, concatenating strings, or merging complex objects. By applying a specified logic, you can distill a large dataset into something manageable and meaningful.

Here's how it works: reduce iterates through an array, applying your logic to an accumulator (a running total or result) and the current item, updating the accumulator with each iteration. The final value of the accumulator is returned as the output:

```
array reduce ((accumulator, item, index) -> transformation, initialValue)
```

Terms used in the code:

accumulator
> The running result of the reduction

item
> The current array element being processed

initialValue
> The starting value for the accumulator

For example, to calculate the total weight of all packages, here is the DataWeave code:

```
%dw 2.0
output application/json
---
{
  totalWeight: [
    {id: 1, weight: 5},
    {id: 2, weight: 10},
    {id: 3, weight: 15}
  ] reduce ((acc, shipment) -> acc + shipment.weight, 0)
```

Here's the output:

```
{
  "totalWeight": 30
}
```

Combining map and filter

You can combine operations for more powerful transformations. The following code block demonstrates the combined use of filter and map functions to transform and refine an array of shipping data into a new structure that highlights express deliveries:

```
%dw 2.0
output application/json
---
{
  expressLabels: [
    {id: 1, deliveryType: "Standard", destination: "New
York"},
    {id: 2, deliveryType: "Express", destination: "Los
Angeles"},
    {id: 3, deliveryType: "Express", destination: "Chicago"}
  ]
    filter ((shipment) -> shipment.deliveryType ==
"Express")
    map ((shipment) -> {label: "EXPRESS SHIP TO: " ++
shipment.destination})
}
```

Here's how it works—the `expressLabels` array contains objects, each representing a shipment with properties:

id
A unique identifier for the shipment

deliveryType
The type of delivery (e.g., standard or express)

destination
The shipment's destination city

You use the `filter` operation:

- The `filter` function selects only those shipments where the `deliveryType` is Express.
- This effectively removes all objects with a `deliveryType` of Standard.

Next, you use the `map` operation:

- After filtering, the `map` function transforms each remaining shipment object into a new object with a single property, `label`.
- The `label` property combines the text "EXPRESS SHIP TO: " with the destination value from each shipment.

The result is an array of objects, each containing the formatted shipping label for express deliveries. With filtering, mapping, and reducing, DataWeave provides essential tools for processing complex shipping and delivery data efficiently:

```
{
  "expressLabels": [
    {"label": "EXPRESS SHIP TO: Los Angeles"},
    {"label": "EXPRESS SHIP TO: Chicago"}
  ]
}
```

The preceding code is a great example of using `filter` to focus on specific data (express shipments) and `map` to restructure that data into a user-friendly format (shipping labels). It's perfect for scenarios where you need to generate targeted outputs based on specific criteria while reshaping the results for further use.

Joining Datasets: Concatenate, Join Functions

At SRL, seamless coordination between shipment, customer, and warehouse data is critical. When preparing dispatch schedules, the logistics team must align orders with customer preferences and regional availability. The shipment and customer records live in different systems—but with DataWeave's join capabilities, these datasets can be merged into a unified view, enabling smarter routing, better communication, and faster delivery.

Joining datasets is a core capability in DataWeave, enabling the merging and restructuring of related data into a unified view. This is especially useful in shipping scenarios, where you may need to combine shipment details, customer information, and carrier schedules to create a seamless workflow. DataWeave offers a variety of functions and operators to join, concatenate, and enrich data just for these purposes. Let's look at the various ways we can achieve this.

Concatenating arrays and strings

The ++ operator is used to concatenate arrays or strings, making it simple to append data or combine textual elements. In shipping, this is useful for creating unified lists or generating labels. Let's combine shipments from multiple warehouses.

Here's the DataWeave code:

```
%dw 2.0
output application/json
---
[
  {shipmentId: 1, warehouse: "East"},
  {shipmentId: 2, warehouse: "West"}
] ++ [
  {shipmentId: 3, warehouse: "North"}
]
```

Here's our output:

```
[
  {shipmentId: 1, warehouse: "East"},
  {shipmentId: 2, warehouse: "West"},
  {shipmentId: 3, warehouse: "North"}
]
```

Now let's create shipment labels. The DataWeave code looks like this:

```
%dw 2.0
output application/json
var shipment = "123456"
var warehouseLocation = "West"


---
"SHIPMENT-" ++ shipment ++ "-WAREHOUSE-" ++  warehouseLocation
```

Here's our output:

```
"SHIPMENT-123456-WAREHOUSE-West"
```

Joining arrays with matching keys

In the bustling world of logistics, a seamless flow of information is key to keeping customers happy and shipments on time. SRL, our example company, manages thousands of daily deliveries. We have two critical datasets: one for shipments and another for customer details. The shipment data includes destinations and carrier assignments, while the customer data contains vital information like names, contact details, and preferred delivery times.

However, these datasets exist in separate silos. The magic of joining arrays in DataWeave bridges this gap, using a common key: customer.customerId in the customer dataset and shipment.customerId in the shipment dataset. This shared key links the two, allowing us to combine the datasets into a unified, enriched structure that you can see in Figure 8-7.

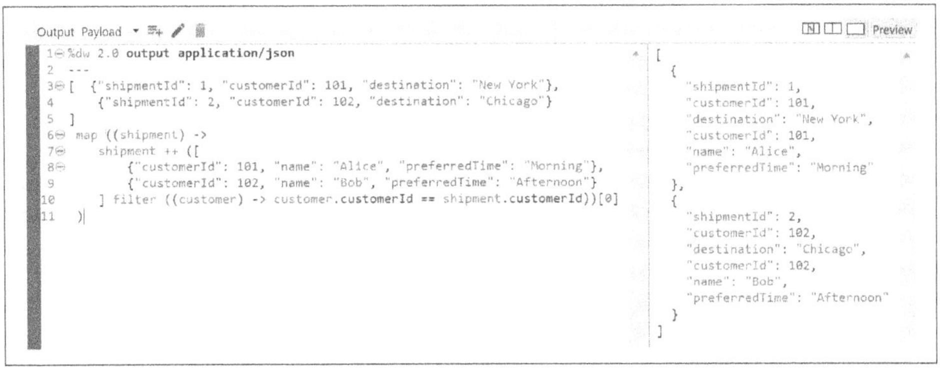

Figure 8-7. DataWeave code and output results

We have an array of shipment data:

```
[
    {"shipmentId": 1, "customerId": 101, "destination": "New York"},
    {"shipmentId": 2, "customerId": 102, "destination": "Chicago"}
]
```

And an array of customer data:

```
[
    {"customerId": 101, "name": "Alice", "preferredTime": "Morning"},
    {"customerId": 102, "name": "Bob", "preferredTime": "Afternoon"}
]
```

Using map and filter, we can merge these arrays, enriching each shipment with customer details:

```
%dw 2.0
output application/json
---
[
```

```
  {"shipmentId": 1, "customerId": 101, "destination": "New York"},
  {"shipmentId": 2, "customerId": 102, "destination": "Chicago"}
] map ((shipment) ->
  shipment ++ ([
    {"customerId": 101, "name": "Alice", "preferredTime": "Morning"},
    {"customerId": 102, "name": "Bob", "preferredTime": "Afternoon"}
  ] filter ((customer) -> customer.customerId == shipment.customerId))[0]
)
```

Here's the output:

```
[
  {
    "shipmentId": 1,
    "customerId": 101,
    "destination": "New York",
    "name": "Alice",
    "preferredTime": "Morning"
  },
  {
    "shipmentId": 2,
    "customerId": 102,
    "destination": "Chicago",
    "name": "Bob",
    "preferredTime": "Afternoon"
  }
]
```

The results of the enriched dataset allow us to do the following:

- Address customers personally (for example, "Alice, your shipment to New York is on the way!")

- Plan deliveries according to customer preferences (morning for Alice, afternoon for Bob)

- Ensure better communication and a more personalized shipping experience

Merging objects (key-value pairs)

The ++ operator can also merge objects by combining key-value pairs into a single object. This is helpful when integrating additional data, like tracking information, into shipment records.

We have an object of shipment data:

```
{
  "shipmentId": 1,
  "destination": "New York",
  "weight": "5kg"
}
```

And an object of tracking data:

```
{
  "trackingNumber": "TRACK12345",
  "status": "In Transit",
  "lastUpdated": "2024-12-24T10:00:00Z"
}
```

With the power of the ++ operator, we can merge these two objects into a single, enriched dataset. This creates a comprehensive view of the shipment, combining the static details (like destination and weight) with dynamic tracking updates (see Figure 8-8).

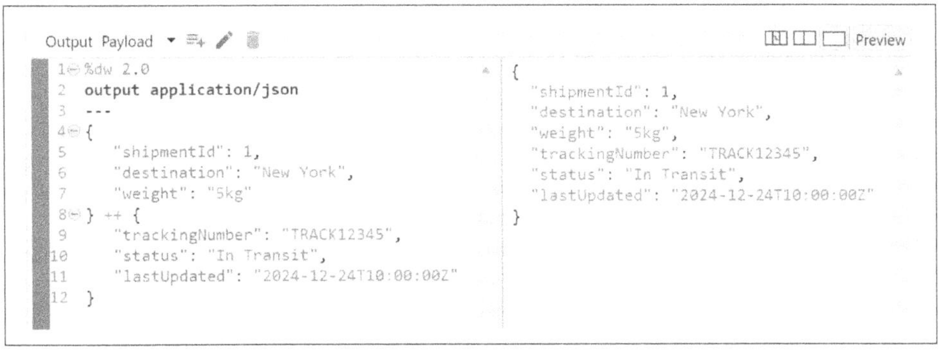

Figure 8-8. DataWeave code and output results for ++

Here's our DataWeave code:

```
%dw 2.0
output application/json
---
{
  "shipmentId": 1,
  "destination": "New York",
  "weight": "5kg"
} ++ {
  "trackingNumber": "TRACK12345",
  "status": "In Transit",
  "lastUpdated": "2024-12-24T10:00:00Z"
}
```

And here's the output:

```
{
  "shipmentId": 1,
  "destination": "New York",
  "weight": "5kg",
  "trackingNumber": "TRACK12345",
  "status": "In Transit",
  "lastUpdated": "2024-12-24T10:00:00Z"
}
```

This single, enriched object gives the SRL team the clarity it needs. With one glance, the team knows the shipment's destination, weight, tracking number, current status, and the last time it was updated. This consolidated data empowers both their operations team and their customers.

Handling null and missing data

SRL's shipment data sometimes arrives incomplete; when this happens, it can cause errors. The second shipment lacks carrier information, and the third shipment lacks a destination. Downstream systems and users might experience errors or confusion without handling these gaps. Here is our shipment data:

```
[
  {"shipmentId": 1, "destination": "New York", "carrier": "FedEx"},
  {"shipmentId": 2, "destination": "Chicago", "carrier": null},
  {"shipmentId": 3, "destination": null, "carrier": "UPS"}
]
```

DataWeave's `default` function allows you to replace null values with predefined defaults, ensuring the data remains consistent and meaningful.

Here's the DataWeave code:

```
%dw 2.0
output application/json
---
[
  {"shipmentId": 1, "destination": "New York", "carrier": "FedEx"},
  {"shipmentId": 2, "destination": "Chicago", "carrier": null},
  {"shipmentId": 3, "destination": null, "carrier": "UPS"}
] map ((shipment) -> shipment ++ {
  destination: shipment.destination default "Unknown Destination",
  carrier: shipment.carrier default "Unknown Carrier"
})
```

And here's the output:

```
[
  {"shipmentId": 1, "destination": "New York", "carrier": "FedEx"},
  {"shipmentId": 2, "destination": "Chicago", "carrier": "Unknown Carrier"},
  {"shipmentId": 3, "destination": "Unknown Destination", "carrier": "UPS"}
]
```

The results of providing fallback values with `default` ensures the following:

Data integrity
Null values are replaced with meaningful defaults, preventing errors.

User clarity
Information gaps are indicated, helping customers and support teams understand incomplete data.

System compatibility
Downstream systems can process data without disruptions caused by null fields.

The join function: merging data for seamless integration

The `join` function in DataWeave is a powerful tool that allows you to merge datasets by matching elements based on specific criteria. It simplifies the process of combining arrays, especially when each dataset has its unique structure but shares a common key. This is invaluable for logistics companies like SRL when aligning shipment records with customer, carrier, or warehouse data.

The `join` function works by iterating through two arrays and matching their elements based on a provided condition. This creates a new array containing merged objects that align with your business requirements.

We have two datasets: one for shipments and another for customers. Both contain a shared key, `customerId`, that links the two. While we can use the ++ concatenation to achieve this, the following code shows how you can use the `join` function.

The shipment data contains information about shipments, including a `shipmentId`, `customerId`, and `destination`:

```
[
  {"shipmentId": 1, "customerId": 101, "destination": "New York"},
  {"shipmentId": 2, "customerId": 102, "destination": "Chicago"}
]
```

The customer data contains customer details, including a `customerId` and `name`:

```
[
  {"customerId": 101, "name": "Alice"},
  {"customerId": 102, "name": "Bob"}
]
```

Here's how it works:

1. The `join` operation combines elements from two arrays based on a matching condition.

2. In this case, the condition on `$.customerId == $$.customerId` ensures that each shipment is correctly linked to its corresponding customer:

   a. `$` refers to the current item in the first array (shipment data).

   b. `$$` refers to the current item in the second array (customer data).

   c. The condition specifies that the `customerId` in both arrays must match.

Here's the DataWeave code:

```
%dw 2.0
output application/json
---
(
  [
    {"shipmentId": 1, "customerId": 101, "destination": "New York"},
    {"shipmentId": 2, "customerId": 102, "destination": "Chicago"}
  ] join (
    [
      {"customerId": 101, "name": "Alice"},
      {"customerId": 102, "name": "Bob"}
    ]
  ) on $.customerId == $$.customerId
)
```

And here's the output:

```
[
  {
    "shipmentId": 1,
    "customerId": 101,
    "destination": "New York",
    "name": "Alice"
  },
  {
    "shipmentId": 2,
    "customerId": 102,
    "destination": "Chicago",
    "name": "Bob"
  }
]
```

The `join` function can also handle more complex conditions, such as joining based on multiple fields or applying transformations to the merged data. To test this out, let's do a `join` with multiple keys because shipments need to match `customerId` and a new field, `region`, in the customer dataset.

The condition for this join is more specific than a simple key match:

```
on ($.customerId == $$.customerId and $.region == $$.region)
```

Here is the interpretation:

- $ refers to the current object from the first array (shipment data).
- $$ refers to the current object from the second array (customer data).
- The join occurs only if both customerId and region match between the two objects.

Here's how it works:

- For each object in the shipment data array, the join function searches for a matching object in the customer data array.
- A match is determined when both the customerId and region fields are equal.

Here's the DataWeave code:

```
%dw 2.0
output application/json
---
(
  [
    {"shipmentId": 1, "customerId": 101, "region": "East",
"destination": "New York"},
    {"shipmentId": 2, "customerId": 102, "region": "West",
"destination": "Chicago"}
  ]
  join (
    [
      {"customerId": 101, "region": "East", "name": "Alice"},
      {"customerId": 102, "region": "West", "name": "Bob"}
    ]
  ) on ($.customerId == $$.customerId and $.region ==
$$.region)
)
```

Here's the output:

```
[
  {
    "shipmentId": 1,
    "customerId": 101,
    "region": "East",
    "destination": "New York",
    "name": "Alice"
  },
  {
    "shipmentId": 2,
```

```
    "customerId": 102,
    "region": "West",
    "destination": "Chicago",
    "name": "Bob"
  }
]
```

The result of joining datasets is a fundamental aspect of effective data integration, enabling the seamless consolidation of information from diverse sources. Whether you are concatenating arrays to build unified lists, merging objects with the ++ operator for enriched insights, or leveraging the join function to align datasets based on shared keys, DataWeave provides powerful tools to tackle complex integration challenges. By combining these functions with thoughtful handling of null or missing data, you can create robust, reliable data pipelines that drive smarter operations and better decision making. These techniques are essential for transforming raw, fragmented data into cohesive, actionable outputs that meet the needs of modern business applications.

Improving Performance: SRL's DataWeave Transformation Success Story

As SRL expanded its operations, it faced growing challenges in processing shipment data efficiently. Their DataWeave scripts, critical to integrating shipments, customer details, and carrier schedules, started to slow under the weight of high data volumes. Determined to maintain its reputation for reliability, SRL embarked on a journey to optimize its transformations. Through five core strategies, it turned performance roadblocks into opportunities for innovation.

Processing smarter with filters and streaming

SRL realized that much of the processed data wasn't relevant to their immediate needs. For instance, shipment manifests covered all regions, but operations often focused on specific areas, like the East region. By filtering early and enabling streaming, they ensured that only relevant data was processed, while keeping memory usage minimal.

Streaming data processes large datasets efficiently by reading them in chunks instead of loading everything into memory, preventing slowdowns or crashes—perfect for massive shipment logs or sensor data:

Purpose
Setting the streaming option to true in readUrl ensures that data is processed incrementally rather than loading the entire file into memory. This is crucial for handling large files (such as massive shipment manifests) without consuming excessive system resources.

Benefit
Reduces memory usage and allows the script to process large datasets efficiently.

Filtering data helps focus on what matters by selecting only the relevant entries, like picking shipments from a certain region while skipping the rest—think of it as skimming emails for the important ones:

Purpose

The `filter` function iterates through the data and selects only shipments where the region equals `"East"`.

Condition

`(shipment) -> shipment.region == "East"` is a lambda function that evaluates each shipment object. If the condition is `true`, the shipment is included in the output.

Let's look at an example for filtering shipments for the East region using streaming. The input, *largeShipmentManifest.json*, contains the following data:

```
[
  {"shipmentId": 1, "region": "East", "destination": "New York"},
  {"shipmentId": 2, "region": "West", "destination": "Chicago"},
  {"shipmentId": 3, "region": "East", "destination": "Boston"}
]
```

Here's the DataWeave code:

```
%dw 2.0
output application/json
---
readUrl("file:///largeShipmentManifest.json",
"application/json", {
  streaming: true
})
filter ((shipment) -> shipment.region == "East")
```

The result is that processing large manifests became efficient, allowing real-time transformations without performance bottlenecks.

Here's how it works:

1. *Read the file.* The `readUrl` function streams the data from the file *largeShipment-Manifest.json*.

2. *Filter the data.* The `filter` function processes each object in the array, checking whether the region is `"East"`. Only shipments that meet this condition are included in the output.

The output is the filtered shipments in JSON format:

```
[
  {"shipmentId": 1, "region": "East", "destination": "New York"},
  {"shipmentId": 3, "region": "East", "destination": "Boston"}
]
```

The result efficiently narrows a large dataset to only the relevant records (shipments for the East region). By combining filtering with streaming, SRL avoids memory overload and improves processing speed, making it ideal for high-volume logistics data.

Simplifying transformations

One of the most effective ways to optimize DataWeave transformations is by replacing nested loops with a combination of `filter` and `map`. We created this in an example earlier in this chapter. This approach simplifies the logic, reduces processing time, and makes scripts easier to maintain. Using the `filter` function, we narrow the dataset to only the relevant records, ensuring that we work with a smaller and more focused subset of data. Then we transform each element with the `map` function, adding or modifying key-value pairs as needed.

This streamlined method eliminates redundancy and handles data enrichment efficiently. Focusing on these two powerful functions achieves cleaner, faster, and more scalable transformations without the overhead of complex nested operations.

Optimizing with data structures and built-in functions

Choosing the right data structures and leveraging built-in DataWeave functions are key to creating efficient and maintainable transformations. Objects, with their fast lookup capabilities, are ideal for tasks like mapping shipment IDs to carriers, whereas arrays are better suited for sequential processing. Selecting the appropriate data structure—objects for lookups, and arrays for sequential processing—ensures the data structure aligns with the task, optimizing performance and reducing overhead.

Built-in functions like `orderBy`, `groupBy`, and `reduce` simplify common operations and are optimized for performance. For example, sorting shipments by destination using `orderBy` is faster, cleaner, and more readable than custom logic. Similarly, `groupBy` can effortlessly categorize shipments by region or carrier.

This strategy reduces script complexity, improves processing speed, and enhances readability. Selecting appropriate data structures and using preoptimized functions ensures that transformations are both effective and efficient, ready to handle real-world demands.

Let's take a closer look at this example. SRL needs to prepare a delivery schedule that does the following:

- Sorts shipments alphabetically by destination
- Groups shipments by their assigned region (for example, East, West)
- Combines `orderBy` and `groupBy` to efficiently organize and categorize the data in one clean transformation

Our input data includes shipments with `shipmentId`, `destination`, `region`, and `customerId`:

```
[
  {"shipmentId": 1, "destination": "Chicago", "region":
  "Midwest", "customerId": 101},
  {"shipmentId": 2, "destination": "New York", "region":
  "East", "customerId": 102},
  {"shipmentId": 3, "destination": "Boston", "region": "East",
  "customerId": 103},
  {"shipmentId": 4, "destination": "Los Angeles", "region":
  "West", "customerId": 104},
  {"shipmentId": 5, "destination": "Denver", "region":
  "Midwest", "customerId": 105}
]
```

Here's the DataWeave code using `orderBy` and `groupBy`:

```
%dw 2.0
output application/json
---
(
  [
    {"shipmentId": 1, "destination": "Chicago", "region":
    "Midwest", "customerId": 101},
    {"shipmentId": 2, "destination": "New York", "region":
    "East", "customerId": 102},
    {"shipmentId": 3, "destination": "Boston", "region": "East",
    "customerId": 103},
    {"shipmentId": 4, "destination": "Los Angeles", "region":
    "West", "customerId": 104},
    {"shipmentId": 5, "destination": "Denver", "region":
    "Midwest", "customerId": 105}
  ]
  orderBy $.destination
  groupBy $.region
)
```

Here's how `orderBy` works:

- Sorts shipments alphabetically by the `destination` field within each `region`
- Reorders the array of shipments based on the `destination` key

And here's how `groupBy` works:

- Groups the sorted shipments by their `region` field
- Creates a new object where each key represents a unique `region`, and its value is an array of shipments belonging to that `region`

Here's the output:

```
{
  "East": [
    {"shipmentId": 3, "destination": "Boston", "region":
  "East", "customerId": 103},
    {"shipmentId": 2, "destination": "New York", "region":
  "East", "customerId": 102}
  ],
  "Midwest": [
    {"shipmentId": 1, "destination": "Chicago", "region":
  "Midwest", "customerId": 101},
    {"shipmentId": 5, "destination": "Denver", "region":
  "Midwest", "customerId": 105}
  ],
  "West": [
    {"shipmentId": 4, "destination": "Los Angeles", "region":
  "West", "customerId": 104}
  ]
}
```

The results are as follows:

Efficient sorting

Using orderBy ensures that the shipment data is neatly organized by destination within each region.

Structured grouping

groupBy allows the data to be categorized by region, making it easier to analyze and act upon.

Scalability

This combined approach works seamlessly for larger datasets, handling both sorting and grouping in a single transformation.

> The question is whether to apply groupBy or orderBy first—it depends on the use case. Generally, applying groupBy first is best when categorizing data into meaningful groups before sorting within them, such as grouping shipments by region before ordering them by delivery date. However, in cases where sorting affects how data should be grouped, applying orderBy first makes more sense, like sorting transactions by date before grouping them by customer to maintain chronological order. If categorization is the primary goal, groupBy should come first, but if sorting is crucial before grouping, orderBy should take precedence.

Handling large data with pagination and parallel processing

When dealing with massive datasets, performance can become a significant challenge. To efficiently manage large volumes of data, you can use a combination of pagination to process data in manageable chunks and parallel processing to execute multiple tasks simultaneously. This strategy reduces memory usage and speeds up execution, ensuring that the system remains responsive even under heavy loads.

Pagination does the following:

- Breaks data into smaller, manageable chunks for processing
- Prevents memory overload by processing only a subset of data at a time
- Is ideal for use cases like retrieving shipments or invoices in batches

Parallel processing does the following:

- Executes multiple independent tasks simultaneously
- Utilizes system resources more effectively, reducing overall processing time
- Is useful for tasks like updating multiple shipment statuses or processing invoices across regions

The first example uses pagination to process a large dataset of shipments in smaller, manageable chunks. This approach ensures efficient memory usage and avoids overloading the system with massive datasets.

Here is the input dataset of shipment records:

```
[
  {"shipmentId": 1, "destination": "New York"},
  {"shipmentId": 2, "destination": "Chicago"},
  {"shipmentId": 3, "destination": "Boston"},
  {"shipmentId": 4, "destination": "Los Angeles"}
]
```

The goal is to divide this dataset into two batches of two shipments each for processing (of course, in a real-world example this would be much larger). Here's the DataWeave code:

```
%dw 2.0
output application/json
---
{
  batches: [0, 2] map ((batchStart) ->
    readUrl("shipments.json", "application/json")
    slice(batchStart, 2)
  )
}
```

And here's how it works:

batches *array*

The batches key defines a series of starting points for slicing the dataset into chunks of two.

[0, 2] represents the starting indexes for each batch:

- Batch 1 starts at index 0.
- Batch 2 starts at index 2.

readUrl *function*

Simulates reading the dataset from a file called *shipments.json*.

In a real-world scenario, this would retrieve data from an external source.

slice *function*

Extracts a subset of the dataset starting from batchStart, and includes two records in each batch.

For example:

- For batchStart = 0, it retrieves the first two records.
- For batchStart = 2, it retrieves the next two records.

map *function*

Iterates over each value in [0, 2] (the starting indexes) to apply the slicing logic.

This generates an array of batches.

Here's the output:

```
{
  "batches": [
    [
      {"shipmentId": 1, "destination": "New York"},
      {"shipmentId": 2, "destination": "Chicago"}
    ],
    [
      {"shipmentId": 3, "destination": "Boston"},
      {"shipmentId": 4, "destination": "Los Angeles"}
    ]
  ]
}
```

The results are as follows:

Efficient memory usage
Instead of loading the entire dataset into memory, smaller chunks are processed individually, reducing the risk of memory overload.

Scalable design
This approach can handle datasets of any size by adjusting the batch size and iterating over more starting indexes.

Improved performance
Breaking data into smaller batches allows for parallel processing and better responsiveness in high-volume systems.

This next example uses parallel processing to process data from multiple regions simultaneously. This technique leverages the system's ability to execute independent tasks concurrently, significantly reducing overall processing time.

The objective is to process shipment data from two different regions (region1 and region2) in parallel and update the shipment status to "Processed". Each region has its own dataset.

The first dataset is *region1_shipments.json*:

```
[
  {"shipmentId": 1, "destination": "New York"},
  {"shipmentId": 2, "destination": "Chicago"}
]
```

The second dataset is *region2_shipments.json*:

```
[
  {"shipmentId": 3, "destination": "Boston"},
  {"shipmentId": 4, "destination": "Los Angeles"}
]
```

Here's the DataWeave code:

```
%dw 2.0
output application/json
---
parallel([
  readUrl("region1_shipments.json", "application/json"),
  readUrl("region2_shipments.json", "application/json")
]) map ((regionData) ->
  regionData map ((shipment) -> shipment ++ {status: "Processed"})
)
```

And here's how it works:

parallel *function*

  Executes multiple independent tasks simultaneously

  Takes input as an array of tasks, in this case readUrl functions for region1 and region2

  Executes by reading data from *region1_shipments.json* and *region2_shipments.json* concurrently

map *over regions*

  Processes the results from each region independently

  Iterates over each region's shipment data and applies the next transformation step

Inner map *over shipments*

  Updates each shipment record within a region

  Adds the key-value pair {status: "Processed"} to each shipment using the ++ operator, which merges objects

The output combines the processed data from both regions into a single array:

```
[
  [
    {"shipmentId": 1, "destination": "New York", "status": "Processed"},
    {"shipmentId": 2, "destination": "Chicago", "status": "Processed"}
  ],
  [
    {"shipmentId": 3, "destination": "Boston", "status": "Processed"},
    {"shipmentId": 4, "destination": "Los Angeles", "status": "Processed"}
  ]
]
```

The results are as follows:

Concurrency

  Both regions are processed simultaneously, reducing the time it would take to process them sequentially.

Efficiency

  Independent datasets (such as shipments from different regions) are ideal for parallel processing, as they have no dependencies.

Scalability

  This approach can handle multiple regions or datasets in parallel, making it suitable for large-scale integrations.

Combining pagination and parallel processing is key to improving a large dataset's performance. Pagination processes data in smaller, manageable chunks, reducing memory usage and keeping systems responsive. Parallel processing executes multiple tasks simultaneously, significantly saving time. Together, these techniques enhance performance, scalability, and efficiency, making them essential for high-volume data integration tasks like processing shipments or updating regional data.

Leveraging caching and reuse for improved efficiency

SRL faces a common challenge: our system repeatedly fetches carrier details for each shipment, causing delays and putting unnecessary strain on the database. Determined to streamline operations, they turn to caching.

We create a *carrier cache*—a simple in-memory store containing carrier information. Instead of querying the database for every shipment, we enrich the shipment data by pulling carrier details directly from the cache. For instance, a shipment assigned to Carrier A no longer triggers a database call; the system instantly retrieves the carrier's name and contact info from the cache. The result is faster processing and a significantly reduced database load.

But we also notice another inefficiency: repetitive calculations for total shipping costs. We recalculate the cost for every shipment based on weight, rates, and taxes. To solve this, we introduce reusable variables. By defining a reusable `totalCost` function, we calculate shipping costs once and reuse the logic throughout our transformations.

This dual strategy of caching and reusing variables transforms our workflow. Database queries drop dramatically, shipment processing times improve, and our transformation scripts become easier to read and maintain. What starts as a performance bottleneck evolves into a success story of efficiency and scalability, thanks to the simple yet powerful techniques of caching and reuse.

Let's look at the next example using caching. A shipping system frequently retrieves shipment carrier details; you should cache the carrier data instead of querying the database for each shipment.

Here's the input dataset:

```
[
  {"shipmentId": 1, "carrierId": 201},
  {"shipmentId": 2, "carrierId": 202},
  {"shipmentId": 3, "carrierId": 201}
]
```

And the DataWeave code:

```
%dw 2.0
output application/json
---
{
  // Carrier Cache stored in memory for quick access
  carrierCache: {
```

```
    201: {name: "Carrier A", contact: "111-222-3333"},
    202: {name: "Carrier B", contact: "444-555-6666"}
  },

  // Enriching shipment data by pulling from the cache
  // instead of querying the database
  enrichedShipments: payload map ((shipment) ->
    shipment ++ carrierCache[shipment.carrierId]
  )
}
```

This is how it works:

Carrier cache

We define a `carrierCache` in the script where carrier data is preloaded. This cache eliminates the need to query the database every time a shipment's carrier information is needed.

Enriching shipments

The `map` function iterates over each shipment and merges the carrier information from the cache based on the `carrierId`. Instead of querying the database for every shipment, the system retrieves the data from the cache, greatly speeding up the process.

Here's the output:

```
{
  "enrichedShipments": [
    {"shipmentId": 1, "carrierId": 201, "name": "Carrier A",
  "contact": "111-222-3333"},
    {"shipmentId": 2, "carrierId": 202, "name": "Carrier B",
  "contact": "444-555-6666"},
    {"shipmentId": 3, "carrierId": 201, "name": "Carrier A",
  "contact": "111-222-3333"}
  ]
}
```

The next example is reusable variables: compute and reuse frequently accessed data within a transformation, such as calculating a shipment's total cost.

Here's the input data:

```
[
  {"shipmentId": 1, "weight": 10},
  {"shipmentId": 2, "weight": 20}
]
```

Here's the DataWeave code:

```
%dw 2.0
output application/json
var shippingRate = 5.00
var taxRate = 0.1
```

```
var totalCost = (weight) -> (weight * shippingRate) * (1 + taxRate)
---
payload map ((shipment) -> shipment ++ {totalCost: totalCost(shipment.weight)})
```

And here's how it works:

Variables

    `shippingRate` and `taxRate` are defined once, avoiding redundant declarations in the calculation logic.

    `totalCost` is a reusable function that calculates the total shipping cost based on weight, shipping rate, and tax rate.

Calculating total cost

    The `map` function iterates over each shipment and applies the `totalCost` function to calculate the shipping cost using the predefined rate and tax values. Following the preceding process ensures consistency and avoids recalculating these values multiple times.

Here's the output:

```
[
  {"shipmentId": 1, "weight": 10, "totalCost": 55.0},
  {"shipmentId": 2, "weight": 20, "totalCost": 110.0}
]
```

The results for both caching and reuse are as follows:

Improved performance

    Avoids redundant operations like repeated database queries or API calls. Reduces processing time for transformations.

Resource efficiency

    Minimizes system load by reusing stored data or computed values.

Simplified logic

    Reusable variables make transformations more readable and maintainable.

Scalability

    As data volumes grow, caching and reusable variables help keep the system responsive and efficient, ensuring scalability.

Implementing caching and reusing variables significantly improve performance and efficiency. Caching reduces the need for repetitive database calls, minimizing latency and system load, while reusable variables eliminate redundant calculations, simplifying transformations and reducing processing time. Together, these techniques make data workflows faster, more scalable, and easier to maintain. They provide a reliable foundation for handling large datasets and complex transformations, ultimately driving more efficient and responsive business operations.

Reuse with DataWeave Libraries

DataWeave libraries are collections of reusable functions that help streamline and simplify integration tasks. In the context of a shipping system, libraries can store common logic for tasks such as address formatting, package tracking, and calculating shipping costs. These libraries allow for better modularity, ensuring that transformation logic is consistent across various flows and reducing the need for redundant code. The use of libraries is essential in a shipping system where tasks like transforming addresses or calculating costs are repeated across different carrier integrations. By centralizing these common functions in libraries, developers can ensure that all transformations are handled uniformly, improving both efficiency and maintainability.

You can include libraries directly in your project's file structure, but for greater reusability, consistency, and collaboration, publishing them to Exchange is the better approach. This allows multiple projects to share and access the same libraries without duplication, ensures updates are centrally managed, and keeps teams working with the latest versions without manual file transfers. By using Exchange, developers gain better visibility and control over dependencies, making it easier to maintain, scale, and standardize integrations across different systems.

Why reuse matters

Reusing functions through libraries significantly boosts efficiency by eliminating redundant code. In shipping systems, for example, address formatting and cost calculations are often required for multiple carriers. By reusing these functions across different integration flows, developers save time and reduce the chance of errors. Furthermore, reuse leads to better maintainability. If business rules or regulations change, updates made to a central library automatically propagate across all integration flows, avoiding the need to change code in every instance manually. Additionally, this approach supports scalability. As new carriers or shipping features are added, the logic in reusable libraries can be extended rather than rewritten, making it easier to scale the integration system.

Creating DataWeave libraries

Creating a DataWeave library involves writing functions that solve specific problems or handle repeated tasks. This could mean creating libraries for address formatting, calculating shipping cost, or validating tracking numbers in a shipping system. For example, a library might include a function to format a shipping address for UPS or a function to calculate shipping costs based on the weight and distance of a package. By organizing functions in a library, developers can ensure that these transformations are handled centrally without duplicating the logic in every flow. This modular approach ensures that each function focuses on a single responsibility, simplifying testing and future updates.

Let's create a DataWeave shipping library. It contains functions for common transformations such as these:

Address formatting
Standardizing shipping addresses for different carriers.

Tracking number validation
Ensuring the tracking number is valid for each shipping carrier.

Shipping cost calculation
Shipping costs are based on weight, distance, and carrier.

Here's the sample library code:

```
%dw 2.0
output application/java

// Library function to format shipping address for UPS
fun formatAddressForUPS(street: String, city: String, zip:
String,
country: String): String =
street ++ ", " ++ city ++ ", " ++ zip ++ ", " ++ country

// Library function to calculate shipping cost for FedEx based on weight
fun calculateShippingCost(weight: Number,
distance: Number): Number = (weight * 0.6) + (distance
* 0.3)
```

Let's organize the libraries into specific categories:

AddressUtils.dwl
For address-related transformations

TrackingUtils.dwl
For tracking number handling

ShippingCostUtils.dwl
For shipping-related calculations

To create *AddressFormatting.dwl*:

```
%dw 2.0
output application/java

// Function to format the address for FedEx
fun formatAddressForFedEx(street: String, city: String,
zip: String,
 country: String): String =
   street ++ ", " ++ city ++ ", " ++ zip ++ ", " ++ country
```

To create *ShippingCost.dwl*:

```
%dw 2.0
output application/java

// Function to calculate shipping cost for FedEx
fun calculateShippingCost(weight: Number, distance: Number): Number =
    (weight * 0.6) + (distance * 0.3
```

Importing and using libraries

Once a DataWeave library is created, it can be easily imported into any integration flow that requires its functionality. Using the `import` statement, a developer can pull in the necessary libraries and access their functions, making it easy to reuse code without redundancy. For instance, when working with UPS, a library that formats addresses can be imported, and its function can be called directly to ensure consistency in the address format across different flows. By importing libraries, developers save time and avoid errors since they are using pretested and reliable functions, ensuring that all shipping-related transformations adhere to the same standards.

To reuse a library in a shipping integration, you import it using the `import` statement. This example imports both libraries and reuses their functions across different flows:

```
%dw 2.0
import addressFormat from 'AddressFormatting.dwl'
import shippingCost from 'ShippingCost.dwl'
output application/json
--
{ formattedAddress:
addressFormat.formatAddressForFedEx("456 Elm St",
    "Chicago", "60616", "USA"),
shippingCost: shippingCost.calculateShippingCost(5.0,
150.0)
}
```

Best practices for DataWeave libraries

To ensure that DataWeave libraries are effective, keeping them small and focused on specific tasks is essential. Each library should address a particular domain of the shipping process—such as address formatting, cost calculation, or tracking number validation—making it easier to maintain and test. Version control is also critical in a shipping system where APIs and business rules change frequently. By versioning libraries, developers can ensure that logic or shipping rules updates don't break existing functionality. Documenting each function is also essential, as it helps developers understand how to use the library properly. Proper documentation should include descriptions of the function's purpose, input parameters, and output to ensure everyone on the team can use the library efficiently and consistently.

Key takeaways. By reusing DataWeave libraries, shipping integrations can become more efficient and maintainable. Centralizing logic such as address formatting, tracking number validation, and shipping cost calculations into libraries allows teams to focus on more complex, unique tasks while maintaining consistency across multiple workflows.

Encouraging best practices. Encourage using modular libraries, version control, and proper documentation. This helps ensure that shipping systems evolve smoothly and scale efficiently as business requirements change.

At SRL, adopting these best practices paid off quickly. By modularizing their Data-Weave libraries—like a shared cost calculator and address formatter—they reduced onboarding time for new carriers by 40% and cut down on maintenance overhead. Versioning helped SRL adapt to evolving carrier APIs without disrupting operations, while clear documentation ensured that new developers could hit the ground running with confidence.

Testing and debugging libraries

Testing DataWeave libraries is crucial, especially when they handle sensitive operations like address formatting or cost calculations in a shipping system. Thorough testing ensures that the functions work as expected in various scenarios, such as when the input is in a different format or when handling edge cases. For example, testing the address formatting function with different international addresses ensures that the library can handle a variety of address formats. Debugging libraries involves checking for issues like invalid inputs or errors in logic. MuleSoft's built-in debugger can help developers trace function calls and check the outputs at each step, making pinpointing and resolving problems easier.

Use case: Implementing a reusable shipping transformation logic

In a shipping integration, reusable libraries can simplify tasks such as address formatting and shipping cost calculation, ensuring consistency across all workflows. For example, consider an integration with multiple shipping carriers like UPS, FedEx, and DHL. Each carrier requires a different address format, but by creating reusable functions in a library, developers can standardize address formatting for all carriers. Similarly, shipping costs often depend on weight and distance, so having a library function to calculate these costs based on the carrier's rules helps avoid duplication. These reusable functions ensure that logic is consistently applied across different flows and carriers. For example, by importing and using the *AddressFormatting.dwl* and *ShippingCost.dwl* libraries, developers can ensure that all shipping information is processed correctly, with minimal redundancy and maximum consistency.

Reusing DataWeave libraries in shipping integrations offers several key benefits: efficiency, maintainability, and scalability. Developers can save time, reduce errors, and ensure consistent behavior across all integration flows by centralizing everyday tasks like address formatting, cost calculation, and tracking number validation in libraries. This approach simplifies development and ensures that the system remains flexible and adaptable as new carriers and shipping requirements are introduced. By following best practices such as keeping libraries focused, versioning them, and documenting them thoroughly, teams can create robust, reusable components that streamline the integration process and improve the overall quality of the shipping system.

Summary

Throughout this chapter, we continued working alongside SRL as our real-world example. Their shipping use cases brought DataWeave's capabilities to life—showing how powerful transformations support operations at scale, from streamlining delivery data to personalizing customer interactions.

This chapter dove deep into the world of DataWeave, MuleSoft's powerful tool for transforming data across various formats. It explored how DataWeave simplifies complex tasks with its functional programming principles, including immutability, declarative logic, and pure functions, making data transformations both efficient and intuitive. Through practical examples, you saw how DataWeave empowers you to convert, reshape, and merge data with precision—whether it's turning JSON into XML for shipping use cases or working with dynamic data structures.

A key focus was on DataWeave libraries, where we looked at how reusing functions across multiple flows boosts efficiency, consistency, and maintainability. By centralizing common logic like address formatting or cost calculations into reusable libraries, you reduce redundancy, streamline workflows, and ensure scalability as your integration needs grow.

SRL is a great example of how DataWeave can be used in real-world logistics to transform fragmented data into fast, reliable, and scalable processes. From streamlining shipment schedules to enriching customer records and optimizing performance with advanced techniques like caching and parallel processing, SRL's journey shows what's possible when you harness the full power of DataWeave in a modern integration strategy.

With this solid foundation, you're now ready to dive into Chapter 9 on testing. Here, we'll explore best practices for ensuring the reliability of our transformations, using MUnit for unit testing, mastering error handling, and utilizing Postman collections to test APIs and integrations. This is where you can take your transformations to the next level, turning them into robust, production-ready solutions.

Testing

In MuleSoft API testing, the goal is to catch defects and ensure the API meets its requirements. But, realistically, you can't test everything. It's not because of tool limitations; exhaustive testing would just take endless resources, which isn't practical. So, a strategic, risk-based approach is needed to make sure the APIs are reliable and deliver what you expect.

Beyond just writing tests, effective unit testing means striving for the best return on the time you invest. It's all about minimizing effort while maximizing impact, which isn't always easy to achieve. With a risk-based approach, you start by focusing on the most critical areas, catching high-impact issues early. You begin by identifying risks in the API, like complex flows, core features, or recurring issues you've seen in past projects.

Once you know the risks, you can prioritize. This lets you focus on high-risk areas where issues would have the most impact, helping you make the best use of your testing time and resources. With these priorities in place, the focus should be to design test cases to target the riskiest areas early in the cycle. For the most crucial tests, it's worth adding more detail, extra test cases, or putting your most experienced testers on them. Finally, you should keep things flexible, adapting as new risks emerge or priorities shift, and staying focused on what matters most throughout the project. By balancing efficient testing with thoughtful prioritization, as shown in Figure 9-1, you can achieve more with less and make every testing effort count.

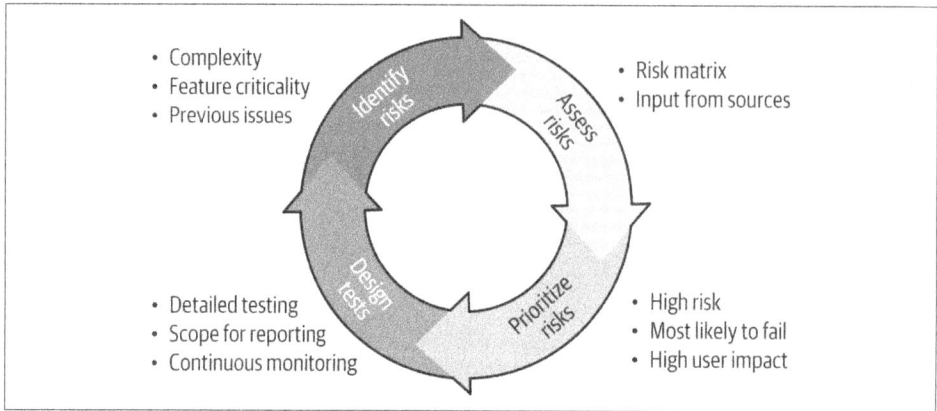

Figure 9-1. A risk-based approach to unit testing

In this chapter, you will learn how to write unit tests in Anypoint Studio and ACB. You will explore the different MUnit processors available, such as the Mock, Spy, and Assert processors, and how to use them effectively. Additionally, we will cover best practices so that your tests are robust, reliable, and maintainable.

MUnit

MUnit is a testing tool for Mule applications that makes it easier to create and run both unit and integration tests for Mule flows and APIs. You can create tests in both Anypoint Studio and ACB, allowing you to design tests using visual tools or XML in the same interface for both development and testing.

MUnit's ability to integrate with CI/CD systems allows you to apply your organization's testing policies so that unit tests are run before deployments to ensure code quality. It works with tools like Maven, Jenkins, Sure-fire Computing, and Sonar-Qube, making it simple to add automated tests to your development process. MUnit can also automatically create basic tests from RAML files, giving you a quick starting point that you can adjust to fit your needs.

MUnit provides detailed reports on test coverage. You can view these reports directly in Anypoint Studio or export them in JSON format for other reporting tools, giving you clear insight into how complete your tests are. Additionally, MUnit has built-in modules for testing FTP, SFTP, databases, and mail servers locally. This setup reduces reliance on external systems, making testing faster and easier, while keeping everything organized and efficient.

When you write MUnits, you should aim to get the best value from your testing time, minimizing effort while maximizing benefits. This balance can be hard to achieve, but projects that do so often grow smoothly, need little maintenance, and adapt quickly to customer needs. On the other hand, projects that struggle to find this balance might have many unit tests but still face slow progress, numerous bugs, and high maintenance costs. The difference comes from the effectiveness of the testing methods used—some methods lead to good results and maintain software quality, while others result in tests that break often and require a lot of upkeep.

Here are the steps to follow to write unit tests in MuleSoft:

1. Launch Anypoint Studio and open the Mule project you wish to test.

2. If it doesn't already exist, create a new folder named *src/test/munit* in your project directory. This is where your MUnit test files will reside, as shown in Figure 9-2.

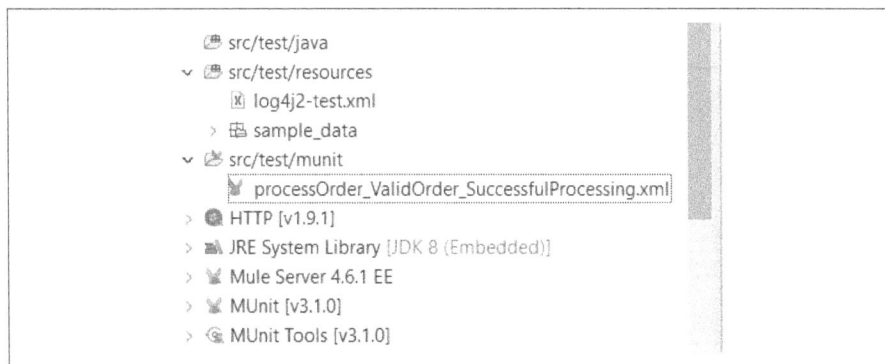

	src/test/java
∨	src/test/resources
	log4j2-test.xml
>	sample_data
∨	src/test/munit
	processOrder_ValidOrder_SuccessfulProcessing.xml
>	HTTP [v1.9.1]
>	JRE System Library [JDK 8 (Embedded)]
>	Mule Server 4.6.1 EE
>	MUnit [v3.1.0]
>	MUnit Tools [v3.1.0]

Figure 9-2. Test folder structure

3. Right-click the *src/test/munit* folder and select New > MUnit Test.

4. In the MUnit test suite window, provide a name for your test suite, as shown in Figure 9-3.

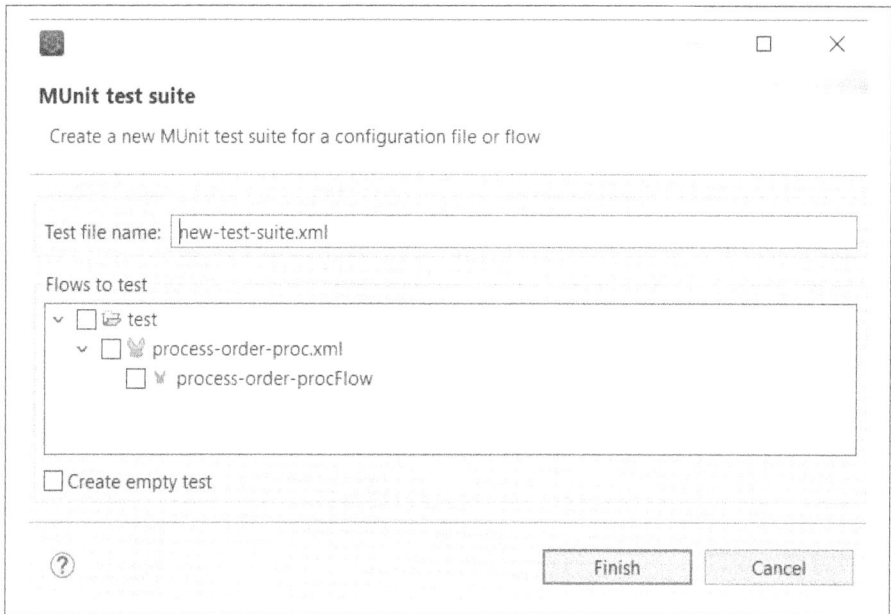

Figure 9-3. MUnit test suite dialog box

5. Choose the flows you want to test from your project's list of available flows.

6. Click Finish to create the test suite.

7. Open the newly created MUnit test suite file.

8. Using the Mule Palette, drag and drop components into the test flow to simulate the behaviors of your Mule application.

9. Configure the MUnit processors such as Mock, Spy, Assert, and so on to define expected outcomes and behaviors. The processors are explained in detail in "MUnit Processors" on page 248.

10. Right-click your MUnit test suite file and select MUnit > Run Test. Alternatively, you can run the test directly from the message flow by right-clicking the test flow and selecting "Run MUnit suite".

11. Add breakpoints in the Message Flow to debug your tests effectively.

12. Right-click your MUnit flow test and select "Debug MUnit test" to analyze the test at each breakpoint.

13. After running the tests, review the results in the Console tab and the MUnit window to verify that all tests pass.

14. If any errors are found, the build will fail, allowing you to inspect and correct issues.

Now let us apply this to test our order-processing Mule application.

Writing and managing MUnit tests in ACB requires a slightly different approach than in Anypoint Studio. Here are the steps to help you get started:

1. Launch ACB and open the Mule project you want to test, such as an order-processing application for an ecommerce platform. In Visual Studio Code, find the Testing tab in the Activity bar on the left. This tab displays all available MUnit tests within your Mule project.

2. While ACB doesn't allow you to create MUnit tests from scratch, you can modify existing MUnit tests in the XML editor. For instance, if you have MUnit tests from Anypoint Studio for order-processing flows (like checkStock, reserveItems, and processPayment), you can migrate these to ACB and adapt them as needed.

3. In the Testing tab, click the Run Tests button at the top to execute all tests in the project or select individual tests to run. For example, you can run tests specifically for the checkStock flow to validate order-processing flows to confirm item availability handling.

4. Use the Debug Tests button to step through your tests in detail. This feature is especially useful for analyzing flows like process payment, where you might want to check if the correct order ID and payment amount are being passed to the payment gateway.

5. After running the tests, view the results in the Testing tab to see which tests passed or failed. This will help you verify that each flow (for example, checking stock, reserving items, and processing payments) performs as expected.

6. For detailed test results, click Show Output to inspect specific errors or messages generated by failed tests. This output helps you troubleshoot specific issues, such as the checkStock flow mistakenly approving out-of-stock items.

MUnit Processors

MUnit provides several processors to help you create comprehensive tests for your Mule applications. This section discusses some of the key MUnit testing processors, as shown in Figure 9-4, and their functions.

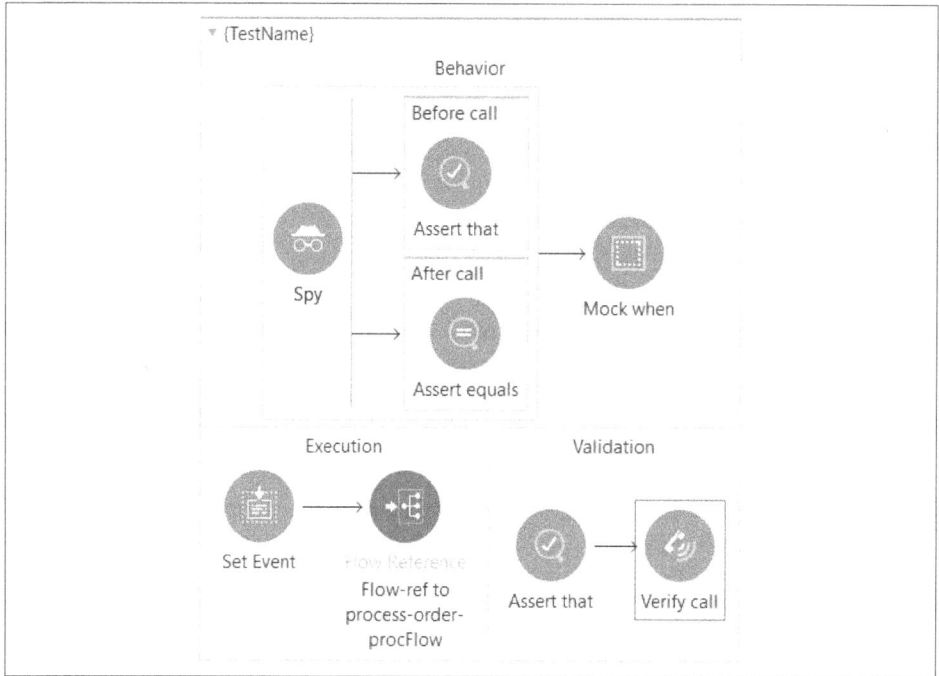

Figure 9-4. MUnit processors

Set Event

The Set Event feature in MUnit is perfect when you want to kick off a test with a specific setup. It lets you set up the Mule event just the way you need, with control over the payload, attributes, and variables to recreate different scenarios. This means you can simulate all kinds of real-world conditions and interactions by configuring the exact data or situation you want for your test. It's super flexible and gives you total control over the testing environment (see Figure 9-5).

```
<munit:set-event doc:name="Set Event" doc:id="20e036a3-bcdb-47d2-9ca6-8c61f58ecdb3" >
    <munit:payload value="#[{'key': 'value'}]" mediaType="application/json" />
    <munit:attributes value="#[{'header': 'value'}]" />
</munit:set-event>
```

Figure 9-5. Set Event

Mock When

The Mock When feature in MUnit is useful when you want to test just a specific part of your flow without bringing in all the external systems. With it, you can "pretend" certain processors are responding a certain way, so you can focus on testing the flow's main logic without getting sidetracked by dependencies. It's a great way to simulate what's happening around the flow and zero in on the part you're interested in (see Figure 9-6).

```
<munit-tools:mock-when doc:name="Mock when" doc:id="26110c3a-6f6f-4489-abbb-86f14aa0b43b" processor="http:request">
    <munit-tools:with-attributes >
        <munit-tools:with-attribute whereValue="GET" attributeName="method" />
    </munit-tools:with-attributes>
    <munit-tools:then-return >
        <munit-tools:payload value="#[{'mocked': 'response'}]" mediaType="application/json" />
    </munit-tools:then-return>
</munit-tools:mock-when>
```

Figure 9-6. Mock When

Assert That

The Assert That feature in MUnit is your go-to for checking that everything in your Mule flow is working as expected. It lets you set conditions that should be true at specific points, helping you validate the output against what you anticipate. So, if you need to make sure your flow's result matches a certain value, Assert That has you covered, giving you confidence that everything's functioning just as it should (see Figure 9-7).

```
<munit-tools:assert-that doc:name="Assert that" doc:id="9a687526-a608-41ce-8c2c-b3e9bbd3a14" is="#[#[equalTo({'key': 'value'})]]]" expression="#[payload]"/>
```

Figure 9-7. Assert That

Verify Call

The purpose of this check is to verify that a specific processor was called during the execution of the flow. This is helpful in testing that certain parts of your flow are executed as expected. For example, you might use this to confirm that a logging processor was triggered when a message passed through a particular point in your flow. This helps in validating that the flow behaves correctly and that all necessary steps are performed during its execution, as shown in Figure 9-8.

```
<munit-tools:verify-call doc:name="Verify call" doc:id="1dd42b87-cdf3-44f2-b28d-7bbb29e8accd" processor="http:request">
    <munit-tools:with-attributes >
        <munit-tools:with-attribute whereValue="POST" attributeName="method" />
    </munit-tools:with-attributes>
</munit-tools:verify-call>
```

Figure 9-8. Verify Call

Here are some of the ways you can use the Verify Call processor:

Validating call counts

This is useful in scenarios like loops or repeated calls (e.g., retry mechanisms or batch processing). You can use it to verify how many times a specific processor or connector is invoked in a flow, as shown in this example:

```
<munit:test name="testRetryDatabaseOperation">
    <munit:behavior>
        <munit-tools:verify-call processor="db:select" times="3"/>
    </munit:behavior>
    <flow-ref name="yourFlow"/>
</munit:test>
```

Ensuring conditional calls

If a flow includes conditional logic that calls a processor only under specific conditions, Verify Call can help you confirm that the processor is triggered (or skipped) based on those conditions, as shown in this example:

```
<munit:test name="testConditionalProcessor">
    <munit:behavior>
        <munit-tools:verify-call processor="choice" times="0"/>
    </munit:behavior>
    <flow-ref name="yourFlow"/>
</munit:test>
```

Testing external system calls

For cases where a flow connects to an external service or database, use Verify Call so that that requests are being made as expected without affecting the external system, which can be helpful in integration or mock testing, as shown here:

```
<munit:test name="testHttpRequest">
    <munit:behavior>
        <munit-tools:verify-call processor="http:request" times="1"/>
    </munit:behavior>
    <flow-ref name="yourFlow"/>
```

Validating retry or error-handling logic

In flows with error-handling logic or retries, Verify Call can confirm that a processor is retried the expected number of times when an error occurs or verify that the error-handling path is triggered as expected.

Using the Verify Call processor ensures that the logic in your Mule flows operates as intended, especially in cases where exact call counts, conditions, and retry mechanisms are crucial for application functionality and reliability.

Spy

The Spy processor in MUnit allows you to observe and validate the behavior of a Mule event processor in a nonintrusive way. By using Spy, you can run assertions or checks before and/or after a processor is called, ensuring certain conditions are met at specific points in the flow without altering its execution. This is ideal for verifying data transformations and processor behaviors throughout the flow, as shown in this example:

```
<munit:spy processor="logger" doc:name="Spy">
    <munit:with-attributes>
        <munit:with-attribute key="level" value="INFO"/>
    </munit:with-attributes>
</munit:spy>
```

The Spy processor is used for various purposes, including validation, where it checks the state of the Mule event—such as payload, attributes, or variables—before and after a processor runs. It is also useful for nonintrusive testing, allowing you to monitor a processor's behavior without altering the flow logic. Spy is very useful in testing flows that have a Transform Message processor. It helps with debugging by providing insights into how data transforms across different stages in the flow:

Using spy to validate payload

Suppose you have an HTTP request in your flow and want to confirm that the payload is null before the request and populated afterward, as shown in this example:

```
<munit:test name="testHttpRequest">
    <munit:behavior>
    <munit-tools:spy processor="http:request">
        <munit-tools:before-call>
        <munit-tools:assert-that expression="#
[payload]" is="#[MunitTools::nullValue()]"/>
        </munit-tools:before-call>
        <munit-tools:after-call>
        <munit-tools:assert-that expression="#
[payload]" is="#[MunitTools::notNullValue()]"/>
        </munit-tools:after-call>
    </munit-tools:spy>
    </munit:behavior>
    <flow-ref name="yourFlow"/>
</munit:test>
```

Using Spy for nonintrusive testing

Database operations are common in projects; you might want to verify that specific attributes are set accurately before and after a database call, as shown here:

```
<munit:test name="testDatabaseOperation">
    <munit:behavior>
    <munit-tools:spy processor="db:select">
        <munit-tools:before-call>
            <munit-tools:assert-that expression="#
[attributes.query]" is="#[equalTo('SELECT * FROM
users')]"/>
        </munit-tools:before-call>
        <munit-tools:after-call>
            <munit-tools:assert-that expression="#
[attributes.query]" is="#[equalTo('SELECT * FROM
users')]"/>
        </munit-tools:after-call>
    </munit-tools:spy>
    </munit:behavior>
    <flow-ref name="yourFlow"/>
</munit:test>
```

Using Spy to debug

You may want to confirm that a specific variable has a defined value before and after a transformation, as shown in this example:

```
<munit:test name="testVariableValue">
    <munit:behavior>
    <munit-tools:spy processor="set-variable">
        <munit-tools:before-call>
            <munit-tools:assert-that expression="#
[vars.myVar]" is="#[nullValue()]"/>
        </munit-tools:before-call>
        <munit-tools:after-call>
            <munit-tools:assert-that expression="#
[vars.myVar]" is="#[equalTo('expectedValue')]"/>
        </munit-tools:after-call>
    </munit-tools:spy>
    </munit:behavior>
    <flow-ref name="yourFlow"/>
</munit:test>
```

Using the Spy processor enhances the robustness and reliability of MUnit tests by providing a clear view of your flow's behavior at various stages, ensuring data integrity and expected outcomes throughout.

MUnit Structure

This section will show you how to structure unit tests using the Arrange-Act-Assert pattern. Figure 9-9 shows a blank test suite in Anypoint Studio.

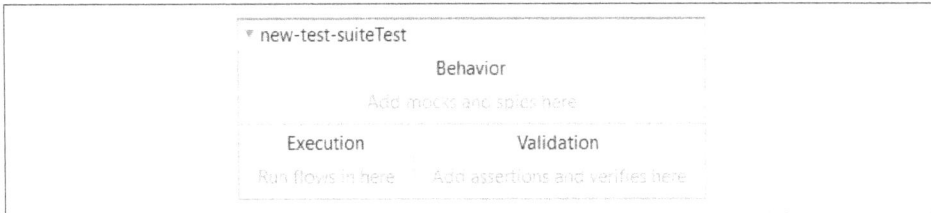

Figure 9-9. Test pattern

Behavior Scope (Arrange)

This scope sets up the initial conditions and inputs for your test. That includes configuring mock processors, setting initial payloads, and preparing the environment, as shown in this example:

```
<munit:behavior>
    <!-- Mock processors and set preconditions -->
    <munit:mock-when processor="db:select">
    <munit:with-attributes>
        <munit:equal-to name="doc:name"
value="Select Order from DB"/>
    </munit:with-attributes>
    <munit:then-return>
        <munit:payload value="#[['orderId': '123',
'status': 'NEW']]"/>
    </munit:then-return>
    </munit:mock-when>
    <munit:set payload="#['{ \"orderId\": \"123\",
\"status\": \"NEW\" }']" doc:name="Set Payload"/>
</munit:behavior>
```

Execution Scope (Act)

This is where you trigger the flow and capture the output, as shown in the following example:

```
<munit:execution>
    <flow-ref name="processOrderFlow"/>
</munit:execution>
```

Validation Scope (Assert)

This involves checking that the flow processed the order correctly and produced the expected results, as shown here:

```
<munit:validation>
    <munit:assert-that expression="#[payload.status]"
is="#[equalTo('PROCESSED')]"/>
</munit:validation>
```

Creating an MUnit template for organizational reuse is a great way to maintain consistency and improve testing efficiency across teams. By standardizing a template, you can establish a consistent structure for MUnit tests, enforce best practices, and ensure that all tests meet organizational requirements.

Best Practices

This section discusses best practices that will help you develop MUnit tests that have the greatest possible value and protection against regressions. Consistent testing not only improves the reliability of the software but also streamlines the development process, allowing teams to identify and resolve issues more efficiently. We will show how to create base templates for MUnits, use MUnit components, and socialize the template for reuse.

Agree on Standards

This next section outlines critical standards that should be agreed upon by all team members, including the structure of tests, naming conventions, error-handling procedures, and the proper use of assertions:

Structure

It is essential to establish a consistent and organized structure for all testing procedures. One effective approach is the AAA format, which stands for Arrange, Act, and Assert. This structure helps to clearly define the steps of the test: first, prepare the necessary conditions and inputs (Arrange), then execute the functionality being tested (Act), and finally, verify that the results meet the expected outcomes (Assert).

Naming conventions

Implementing a clear and systematic naming convention for test suites, test cases, and related files is crucial for maintaining readability and organization. This naming convention should reflect the specific functionalities or processes being tested, making it easy for team members to identify the purpose of each test at a glance. For example, names could incorporate the feature being tested, the expected behavior, and the specific scenario (for example, `UserLogin_Valid Credentials_Success`).

Error handling

A defined standard for error handling in tests is vital for reliability. This should include procedures for testing various error responses that the application may return and verifying that the system handles errors gracefully. Additionally, it is important to include mechanisms for retrying operations when appropriate, which can help to confirm that transient errors do not affect overall functionality. By outlining specific error conditions to test, you create a more resilient suite of tests.

Assertions

Developing clear guidelines for the usage of assertions is important so that all key business logic and processes are thoroughly validated. Assertions should not only check that the main results of a test are correct but should also validate any relevant payloads or specific attributes involved in the operation. This includes confirming that data returned from the system meets predetermined criteria, which enhances the quality and reliability of the testing process. Aim to cover all critical paths with assertions to provide comprehensive test coverage.

Naming Test Cases

Naming test cases effectively is crucial for maintaining clarity and organization in your testing process. To achieve this, ensure that the name clearly describes what the test is verifying, helping anyone reading the test understand its purpose immediately. Consistently use a naming convention, such as prefixing with *test* or using camelCase to make it easier to identify and manage test cases.

Keep names short and simple, since concise names are easier to read and understand. Incorporate the expected outcome in the test name to provide a quick reference to what the test is supposed to validate. Avoid including unnecessary details that do not add value, focusing instead on the key aspects of what the test is checking. Use human-readable titles, avoiding codes or abbreviations that might be unclear. Ensure that each test case name is unique to avoid confusion and make each test easily distinguishable. Follow a consistent structure for naming, such as *processOrder_ValidOrder_SuccessfulProcessing*, to help in organizing and locating tests. For example:

processOrder
> Indicates the method or flow being tested

ValidOrder
> Describes the state or condition being tested

SuccessfulProcessing
> Specifies the expected outcome of the test

This naming convention clearly indicates that the test is verifying the *processOrder* method using a valid order and expects successful processing. It follows the structure of *MethodName_StateUnderTest_ExpectedBehavior*, which helps someone understand the purpose of the test at a glance.

Create a Base MUnit Template

Here are the steps to create a base MUnit template:

1. Open Anypoint Studio or ACB and create a new test file in *src/test/munit*.

2. Set up the basic structure in XML to serve as a blueprint, including placeholders for flow names, configurations, and assertions. For example:

```
<munit:test name="{Test_Name}" description="
{Description}">
    <munit:behavior>
    <!-- Setup common stubs or mocks here -->
    <munit-tools:mock-when processor="
{Processor_to_Mock}">
        <munit-tools:with-attributes>
        <munit-tools:with-attribute key="method"
value="GET"/>
        </munit-tools:with-attributes>
        <munit-tools:then-return payload="#
[{Default_Payload}]" />
    </munit-tools:mock-when>
    </munit:behavior>

    <munit:execution>
    <!-- Trigger the actual flow to be tested -->
    <flow-ref name="{Flow_Name}"/>
    </munit:execution>

    <munit:validation>
    <!-- Add assertions for expected payload, variables,
and attributes -->
    <munit-tools:assert-that expression="#[payload]"
is="#[equalTo({Expected_Payload})]"/>
    <munit-tools:verify-call processor="
{Processor_to_Verify}" times="1"/>
```

```
        </munit:validation>
      </munit:test>
```

Include Common Components and Mocks

Common components and mocks make it easier to maintain and update code. When testing, you might be dealing with external environments that produce variable responses. It's important to test for consistency and reliability to create higher-quality applications:

Reusable mocks

Set up reusable mocks for commonly utilized connectors or processors, such as HTTP requests and database interactions. This practice streamlines the testing process by eliminating the need for repetitive configurations each time a test is run. By creating standardized mocks, you can ensure consistency across tests and improve the maintainability of your testing framework.

Spy processors

Integrate a Spy processor into your template to monitor and capture the state of payloads, variables, or attributes during crucial stages of processing. This allows you to gain insights into the flow of data within your application, making it easier to debug and analyze the behavior of your workflows. Spy processors can be invaluable for tracking how data transforms through each step and identifying any issues that may arise.

Global properties

Utilize global properties to manage dynamic values such as URLs, database names, and API keys. By referencing these properties from a central configuration file (such as *mule-app.properties*), you streamline the process of updating these values when necessary. This approach not only reduces the risk of inconsistencies across different environments but also enhances security and simplifies deployment by managing sensitive information in one place.

Define Setup and Teardown Logic

Setting up tests and incorporating tear-down logic helps to create test runs in a clean and controlled environment:

Setup

In the testing environment, utilize a standard *munit:before-test* processor so that all necessary resources are prepared prior to executing the tests. This may involve initializing variables that will be used throughout the test cases, loading specific datasets that the tests depend on, or configuring any external services that are required for the tests to run smoothly. Proper setup is crucial for ensuring consistency and reliability across all test scenarios.

Teardown

After each test case, it is essential to implement a *munit:after-test* processor for thorough cleanup. This step should involve resetting any modified variables back to their original values and clearing out test data that may interfere with subsequent tests. By performing these cleanup operations, you can avoid conflicts between test cases and ensure a clean slate for each individual test run, which contributes to the overall integrity of the testing process.

Automate verification

Automated verification is a process where you systematically validate your application's behavior to compare and check that it aligns with expected results. MUnit has many tools to help this process:

- Add standard assertions for payloads, variables, and attributes. For example, verify payload content, the existence of required variables, or attributes set by specific processors.

- Use Verify Call processors in the template to enforce that critical processors are called the correct number of times, ensuring that workflows execute as expected.

Troubleshoot

Include logging at strategic points within the test template, especially in the execution and validation phases, to make it easier to troubleshoot failed tests.

Reuse

We have seen organizations where in every project the MUnits are styled differently. To avoid this and maintain uniformity, it's important to create templates for reuse:

- Store the template in a version-controlled repository, such as Git, that is easily accessible to all teams within the organization. This setup will enable team members to efficiently pull the latest version of the template and make updates as necessary, ensuring that everyone is working with the most current resources.

- Provide comprehensive documentation to guide users on how to effectively utilize the template. This documentation should include detailed explanations of any placeholders within the template, customization options available to users, and a list of best practices to follow for optimal results. Additionally, consider adding an FAQ section to address common questions or issues that may arise.

- Include a set of sample tests that showcase the template's functionality in a variety of scenarios. These tests should cover important areas such as making HTTP calls, performing database operations, and executing other relevant tasks. By providing these examples, other users can gain a better understanding of how to implement the template in real-world applications and make sure it meets their specific needs.

Socialize the Template

Create a comprehensive guide on how to effectively utilize the template. The template must be maintained as a reusable asset within a version control system, such as Git. Regularly review and update the template to incorporate any changes in testing standards, best practices, or new versions of Mule. Include detailed commit messages to track the evolution of the template and facilitate collaboration among team members. Establish a routine for teams to review the template at regular intervals, such as quarterly or biannually. Encourage team members to provide constructive feedback on the template's effectiveness, clarity, and relevance in light of current practices. This feedback loop is essential for continuous improvement and ensures that the template evolves to meet the needs of the team and enhances the quality of the testing process.

With this MUnit template, your organization can ensure that tests are consistently written, reliable, and easily maintained across projects.

Integration Testing

Using MUnit for integration testing in Mule applications enables you to validate interactions between various components, connectors, and external systems, ensuring that the entire Mule flow or service functions as expected when the parts work together. MUnit's tools—such as mocking, spies, and assertions—are especially useful for simulating external dependencies and observing data transformations, making integration tests reliable and repeatable.

The following section describes how to set up effective integration tests with MUnit.

Identify Test Scenarios

Test scenarios are overarching descriptions of what needs to be tested. They detail the functionalities, features, and conditions that must be validated to ensure the application fulfills its requirements. By systematically identifying test scenarios, you can create high-quality applications:

Integration points

Identify and document the specific points at which your Mule application interfaces with external systems. These may include various types of connections, such as HTTP APIs for your service calls, databases for data retrieval and storage, and FTP servers for file transfers. For each integration point, specify the protocol used, the expected input and output formats, and any authentication or security mechanisms in place.

Data flow validations

Develop a comprehensive set of scenarios designed to validate the flow of data between different components of your application. This includes not only checking that the data is transformed correctly according to defined mappings but also verifying that it maintains its integrity throughout the entire process. Consider edge cases, such as varying data sizes and formats, so that all possible variations are handled appropriately.

Error paths

Plan for the testing of error-handling mechanisms and the implementation of retry logic within your application. This involves simulating various failure scenarios, such as retry exhausts, database unavailability, or unexpected input conditions, to confirm that your application behaves as expected under these circumstances. Ensure that proper logging and alerting are in place, and evaluate how the system recovers from errors to maintain overall reliability and user experience.

Environment Setup

Each test case should concentrate on a particular integration scenario so that there is comprehensive coverage of the system's functionality. For example, one test case could examine a successful API call, verifying that the expected data is correctly returned and that the response matches the defined specifications. Another test case might focus on fetching data from Anypoint MQ, ensuring that the correct records are retrieved and the system handles various query parameters appropriately. Additionally, test cases should also cover error scenarios, such as handling invalid API requests or connection failures, to assess how the system manages unexpected issues and returns appropriate error messages. As discussed in the previous sections, it's very important to cover core logic and test it thoroughly to avoid failures.

Mocking

Mocking allows for simulation of the behavior of certain components or flows in Mule applications during testing. This approach is especially handy for isolating the parts of your flows that you want to dive deeper into, all without needing to rely on external systems or complicated setups. Let's look at two mocking techniques:

Mocking external dependencies

When developing and testing software that relies on external systems, such as databases, HTTP endpoints, or message queues, it is important to use mock objects to simulate the behavior of these systems. Mocking allows developers to create a controlled testing environment without needing the actual systems in place. This isolation ensures that tests can run independently, leading to more accurate and reliable results.

Set up mocks correctly

It is important to configure your mock objects to respond differently based on the various scenarios you want to test. For example, if your software makes an HTTP request, a successful call should be set up to return a valid payload that the application expects. Conversely, if you're testing how your application handles errors, you should configure the mock to return a 500 status code, which signifies an internal server error. This way, you can comprehensively test how your software reacts to both success and failure scenarios, ensuring robust performance in real-world situations. For example:

```
<munit:test name="testHttpIntegration">
    <munit:behavior>
    <munit-tools:mock-when
processor="http:request">
        <munit-tools:with-attributes>
        <munit-tools:with-attribute key="method"
value="POST"/>
        </munit-tools:with-attributes>
        <munit-tools:then-return payload="#
[{\"status\":\"success\"}]" statusCode="200"/>
    </munit-tools:mock-when>
    </munit:behavior>
    <flow-ref name="myHttpFlow"/>
    <munit:validation>
    <munit-tools:assert-that expression="#[payload]"
is="#[equalTo({\"status\":\"success\"})]"/>
    </munit:validation>
</munit:test>
```

To mock a JMS Publish you can use this example:

```
<munit:mock-when processor="jms:publish">
    <munit:with-attributes>
        <munit:with-attribute key="destination" value="queue://testQueue"/>
    </munit:with-attributes>
    <munit:then-return>
        <munit:payload value="#[ 'Message Published' ]"/>
    </munit:then-return>
</munit:mock-when>
```

You can also mock errors to test how your flow handles exceptions. This is done using the <munit:fail> element within your mock configuration. The following example shows how to mock a database error:

```
<munit:mock-when processor="db:select">
    <munit:with-attributes>
        <munit:with-attribute key="config-ref"
value="Database_Config"/>
    </munit:with-attributes>
    <munit:then-return>
        <munit:fail exception="java.sql.SQLException"
message="Database Connection Error"/>
    </munit:then-return>
</munit:mock-when>
```

To mock a user, you can use <munit:set variable="userId" value="#['Dummy User']"/>.

After mocking and executing your flow, you can use various MUnit tools to validate the results, such as <munit-tools:assert-that>.

Spies

Use the Spy processor to monitor the payload, attributes, and variables at different points in the process. This checking helps ensure that data transformations and routing decisions are correct at every stage.

Set up before-call and after-call checks in the Spy to confirm the data state before and after important processors. This ensures that the data is accurate and the system is working as it should, as shown in the following example:

```
<munit:test name="testDataTransformation">
    <munit:behavior>
    <munit-tools:spy processor="choice">
        <munit-tools:before-call>
        <munit-tools:assert-that expression="#
[payload]" is="#[notNullValue()]"/>
        </munit-tools:before-call>
    </munit-tools:spy>
    </munit:behavior>
```

```
        <flow-ref name="dataTransformFlow"/>
    </munit:test>
```

Integrate with CI/CD for Automation

Integrate your MUnit test suite into your CI/CD pipeline by utilizing tools such as Maven or Jenkins. This integration will automate the execution of integration tests with each build process, allowing you to identify and address potential issues early in the development cycle.

To implement this, first ensure that your MUnit tests are properly configured and located within your project structure. Then, within your Maven or Jenkins configuration, set up a build step that triggers the MUnit test execution as part of the build process. This step can be configured to run after compiling the code but before deploying to production environments.

By setting up your pipeline in this way, you can facilitate a continuous feedback loop, reducing the risk of defects and improving the overall quality of your application. Regularly monitoring the test results will also help in maintaining code integrity as new features and updates are introduced.

Example Integration Test for an API Flow

SRL uses a basic Mule flow designed to process an order effectively. The flow begins by capturing the order details, which are then logged for recordkeeping and auditing purposes (see Figure 9-10):

```
<flow name="processOrderFlow">
        <logger message="Processing order: #[payload]"
level="INFO" doc:name="Log Order"/>
            <db:insert doc:name="Insert Order Status">
            <db:sql>INSERT INTO orders (orderId, status)
VALUES (#[payload.orderId], 'PROCESSED')</db:sql>
        </db:insert>
        </flow>
```

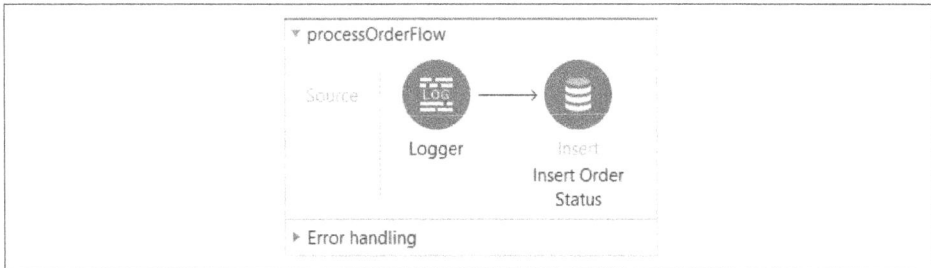

Figure 9-10. Example flow

After the details are logged, the flow updates the order status in a database to reflect the current state of the order, ensuring that all relevant information is there (see Figure 9-11):

```
<munit:test
name="processOrder_ValidOrder_SuccessfulProcessing
" description="Test for processing a valid order">
    <munit:behavior>
        <!-- Arrange -->
        <db:insert doc:name="Insert" doc:id="7c774b81-
4c27-4fc4-9fa8-e005797bac17">
            <db:sql ><![CDATA['{ "orderId\": "123", "status":
"NEW" }']]></db:sql>
        </db:insert>
        <set-payload value="#[payload]" doc:name="Set
Payload" doc:id="76107bd3-d811-4113-b880-
5341dbf00347"/>
    </munit:behavior>

    <munit:execution>
        <!-- Act -->
        <flow-ref name="processOrderFlow"/>
    </munit:execution>

    <munit:validation>
        <!-- Assert -->
        <munit-tools:assert-equals doc:name="Assert
orderId" doc:id="4fc15ed0-8c32-4b5b-9265-1ff81ece2f1c"
actual="#[payload.orderId]" expected="#[123]"/>
        <munit-tools:assert-equals doc:name="Assert
status" doc:id="6b865279-9a40-42b4-bf7d-
3145e0a1cf83" actual='#[payload.status]' expected="#
['PROCESSED']"/>
        <munit-tools:assert doc:name="Assert expression"
doc:id="b1f943ec-4441-4352-90b3-383f6b58ea4c"/>
    </munit:validation>
</munit:test>
```

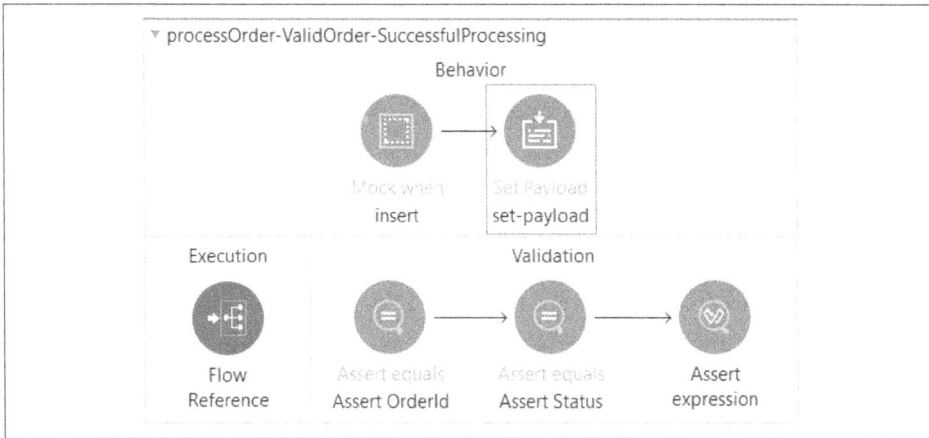

Figure 9-11. Example MUnit

MUnit Test Recorder

The MUnit Test Recorder is a feature in Anypoint Studio that allows you to record the execution of a Mule flow and automatically generate an MUnit test based on the captured data. This tool captures real data as it flows through your application, enabling you to create unit tests without writing code manually. The Test Recorder simplifies the process of creating tests by allowing you to configure necessary mocks and assertions based on the recorded flow execution.

So, what sets manual MUnit testing apart from the Test Recorder? The following is a comparison:

Manual MUnit testing
> Manual MUnit testing offers greater flexibility and control, allowing for highly specialized tests tailored to specific scenarios. It can be intricate and time-consuming, particularly for large workflows. A solid grasp of MUnit and MuleSoft components is essential for effective testing.

MUnit Test Recorder
> The Test Recorder automates the generation of test cases from recorded flows, benefiting beginners or those needing quick setups. In terms of speed, it enables faster initial test setups by capturing real-time data. Its limitations are that it has restrictions, such as not handling flows with Mule errors or complex scenarios effectively, compared to manual testing.

Summary

This chapter discussed the importance of effective testing in MuleSoft API development to identify defects and meet user needs. You should create a strategic, risk-based approach, prioritizing high-risk areas to make the most of limited testing resources. We also introduced the MUnit tool, which is essential for creating unit and integration tests within Anypoint Studio and Anypoint Code Builder.

The chapter outlined best practices for writing robust and maintainable MUnit tests, highlighting the need for integration with CI/CD systems and automated test generation from RAML files. It stressed the importance of balancing testing efforts with meaningful results, suggesting that effective testing methodologies lead to smoother project execution and improved software quality. Finally, the chapter provided a step-by-step guide for writing MUnit tests, from setting up the test suite to executing and debugging tests, ensuring that readers can effectively implement testing strategies for high-quality APIs.

Having successfully built a Mule API using MUnit to ensure its functionality and performance, we are now ready to move on to the deployment phase of our application. This is an important step, as it involves making our API accessible to users and integrating it into the desired environments.

Chapter 10 discusses the various deployment strategies available for MuleSoft APIs, covering topics such as cloud deployment, on-premises deployment, and hybrid options. The chapter also explores best practices for a seamless deployment process, including considerations for environment configurations, version control, and monitoring post-deployment performance.

Deployment

Now that you have completed your implementation, it's time to learn how to deploy and manage your API in CloudHub. There are eight steps to deploying and managing an API:

1. Deploy the API as a web service:

    a. Use Runtime Manager to set up API settings.

    b. Define endpoints to make the API accessible online.

2. Create a proxy application:

    a. Use API Manager to manage API traffic.

    b. Add a layer of security.

3. Set up security and governance policies:

    a. Control user access to the API.

    b. Implement authentication, authorization, and data-handling steps.

4. Monitor and analyze API usage:

    a. Use Runtime Manager and other tools to visualize performance.

    b. Generate activity reports and gather analytics.

    c. Track user feedback to understand changing needs.

5. Troubleshoot issues:

    a. Check logs and diagnose problems to maintain smooth operation.

6. Optimize performance:

    a. Add more resources to handle increased traffic as user access grows.

7. Regularly update the API:

    a. Fix bugs and add new features.

    b. Ensure the API remains relevant and meets user expectations.

This chapter is split into three parts. In the first part, you will learn the different deployment options MuleSoft provides. The second part examines how to deploy Mule applications. In the final part, you will learn how to set up application settings and monitor performance. By the end of this chapter, you will understand how to deploy Mule applications, use API Manager to create API proxies, and implement security to keep your APIs safe.

Deployment Options

There are three primary options for deploying Mule applications, and this section explores all three.

CloudHub

The first and most popular option is a MuleSoft-hosted runtime environment called CloudHub. This platform utilizes *virtual machines* (VMs) on Amazon Web Services (AWS) infrastructure. CloudHub is fully managed, multitenanted, globally available, and highly secure. It simplifies the deployment process because, as a user, you do not have to worry about the underlying infrastructure. This means you can focus on building and managing applications instead of worrying about setting up virtual machines and doing gateway configuration. CloudHub 2.0 is MuleSoft's latest iteration of this cloud-based integration platform, offering advanced features and a reengineered architecture for improved performance and scalability. In this chapter, you will learn how to deploy apps on the CloudHub platform, which remains a robust and reliable choice for many integration needs.

Deploying to CloudHub is a straightforward process, with MuleSoft handling all hardware and software maintenance. The platform provides an infrastructure for the Domain Name System (DNS) and load balancing, and it can scale dynamically during periods of high demand. This simplicity and reliability should give you confidence in your deployment.

When would you use this option? Consider a scenario where you've developed a media streaming API for a company to view shows. By deploying this API on Cloud-Hub, your application benefits from the platform's built-in scalability and global availability. During peak traffic times, such as a Mike Tyson fight on Netflix, or the Super Bowl, CloudHub can automatically scale your API to manage significant traffic spikes while maintaining high performance. This ensures that customers can place orders smoothly without delays, providing a seamless experience even during the busiest moments.

During API deployment, the most important decision you will make is picking the right worker sizes. Having multiple workers and worker sizes is a complex decision that involves looking at the API's different integrations. Multiple workers can complicate state management if your API relies on stateful processing. Deploying more workers is also expensive; avoiding the use of multiple workers might be more cost-effective. Next, we will review how to pick the right workers.

CloudHub workers

CloudHub is hosted on AWS, where a *vCore* represents Amazon's processing power unit. A CloudHub worker is a dedicated instance of Mule that runs a single application. Workers have varying memory capacities and processing power and can operate in different environments. Each worker is a dedicated VM that executes a single Mule application within CloudHub. Every worker runs in its separate VM, allowing for independent deployment and monitoring in a specific geographical region. An application can be deployed across multiple workers, with the flexibility to assign different memory capacities and processing power as needed, facilitating horizontal and vertical scaling.

The memory capacity and processing power of a worker can be tailored to your needs by selecting the right configuration at the application level, allowing for an optimized performance experience.

You have the flexibility to choose from various worker sizes, each offering different compute, memory, and storage capacities. Table 10-1 shows the options available.

Table 10-1. Available memory for each vCore size

vCore Size	Total memory	Heap memory	Storage
0.1	1.2 GB	480 MB	8 GB
0.2	2 GB	1 GB	8 GB
0.5	2.6 GB	1.3 GB	10 GB
1	4 GB	2 GB	12 GB
1.5	6 GB	3 GB	20 GB
2	8 GB	4 GB	20 GB
2.5	9.5 GB	4.75 GB	20 GB
3	11 GB	5.5 GB	20 GB
3.5	13 GB	6.5 GB	20 GB
4	15 GB	7.5 GB	20 GB

For those using workers with 0.1 vCores and 0.2 vCores, these provide modest CPU and I/O capabilities that are perfect for smaller workloads. For example, if you are running a pass-through system API that is sending data from one queue to another, you do not need a lot of processing power. They can also temporarily boost CPU speeds, enhancing application startup times and managing occasional larger tasks if there are infrequent large loads passing through the system. If you're looking for consistent performance, we would encourage you to consider workers with more vCores.

On the other hand, workers with one vCore or more deliver great consistency in performance and are available for Mule version 3.6.2 and later, or API Gateway version 2.0.2 and later. You should use this if you are looking to process consistent large loads, for example, consuming Salesforce data logs and processing them before sending them to Tableau.

Each worker comes with a minimum of 8 GB of storage to support both system and application needs, with about 3 GB allocated for the operating system and Mule components. If your application demands more storage—like verbose logging—opt for a worker with two or more vCores to get the additional capacity you need.

Remember, only running applications are counted toward worker usage.

Customer-Hosted Runtime Environment

The second option is a customer-hosted runtime environment. This is suitable for customers who want to control their deployment setup tightly. This environment can be deployed on bare metal servers or through various cloud service providers such as AWS, Microsoft Azure, and Pivotal Cloud Foundry. This option is ideal for organizations that require specific configurations, have stringent compliance requirements, or prefer to manage their infrastructure. It allows for customization and optimization according to the business's unique needs. Deploying to customer-hosted Mule runtimes also has many benefits. Mule servers are easy to install, require minimal resources, and allow you to run multiple applications within a single server. Though the servers are customer-hosted, you still have the option to manage them using the MuleSoft-hosted Anypoint Platform on CloudHub or the customer-hosted Anypoint Platform Private Cloud Edition.

If your organization operates in a highly regulated industry, such as healthcare or finance, you may have strict data residency regulations that dictate where data can be processed and stored. In this case, you can deploy your Mule applications on AWS servers in a specific geographic region that complies with these regulations. This allows you to ensure all data processing remains within the legal boundaries set by local laws, thereby minimizing the risk of noncompliance.

Anypoint Runtime Fabric

The final option is Anypoint Runtime Fabric, a clustered container service designed to automate and orchestrate the deployment of Mule applications. This service can be used on private cloud infrastructure and on-premises data centers, providing a hybrid deployment model. Anypoint Runtime Fabric leverages containerization technology to ensure consistent and efficient application deployment, scaling, and management. It supports high availability and disaster recovery, making it a robust solution for enterprises looking to modernize their IT infrastructure while maintaining control over their deployment environments.

Anypoint Runtime Fabric is a container service that automates the deployment and orchestration of Mule applications and API proxies. Using this model, MuleSoft still provides cloud services that enable the design, reuse, and management of integrations and APIs. This set of services is collectively known as the *control plane*. In addition, applications, connectors, and Mule runtime instances are deployed within a customer-managed infrastructure such as AWS, Azure, VMs, and bare-metal servers. Together, these deployed components are called the *runtime plane*.

Like CloudHub and customer-hosted Mule runtimes, the model also has its benefits, such as the following:

- Increased security and reliability through application isolation
- Zero-downtime redeployments
- Horizontal scaling, which allows for multiple application replicas and automatic failover
- Ability to run multiple versions of Mule runtime on the same set of resources
- Availability of carefully designed runtime container images supported by MuleSoft for use specifically with Anypoint Runtime Fabric

Each option offers distinct advantages, allowing organizations to choose the deployment strategy that best aligns with their operational requirements and strategic goals. We'll start with how to deploy using the first model: CloudHub.

Deploying Applications to CloudHub

Mule applications can be deployed to CloudHub utilizing two primary methods: an embedded connection to Runtime Manager within Anypoint Studio, or direct navigation to Runtime Manager via the Anypoint Platform. This section provides a detailed overview of both methods.

Method 1: Using Anypoint Studio

Here are the steps to follow when deploying using Anypoint Studio:

1. *Open Anypoint Studio.* Initiate the deployment process by launching Anypoint Studio and opening your specific Mule application project. Before proceeding, confirming that the project functions correctly and without errors is essential.

2. *Configure deployment.* Right-click on the project within the Anypoint Studio workspace and select "Deploy to CloudHub" from the context menu. This action will open the deployment configuration window, as Figure 10-1 shows.

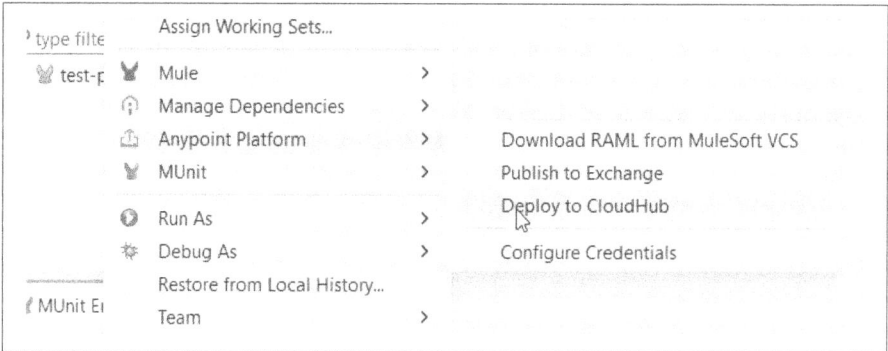

Figure 10-1. Studio deployment

3. *Deployment environment.* Choose the environment for deployment, as shown in Figure 10-2. If you get a dialog asking to enable multifactor authentication, click Not Now.

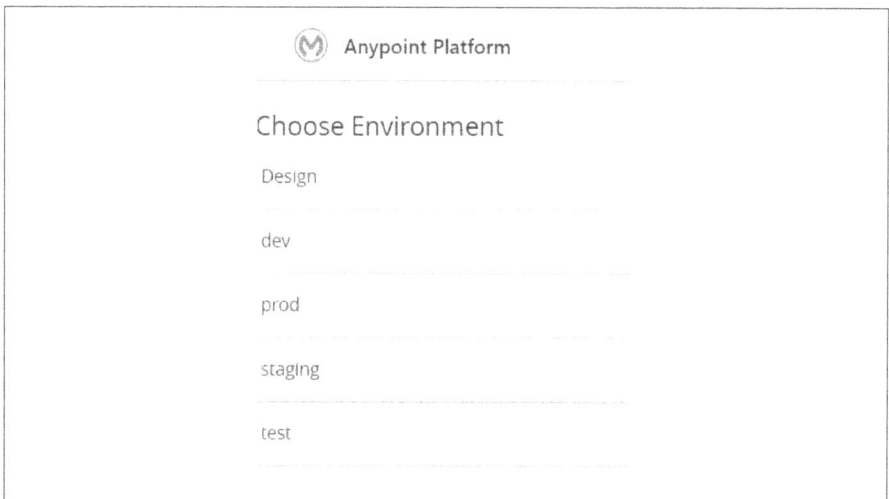

Figure 10-2. Deployment environments

4. *Log in to Anypoint Platform.* If you still need to be authenticated, you will be prompted to enter your Anypoint Platform credentials. This login is critical for accessing CloudHub services.

5. *Specify deployment settings.* Within the deployment configuration window, you must provide several essential details (see Figure 10-3):

   a. *Application name.* Enter a distinctive and descriptive name for your application, which will serve as its identifier within CloudHub. This name will be part of the URL used to access the application on CloudHub. It must be unique across all applications on CloudHub. If the domain is available, you will receive a green check mark.

   b. *Environment.* To ensure proper contextual deployment, select the relevant environment for deployment, such as Development or Production.

   c. *Worker size.* Choose the appropriate worker size based on your application's anticipated resource requirements. Options typically range from small, for lighter workloads, to extra-large, for those necessitating substantial processing capabilities with varying CPU and memory levels.

   d. *Number of workers.* Indicate the workers needed to manage your application's load effectively. Increasing the number of workers can improve performance and enhance redundancy.

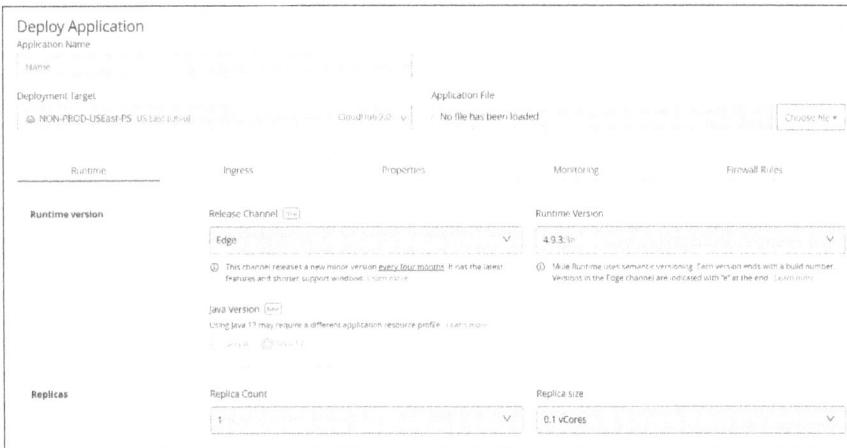

Figure 10-3. Deployment settings

Ensure the runtime version is set to the version your project is using, and the worker size is set to 0.1 vCores. If you don't know what version it uses, look in the Package Explorer and find a library folder named *Mule Server 4.4.0 EE.*

6. *Deploy.* After configuring all settings, click the Deploy button to initiate the deployment process. Anypoint Studio will compile the application package and execute its deployment to CloudHub while providing updates regarding its status.

Method 2: Using Runtime Manager in Anypoint Platform

Here are the steps to follow when deploying using Runtime Manager:

1. *Navigate to Runtime Manager.* Open a web browser and log in to the Anypoint Platform. From the dashboard, proceed to Runtime Manager, where you can monitor all deployed applications.

2. *Create a new deployment.* Click the "Deploy application" button to begin the deployment process, as shown in Figure 10-4.

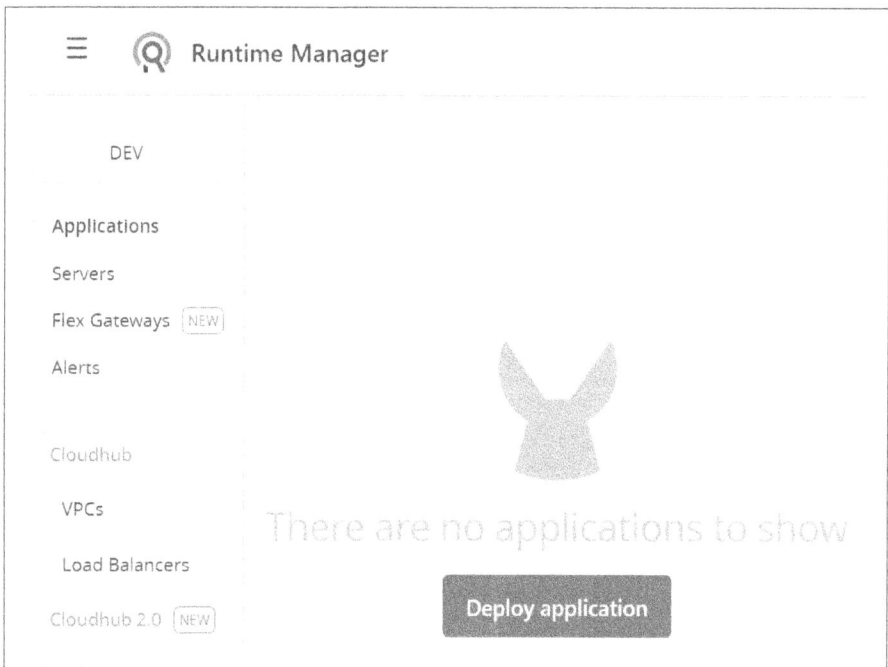

Figure 10-4. Deployment button

3. *Upload application.* You can upload your Mule application package, typically in a *.jar* file, or select an application you have previously published in Exchange, as shown in Figure 10-5.

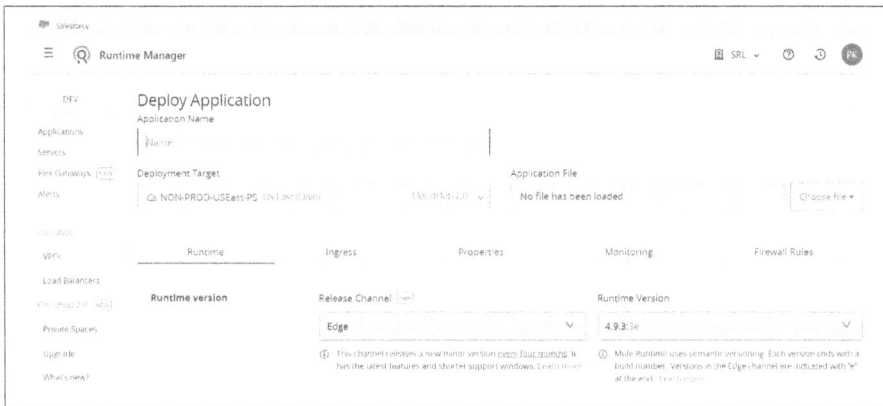

Figure 10-5. Upload application package

4. *CloudHub 2.0.* You can deploy Mule apps to a shared or private space in CloudHub 2.0:

   a. *Shared space.* To deploy to a shared space, select CloudHub 2.0, and then Shared Space for the region from the Deployment Target list.

   b. *Private space.* Select the name of the private or shared space from the Deployment Target list.

Runtime Manager doesn't support deploying an application to CloudHub 2.0 or Runtime Fabric if the asset was previously in Exchange:

1. *Configure deployment settings.* Like the first method, you need to complete the following fields:

   a. *Application Name.* Assign a unique name to your application.

   b. *Environment.* Choose the appropriate environment for deployment.

   c. *Worker Size.* Designate the suitable worker size based on resource needs.

   d. *Number of Workers.* Specify the number of workers allocated for the application.

   e. *Advanced Settings.* To enhance performance and control, you can explore advanced configuration options, including logging preferences, monitoring settings, and custom properties.

2. *Deploy.* Once you have confirmed all deployment details, click the Deploy Application button. Runtime Manager will oversee the deployment process and provide real-time status updates and logs.

Method 3: Using Anypoint Code Builder

You can use ACB to deploy applications to CloudHub:

1. Open any configuration XML file for the Mule app you want to deploy.
2. Click "Deploy to CloudHub," as shown in the drop-down menu in Figure 10-6.

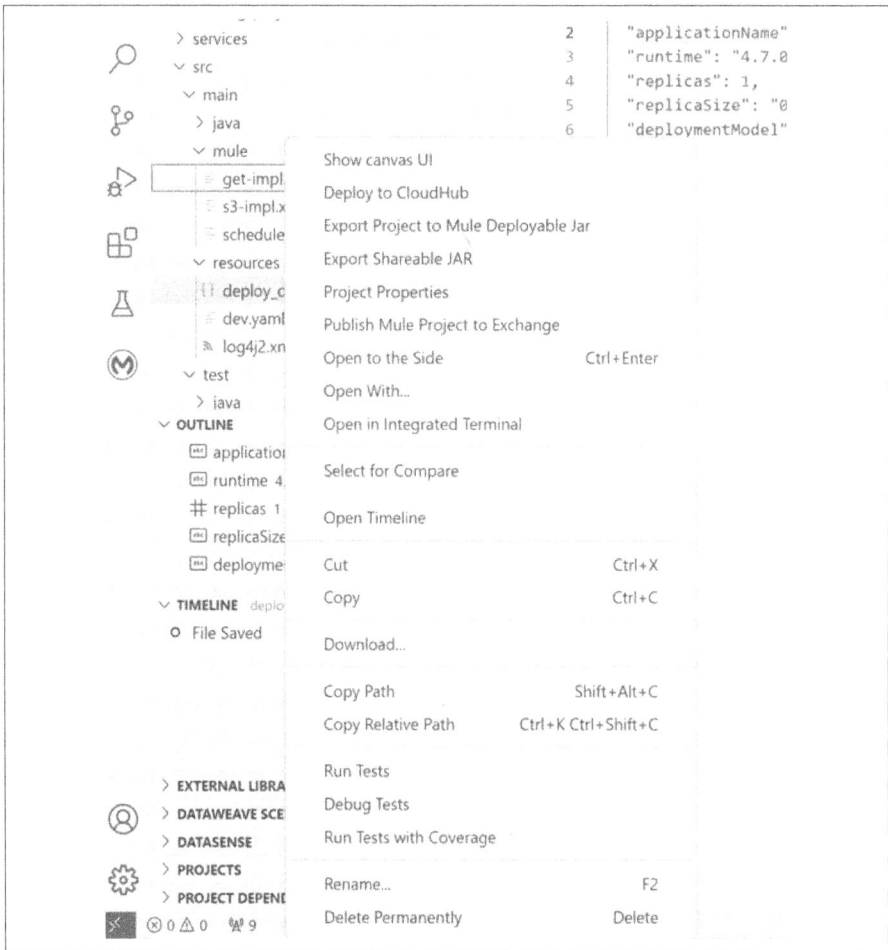

Figure 10-6. "Deploy to CloudHub" from ACB

3. Alternatively, open the command palette and select MuleSoft > "Deploy to CloudHub".

4. If prompted, click "Allow to sign in using Anypoint Platform" and select the Business Group.

5. Choose the Business Group for deployment.

6. When prompted via the VS Code command palette, select the deployment target: CloudHub 2.0 or CloudHub 1.0.

7. If you select CloudHub 2.0, you will be prompted to select the space to deploy your application, e.g., "srl_nonprod".

8. If the project doesn't already have a *deploy.json* or *deploy_ch2.json* file, ACB will create a deployment configuration file and open it for you to review, as shown in Figure 10-7.

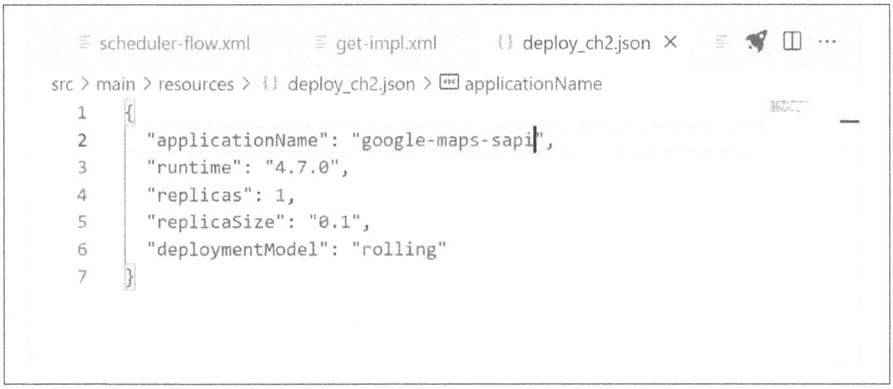

```
  scheduler-flow.xml        get-impl.xml        {} deploy_ch2.json  ×

src > main > resources > {} deploy_ch2.json > ⚙ applicationName
  1    {
  2        "applicationName": "google-maps-sapi",
  3        "runtime": "4.7.0",
  4        "replicas": 1,
  5        "replicaSize": "0.1",
  6        "deploymentModel": "rolling"
  7    }
```

Figure 10-7. ACB deployment configuration file

Managing Deployed Applications

To manage a deployed API, follow these steps:

1. Go to API Manager and select Add API, which opens the page that asks you to select either Flex Gateway or Mule Gateway. Choose Mule Gateway, which opens the page shown in Figure 10-8.

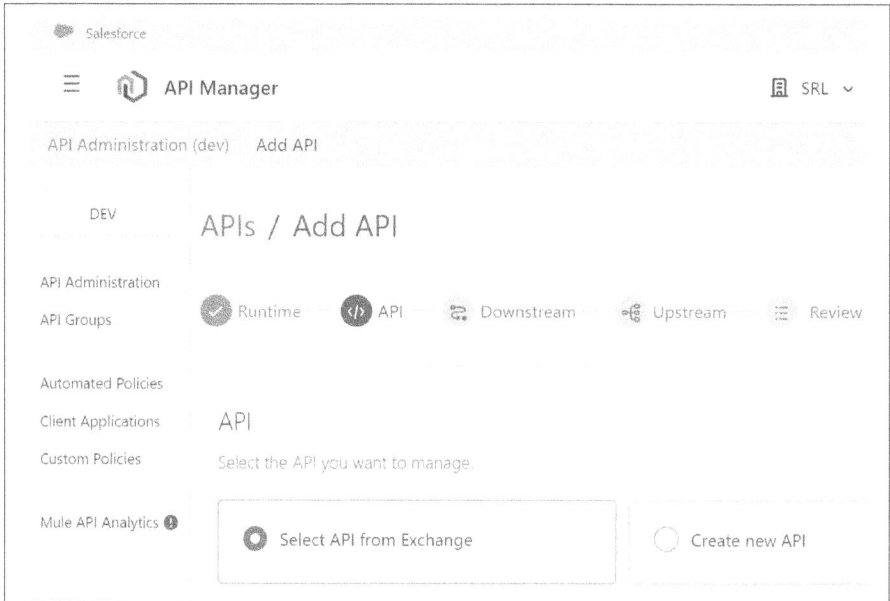

Figure 10-8. Add API to API Manager

2. Next, update downstream details, as shown in Figure 10-9.

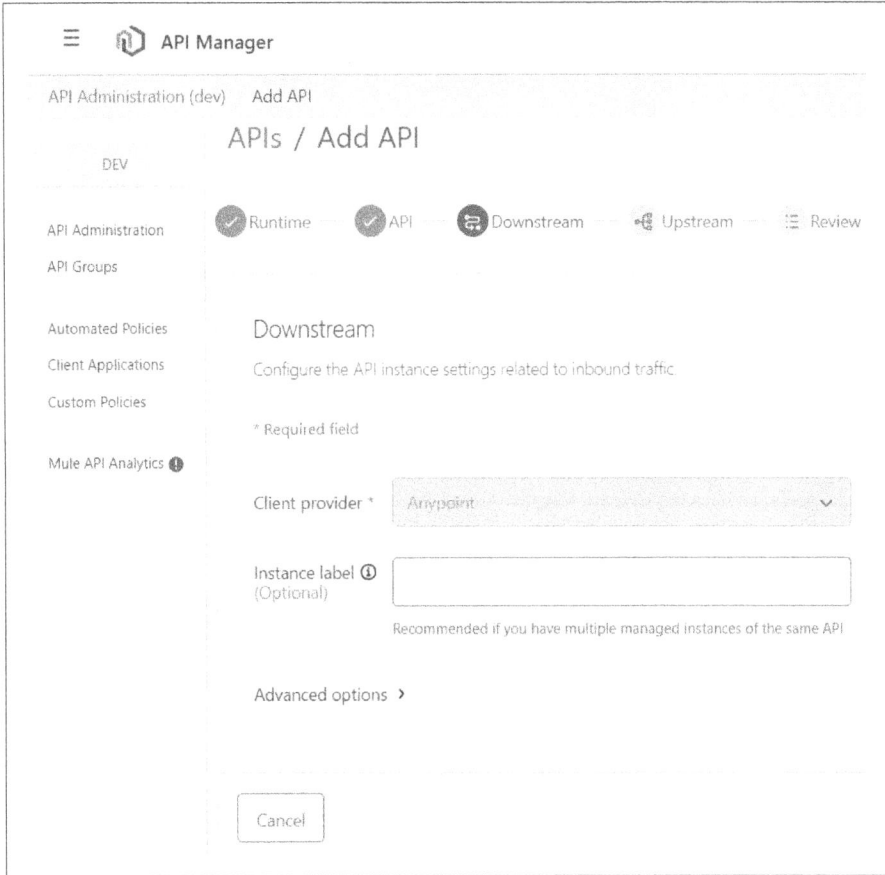

Figure 10-9. Downstream details

3. Finally, update the upstream details, as shown in Figure 10-10; the upstream URL must point to the URL of the API you wish to configure.

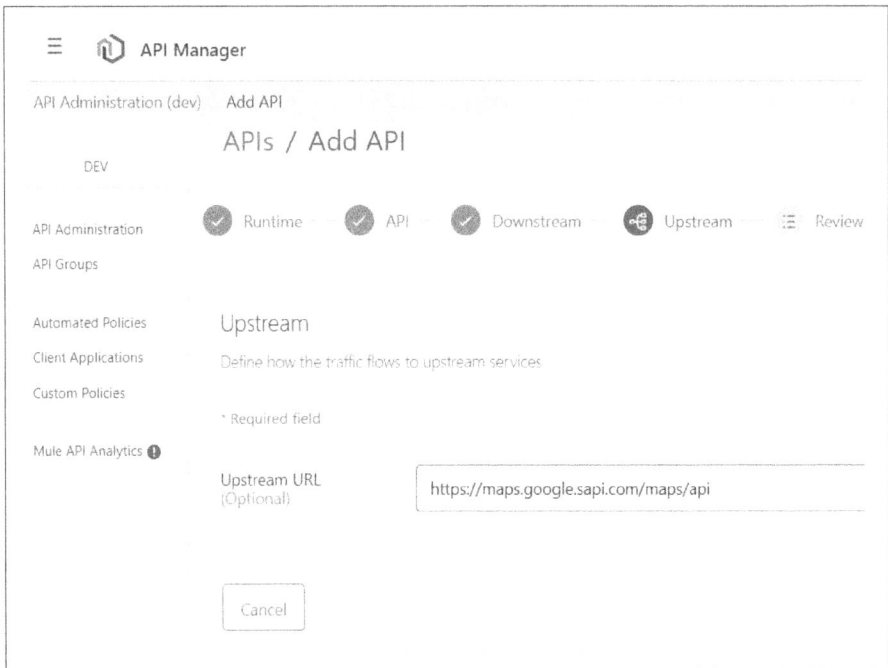

Figure 10-10. Upstream URL

Figure 10-11 shows an API configured using API Manager; notice the API status shows unregistered and has an API instance. You will learn more about this later in the chapter.

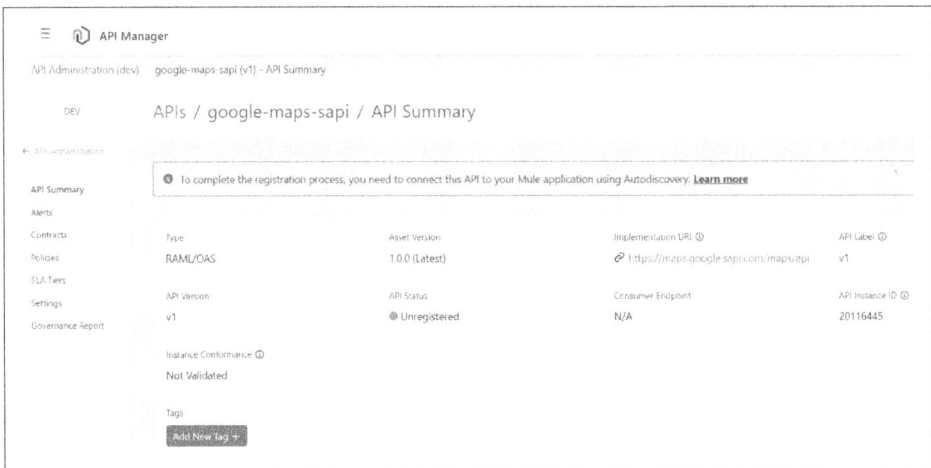

Figure 10-11. API configuration in API Manager

Now that you've seen how to deploy an API and configure it in API Manager, let's look at CloudHub 2.0 efficiently.

Static IPs

You can easily allocate a static IP address to your application using the Static IPs tab, specifically tailored for your deployed region. You can even preconfigure static IPs for multiple regions, which is a great way to enhance your disaster recovery (DR) plans.

Here's how you can set up static IPs for applications deployed on the MuleSoft Anypoint Platform:

1. Log in to the Anypoint Platform and navigate to the Runtime Manager.
2. Choose the application for which you want to set up a static IP.
3. In the application settings, find and click on the Static IPs tab.
4. Check the option to enable static IP for your application. This will assign a fixed IP address to your application.
5. Save the changes and redeploy your application if necessary. This will apply the static IP configuration.
6. Update your firewall and security settings to allow traffic from the new static IP address. This may involve listing the IP in your source and target applications.
7. Verify that the static IP is correctly assigned by checking the application details in Runtime Manager.
8. Test the connectivity to ensure that your application can communicate with other services using the static IP.

CloudHub 2.0

In this section, you will learn about CloudHub 2.0 and compare it with CloudHub 1.0, as shown in Table 10-2. CloudHub 2.0 offers several enhancements over its predecessor, including improved scalability, enhanced security features, better performance, and a more intuitive user interface. It also provides advanced monitoring tools and more robust integration capabilities, making it a superior choice for managing integrations.

Table 10-2. Deployment model comparison between CloudHub 1.0 and CloudHub 2.0

Feature/Capability	CloudHub 1.0	CloudHub 2.0
Deployment model	Fully managed	Fully managed; containerized
Details	Applications are deployed and managed by MuleSoft.	Applications are deployed in containers, providing better isolation and resource management.
Scalability	Limited	Enhanced; supports clustering
Details	Scaling is limited to the number of workers.	Supports horizontal scaling with clustering, allowing for better handling of high-traffic loads.
Performance	Standard	Improved with intelligent self-healing
Details	Standard performance with essential resource management	Improved performance with self-healing capabilities that automatically detect and recover from failures
User interface	Basic	Enhanced; more user-friendly
Details	Basic interface for managing applications	Enhanced UI with a more intuitive and user-friendly design makes managing and monitoring applications easier.
Security	Standard	Advanced, with built-in policies
Details	Standard security features like basic authentication and encryption	Advanced security features, including built-in policies for OAuth, JSON Web Token, and more
Regions	12 geographical regions	12 geographical regions
Details	Supports deployment in 12 regions worldwide	Same regional support with improved infrastructure
Load balancing	Fully managed	Fully managed; supports URL rewriting
Details	Management by MuleSoft load balancing	Enhanced load balancing; support for URL rewriting with better traffic management
TLS support	Up to TLS 1.2	Up to TLS 1.3
Details	Supports up to TLS 1.2 for secure communications	Supports up to TLS 1.3, offering improved security and performance
Virtual private cloud	Fully managed (Anypoint Virtual Private Cloud [VPC])	Fully managed (private space)
Details	Uses Anypoint VPC for network isolation	Uses private spaces, which are easier to configure and manage, providing better network isolation and security
High availability	Fully managed (with two or more workers)	Fully managed (with two or more replicas)
Details	High availability achieved with multiple workers	High availability with various replicas, providing better fault tolerance
Logging	Basic	Enhanced; supports log tailing

Feature/ Capability	CloudHub 1.0	CloudHub 2.0
Details	Basic logging capabilities	Enhanced logging; support for log tailing with troubleshooting issues more manageable
Integration capabilities	Standard	Enhanced, supports advanced integrations
Details	Standard integration capabilities	Enhanced capabilities; supports more complex and advanced integrations
Monitoring	Basic	Enhanced, with built-in notifications
Details	Basic monitoring tools	Enhanced monitoring; built-in notifications, providing better visibility into application performance

Proxy Deployment

Separation of concerns is a key principle in API design. It involves dividing a system into distinct sections, each addressing a specific aspect of its functionality. This approach results in a more maintainable, secure, and scalable API, ultimately enhancing the experience for both developers and users.

One significant advantage of using an API proxy and Gateway setup is the clear separation between orchestration and implementation concerns. This means that the logic for managing API traffic, enforcing policies, and handling security is decoupled from the core business logic of the backend service. This separation allows developers to concentrate on building and maintaining the essential functionality of their services while the API proxy and Gateway manage the operational aspects. It also simplifies updating and scaling the API infrastructure without affecting the backend services.

The primary role of an API proxy is to act as a gatekeeper for your web service. It intercepts incoming API requests, applies security policies, and routes them to the appropriate backend service, ensuring that only authorized and valid requests are processed. The API proxy does this by leveraging an API Gateway. The API Gateway is a specialized runtime environment designed to host APIs or connect to APIs deployed on different runtimes. It provides a centralized point for managing API traffic, enforcing policies, and ensuring security.

The API Gateway can handle authentication, authorization, rate limiting, request and response transformation, and logging tasks. It acts as a mediator between clients and backend services, ensuring that all interactions are secure and efficient. Here are the steps to create a proxy application:

1. *API Manager.* Navigate to the API Manager in the Anypoint Platform. Figure 10-12 shows the API Manager page on the Anypoint platform.

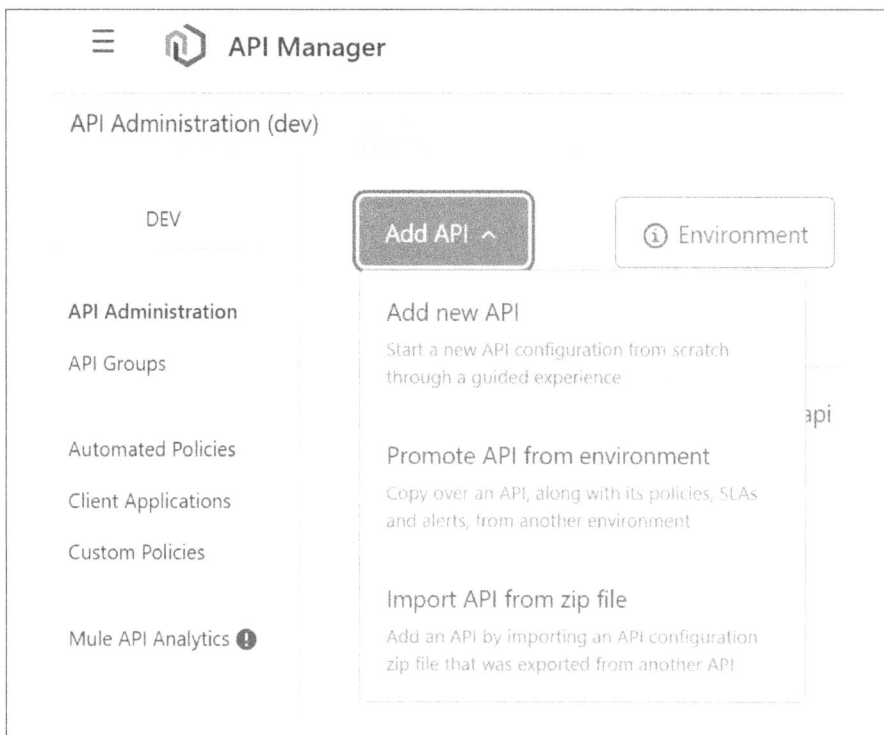

Figure 10-12. Add API in API Manager

2. *Add API.* Click Add API and select "Add New API."

3. *Proxy type.* Choose "Deploy a proxy application" as the proxy type, as shown in Figure 10-13.

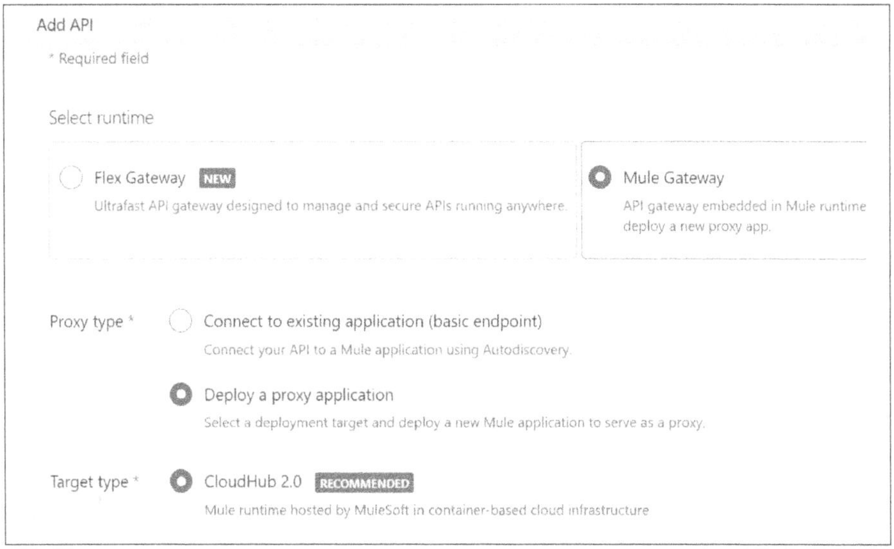

Figure 10-13. Target types

4. *Target type.* Select the target deployment environment (for example, CloudHub, Hybrid, or Self-managed Server) also shown in Figure10-13.

You have successfully deployed an API proxy, which is a simple pass-through. Next, you will learn how to restrict access to the API by implementing policies and filters.

Policy Creation

You can use the API Manager to define service-level access (SLA) tiers and policies that the API Gateway enforces. API Autodiscovery is a feature in MuleSoft's Anypoint Platform that allows a deployed Mule application to automatically connect with API Manager. This connection enables the application to download and manage policies and generate analytics data. With API Autodiscovery, applications can also be configured to act as their API proxy.

To restrict access to the APIs, you can apply out-of-the-box policies for everyday use cases, such as client ID enforcement, data encryption, threat protection, OAuth 2.0, cross-origin resource sharing (CORS), header injection, and basic authentication. You also have the flexibility to create custom policies using XML and YAML files. Multiple policies can be applied simultaneously, and you can specify the order in which they are enforced. Automated policies can also be configured to meet shared security and logging requirements by applying consistent policies to all APIs running within a single environment.

You can also set up SLA to manage the number of requests made to the API within a specified unit of time. Creating an SLA for your API involves defining specific tiers that set the usage limits and access controls for different groups of API consumers. To set this up in the Anypoint Platform, you have to configure SLA tiers in the API Manager by specifying the number of requests allowed per period (such as per minute, hour, or day) for each tier, as shown in Figure 10-14. Once the SLA tiers are defined, you can apply them to your API, and the API Gateway will enforce these limits, automatically restricting access when the limits are exceeded. This setup helps maintain the performance and reliability of your API and provides a structured way to maintain and manage the separation of concerns.

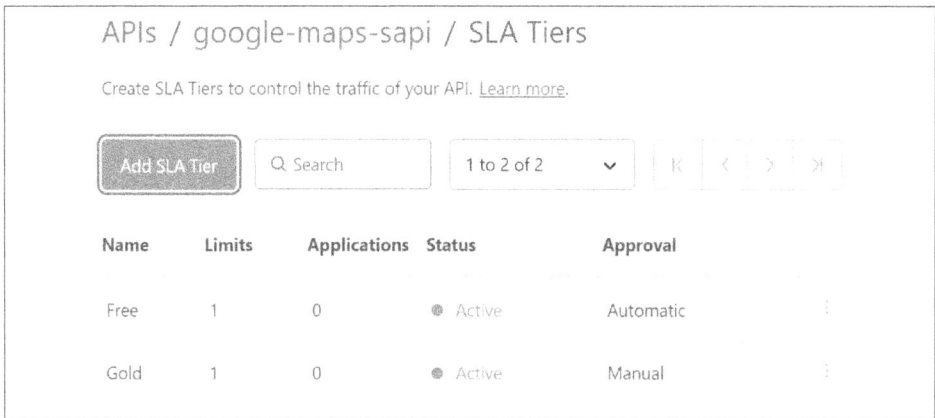

APIs / google-maps-sapi / SLA Tiers

Create SLA Tiers to control the traffic of your API. Learn more.

| Add SLA Tier | Q Search | 1 to 2 of 2 | ⌄ | K ‹ › ⟩ |

Name	Limits	Applications	Status	Approval	
Free	1	0	● Active	Automatic	⋮
Gold	1	0	● Active	Manual	⋮

Figure 10-14. SLA tiers

Let's set policies for our Google Maps system API:

1. Log in to your Anypoint Platform account and navigate to API Manager. Choose the API for which you want to set policies.
2. Click the Policies tab and click "Add policy," as shown in Figure 10-15.

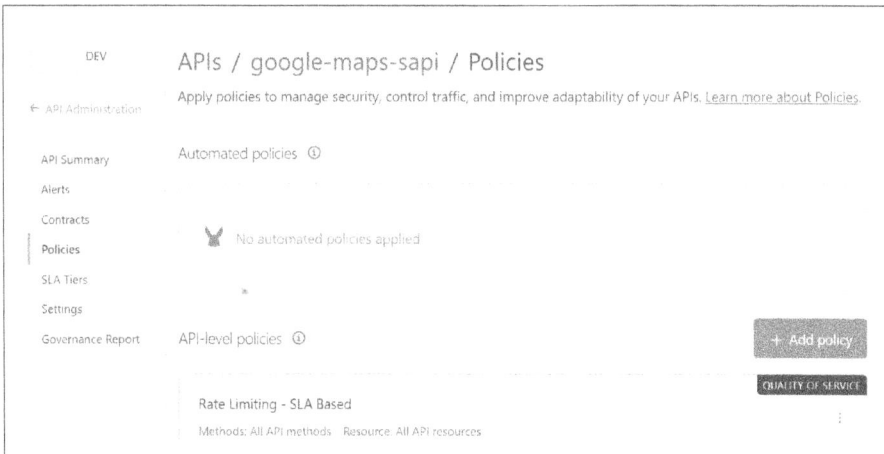

Figure 10-15. Add a policy to Google API

3. Select the policy you want to apply from the list of available policies. These can include security policies (like OAuth 2.0 or IP allowlist), compliance policies (like client ID enforcement), and quality of service policies (like rate limiting). In this case, we are choosing the rate-limiting options, as shown in Figure 10-16.

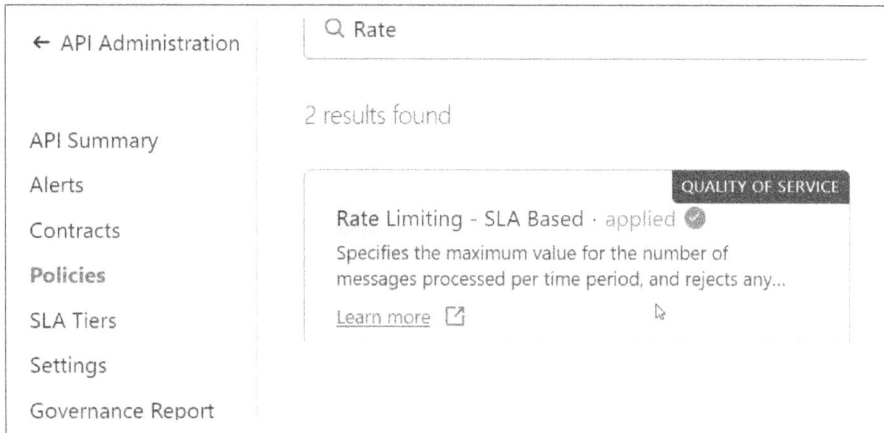

Figure 10-16. Choose rate-limiting options

4. After selecting a policy, configure its settings as needed. This might include setting thresholds for rate limiting, specifying authentication parameters, or defining custom rules. Once configured, save the policy and apply it to your API. The policy will now be enforced for all incoming requests to the API. Figure 10-17 shows a saved policy.

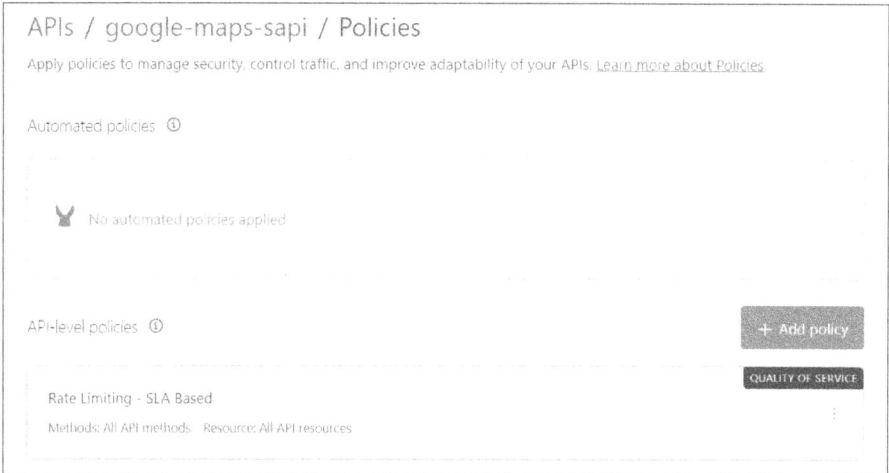

Figure 10-17. Policy applied to an API

After setting up the policy, the next step is to learn how to request and grant access for consuming the API.

Access Provision

To access an API restricted by an SLA-based policy, consumers must register their Exchange application, choose a tier, and request access. Upon approval, they will receive credentials that must be included with each API call. If you go to the API Summary of the Google Maps app, you will see it shows unregistered, as shown in Figure 10-18.

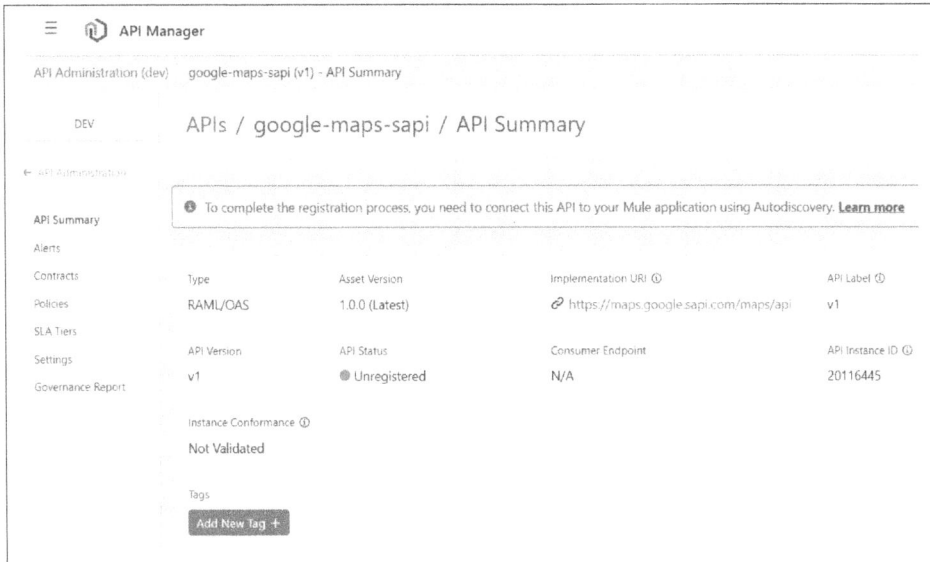

Figure 10-18. Unregistered API

If an SLA-based policy governs an API, a "Request access" button will appear in the API portal, as shown in Figure 10-19.

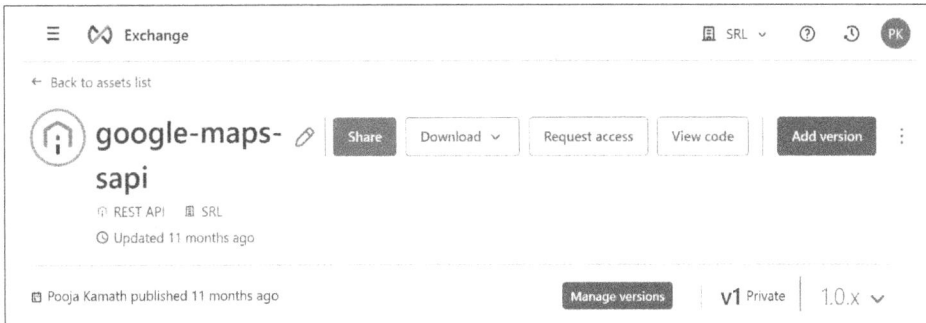

Figure 10-19. "Request access" button

To request access, a developer must be logged in and a member of the Anypoint Platform organization. They must also register or add an application to their Anypoint Platform account and select the appropriate tier, as shown in Figure 10-20.

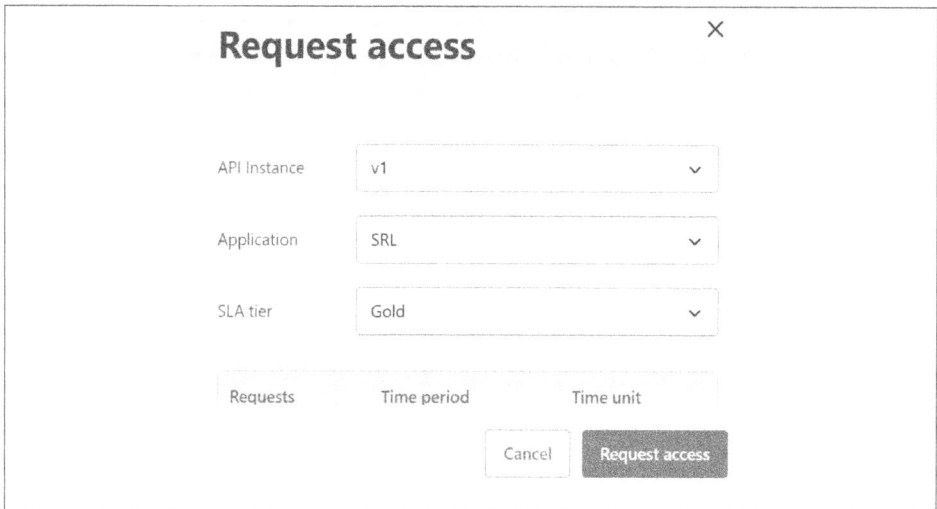

Figure 10-20. Request access dialog box

The SLA-based policy is in place. Now let's see how to add client ID enforcement to your API specification.

Client ID enforcement

Client ID-based policies require the client ID and secret to be provided as headers. You can apply a trait to the resource or methods to enforce this in your API definition. This enforcement ensures that users have the necessary properties in the RESTful connector and headers in the API console to pass the required authentication credentials:

```
Traits:
  client-id-required:
    headers:
      client_id:
        description: The client ID for authentication
        type: string
        required: true
      client_secret:
        description: The client's secret for authentication
        type: string
        required: true

/example-resource:
  is: [client-id-required]
  Get:
    Description: An example endpoint that requires client ID and secret
    Responses:
      200:
        body:
```

```
Application/json:
    example: |
        {
          "message": "Access granted"
        }
```

Anypoint Monitoring

Anypoint Monitoring is a feature of MuleSoft's Anypoint Platform for API analytics. It allows you to do the following:

- Track the performance of your applications and APIs in real-time.
- Create customizable dashboards tailored to your specific needs.
- Set up alerts to notify you of any issues or anomalies.
- Visualize dependencies between different components of your application network.
- Access historical log data to help with troubleshooting and root cause analysis.

Setting up Anypoint Monitoring involves a procedure. First, log in to your Anypoint Platform account and navigate to the Monitoring section from the main dashboard. For CloudHub deployments, monitoring is enabled by default for Mule apps deployed to CloudHub 2.0. Still, you can manually enable it by selecting the appropriate runtime version in the application's settings in Runtime Manager. You must install the Anypoint Monitoring agent on your server for on-premises deployments, sending monitoring data to the Anypoint Monitoring cloud endpoint. Next, configure custom dashboards and alerts to monitor the performance and health of your applications, creating alerts based on specific metrics and thresholds. Use the dependency mapping feature to visualize the relationships between different components of your application network and review historical log data for troubleshooting and root cause analysis. Figure 10-21 shows API Monitoring dashboards.

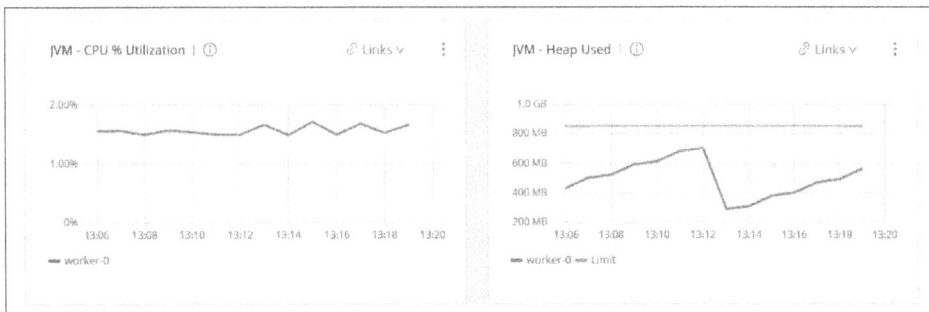

Figure 10-21. API monitoring

Summary

In this chapter, you learned how to deploy Mule applications to CloudHub using Anypoint Studio, the Runtime Manager, and Anypoint Code Builder. You learned to use API Manager to manage a newly created API. You also explored methods to secure and manage your applications using an API proxy. This proxy is hosted and managed through an API Gateway, which helps enforce security policies, manage traffic, and provide monitoring capabilities.

The chapter also compared CloudHub 1.0 and CloudHub 2.0 capabilities for developers familiar with both options. You now know how to deploy, secure, and manage your Mule applications effectively using CloudHub and the API Gateway.

Congratulations on making it to the end of this book! Your dedication and perseverance are truly commendable. We hope the knowledge and insights you've gained will serve you well in your career and projects. Remember, this is just the beginning of your journey. If you have any ideas, questions, or feedback, feel free to contact us at *queries@integrationauthors.com*. We're always here to help and would love to hear from you. Best of luck in all your future endeavors. Woooot, you did it!

Index

E

About the Authors

Pooja Kamath excels at integrating employee and customer insights to drive collaborative success. As president and chief architect of API Insights in Houston, she leads innovative software integration solutions for the travel and transportation industry, establishing the firm as a trusted partner. Her extensive experience includes resolving complex integration challenges and delivering multimillion-dollar MuleSoft projects. Holding a master's in computer science, Pooja leverages her deep technical understanding to advise on and improve integration practices. She actively shares her knowledge through insightful blog posts and presentations at international technology conferences, including Salesforce Dreamforce, focusing on integration and customer experience. Her significant contributions to the MuleSoft community have earned her the distinction of being a three-time MuleSoft community ambassador (2023–2025), recognizing her expertise and dedication to the field.

Diane Kesler is the practice lead at CloudBlazer, a Salesforce consulting firm headquartered in Charlotte, NC. She is also the cofounder of Integration Quest, a modern enablement platform focused on training and mentoring the next generation of integration and automation professionals. With a master's degree in IT management and deep roots in the MuleSoft ecosystem, Diane has built a career at the intersection of integration, automation, and innovation. As a Salesforce certified instructor, she teaches several instructor-led MuleSoft courses and is one of only two certified hyperautomation instructors in the Americas.

Diane's passion for teaching was inspired by her grandmother, a lifelong educator who instilled in her the belief that knowledge should be shared generously. That value has guided her through roles as a MuleSoft community ambassador for the last three years (2022–2025), 2025 Agentblazer Innovator, and 2025 Top Muley AI Advocate MuleSoft Community Award winner.

As a recognized speaker, Diane shares her expertise across industry panels, Dreamforce and World Tours, and Women Who Mule events, often focusing on intelligent automation, inclusive leadership, and real-world integration use cases. At her core, Diane is committed to helping businesses and developers make technology work smarter—not harder—by simplifying complexity and inspiring continuous learning through her work at Integration Quest and CloudBlazer.

In addition to her leadership roles, Diane is a curriculum developer and mentor who actively supports the growth of new talent in the integration space. Through Integration Quest's study groups, hands-on workshops, and enablement programs, she champions the development of future-ready skills in API-led connectivity, automation, and AI. Her writing brings clarity, creativity, and real-world relevance to technical topics, making her a trusted guide for readers navigating the evolving world of integration.

Colophon

The animal on the cover of *Building Integrations with MuleSoft* is a muskrat (*Ondatra zibethicus*).

These semi-aquatic rodents are native to North America but also thrive in large areas of Europe and northern Asia. Despite their name, muskrats are more closely related to voles than to rats. As with all animals, their unique physical characteristics contribute to their survival in the wild. Partially webbed back feet help them move both on land and in water, and their long flat tails also contribute to movement (primarily aquatic) and, to a lesser extent, communication with other muskrats. Specialized lips that close behind their prominent front teeth allow them to chew and swallow underwater. Their waterproof fur also serves them well, keeping their body temperature appropriately regulated.

In addition to being physically distinctive, muskrats are known for their engineering abilities, highlighted through their nest building. For drier banks, they tunnel (above the waterline) to form dry caves, while for more muddy, less stable banks, they build domed structures. The females produce several litters a year and tend to their young until the kits are independent at a few weeks old, at which point the mother can move on to gestating her next litter. While muskrat lifespans are only one to three years long, their rapid and prolific reproduction means that their population is still thriving and "Of Least Concern" on the IUCN conservation scale.

Many of the animals on O'Reilly covers are endangered; all of them are important to the world.

The cover illustration is by Monica Kamsvaag, based on a black-and-white engraving from *Lydekker's Royal Natural History*. The series design is by Edie Freedman, Ellie Volckhausen, and Karen Montgomery. The cover fonts are Gilroy Semibold and Guardian Sans. The text font is Adobe Minion Pro; the heading font is Adobe Myriad Condensed; and the code font is Dalton Maag's Ubuntu Mono.